# Don's Brother

*A Hike of Hope on the Appalachian Trail*

## Mike Stephens

ISBN: 1494753561
ISBN 13: 9781494753566
Library of Congress Control Number: 2013923382
CreateSpace Independent Publishing Platform
North Charleston, South Carolina

# Dedication

For Family: Linda, Sam, and Rachel
Lisa, Brent, and Lori
My mother, Elizabeth
And especially in memory of my brother, Don

# Acknowledgements

There are so many people who need to be thanked. First, I want to express my greatest appreciation to my wife, Linda, who supported me from home and briefly on the trail during the five months and eleven days that I was on the Appalachian Trail. She encouraged me to hike and lifted my spirits when we talked.

I would like to thank the rest of my family, especially my mother, Elizabeth. Still grieving the loss of Don, it was difficult for her to be without her other son for the time I was away. Still she constantly stayed strong and prayed faithfully for my safety and well-being.

Other members of my family, my children, Sam and Rachel, Don's widow, Lisa, Don's son, Brent, and his wife, Lori, all encouraged me throughout the hike. Knowing that I had the support of a caring and loving family sustained me on many occasions.

I would also like to especially thank Karen Duffy, a friend of the Stephens family who assisted with my website, encouraged me as I hiked, and tirelessly advocates for ALS research.

I would like to thank Jenny Horton who used my vision to design the cover for *Don's Brother*.

I would like to thank all of those who helped me during the hike as well as those who assisted with the process of getting this book published. For fear of missing someone, I won't try to list them all.

I would also like to thank all of those who lifted up a prayer for me, especially members of Wynnton United Methodist Church. Always aware of my church family's prayerful concern for my endeavor, I appreciated greatly their many kindnesses while I was away.

Finally, I would like to thank all the other hikers that I met and hiked with along the way. A very special, heartfelt thank you goes out to John "Molar Man" Eichelberger and his wife Diane "Sweet Tooth," Walt "Susquehanna Slim" Krzastek, Doug "Banzai" Douma, Joe "Pilgrim" Estes, and Renea "Speck" Woodard. I could not have made it without all of you.

And in memoriam, I would like to thank my brother, Donald Andrews Stephens. His life and memory kept me going at times when I really didn't think I could make it. Had he not lived, and sadly had he not died, neither the journey nor the book would have become a reality. I faithfully believe that all things happen for a reason. This hike and book mainly occurred because Don loved the woods.

Monday, September 2, 2013.......When Molar Man said he would like to stick with our plans to summit Katahdin on Labor Day, regardless of the weather, I felt just a bit concerned with our decision. With a 90% chance of rain by early afternoon, I seriously wondered if we were doing the smart thing. I had been somewhat apprehensive and a little anxious about the climb for the past week. Due to the potential for a nasty day, my anxiety increased. So with the possibility of no views, and the almost certainty of encounters with wet, slippery rocks, Molar Man and I signed the trailhead register at 6:30 before taking our first steps toward the summit of Katahdin and the end of my thru-hike of the Appalachian Trail.

# Contents

# Preface

# Becoming Don's Brother

On the afternoons that I stayed with my brother Don in the final three months of his life, I often found myself answering the phone. Some of the calls were from solicitors who said they would call back later. Other calls were from family members, or friends of Don's, who usually recognized my voice. When I answered the phone I would simply say, "Hello." The greeting changed, however, the day Don's mother-in-law almost had a coronary, thinking that Don had not only regained his ability to walk to the phone, but also his speech. Henceforth, I answered the phone, "Hello. This is Mike, Don's brother."

So in the summer of 2012, it became very natural to refer to myself this way. After all, most people at various times use an appositive in reference to themselves. I already was the dad, the husband, the son. I also had been the teacher and the coach. At other times I had even been Mike, the runner, and Mike, the hiker. But during those hot summer days of 2012, none suited me like my role of Mike, Don's brother.

On the evening of the visitation prior to Don's following day Memorial Service, I lined up with the rest of our family to greet a multitude of visitors who had come to offer their condolences as well as to show their respect for my brother. Many were friends of the family or members of our church that I already knew. Some, however, were people I had never seen before that evening. So when gentlemen in dark suits or casual attire introduced themselves as having worked with Don, I stated, "Thank you for coming; I'm Mike, Don's brother." When others stated that they had been in a hunting club with Don, I thanked them and said, "I'm Mike, Don's brother." When some said they had fished in tournaments with my brother, again, I offered my appreciation for their coming, followed by, "I'm Mike, Don's brother."

The line of visitors wound down the hallway of the mortuary, out to the parking lot, and around the building. Those who had played on a softball team with Don, one even in uniform, offered their remorse, and I accepted after telling them that I was Mike, Don's brother. Over the three hours that I, along with members of our family, greeted the many who had stood in line to express their love, or respect, or to tell us how much they already missed my brother, I must have identified myself dozens of times as Don's brother. And each time I said it, I became even more proud of indeed being Don's brother.

So as I set out from Springer in March, 2013 to begin the five month journey to Katahdin, I knew that I would carry the memory of my brother Don with me every step of the way. I knew that each time I would admire a fishing pond I would think of Don. I knew that I would watch a deer feeding under a budding tree and remember my brother. Don wouldn't just be in my mind. He would be with me. So as I embarked on the journey, the fulfillment of a dream, the undertaking that would require all the physical, mental, and emotional strength that God would grant me, I knew that the only way to travel toward my destination would be, proudly, as Don's Brother.

# 1

# My Brother Don

My brother Don was one of the healthiest men I knew. Aside from his fishing and hunting, he played on organized softball teams in both the fall and spring seasons for many years. At 53, Don prided himself on still playing with the "younger guys." In fact, he often batted clean-up on very competitive teams and still produced his share of homeruns right up until his last season. He also lifted weights and did numerous sets of push-ups daily to keep in shape. For Don, competing on the softball playing field kept him young, added vigor to his life, and allowed him to stay connected to a sport he had loved and played all his life. And for Don, athletics was just as important a part of life as breathing was.

Having played football, basketball, baseball, as well as having run cross-country and track in high school, Don retained that youthful enthusiasm for competition throughout his adult life. He liked to win, but more importantly he liked the excitement and challenge of competing. He was a true lover of sports in every sense of the word.

As I've already stated, my brother Don was one of the healthiest men I have ever known. That is why it came as such a shock when he called me one night in the spring of 2011 to tell me that he thought he had Lou Gehrig's disease. Amyotrophic Lateral Sclerosis, or ALS, is a neurological disease that eventually completely paralyzes its victims. Those who suffer from this horrible disease lose their ability to use their arms and legs. Over time they also lose their ability to speak, swallow, and breathe. And there is no cure.

How could my healthy, strong, athletic brother have such a crippling disease? Since he had not been officially diagnosed, I thought he must be mistaken. Even though he exhibited symptoms of the illness, there were still many other illnesses that evoked the same or similar symptoms. He would go to his doctor and find out that there was some other reason that he was losing strength in his right hand, was having difficulty throwing and hitting a softball, and falling occasionally for no apparent reason. That night that he called, and for many nights to come, I prayed that indeed what he did have, would not be ALS.

The next few weeks were difficult for all of our family. After many tests, an unnecessary surgery, visits to specialists for second opinions, and a great deal of anxiety, my brother Don was diagnosed with ALS on May 26, 2011. He was told that all cases of ALS are different, but that life expectancy is usually 2 to 5 years. So just a little over a month before his 54th birthday, my brother Don found out that he had five years or less to live. There would be no more softball, and the days spent in nature hunting and fishing were suddenly at a premium. How many remained he had no way of knowing. What he did know was that he would die from ALS.

When I told my brother that I wanted to do a thru-hike of the Appalachian Trail in his honor, he smiled and said, "It won't be in my honor; it will be in my memory." I knew that Don was right when he corrected me; however, at that time I still did not want to think about his death. Even though he had already lost his ability to walk and only had limited use of his left hand, he still communicated fairly well on that late April afternoon. I quickly learned to treasure the conversations we had during those final few months he could speak. Speech is one of those things we so often take for granted. When it's lost, silence can be deafening.

On the occasion that I brought up my idea to hike the Appalachian Trail, Don and I were out on a breezeway overlooking the Chattahoochee River. He had driven out over the weathered wooden boards in his power chair to a spot that afforded a view of the old Eagle Phenix dam. Don loved the river. I'm sure there were times when he thought about other days on the river. Days when he navigated in his bass boat rather than a power chair. Days to meditate on life rather than on death.

Still he smiled and listened as I related my idea of doing a thru-hike of the Appalachian Trail in his honor, or memory, and of attempting to raise awareness of ALS as I hiked. Don knew that I had hiked sections of the trail for several years. He knew that I had often thought about giving a thru-hike a try. Don also knew that I was not an outdoorsman. So the smile that my brother gave me on that afternoon just before sundown was seasoned with what I knew was a bit of incredulity. Don didn't necessarily doubt my intentions; he just realistically viewed the enormity of the pursuit.

I did mention the hike to Don a couple of other times, but we never really discussed my plans in detail. At the time I wasn't even sure when or how the project would become a reality. I just knew that I had to do something for my brother, and a hike of the Appalachian Trail seemed to be an appropriate tribute. Every day that I would spend with nature on the trail would be a day that I would be spending not just for myself, but for both of us. The woods would be our woods to share. I wanted to face the challenges of the trail as bravely as my brother Don faced a debilitating disease. When things weren't going quite as well as I would have liked for them to, I would try not to complain. Because despite his discomfort, his pain, and his facing death, my brother didn't really bemoan his fate. Sure, there were times when he was downright angry at what was happening to him. Don, however, still tried to live a life of dignity even when the crippling effects of the disease were overtaking him.

So what does one do when he finds out he has little time to live? But then again, none of us really knows how many days we have left on this earth. Each day is a gift, and that is how I knew I would view every day that I spent on the Appalachian Trail. I would be grateful for my brother's life and our relationship. As I hiked I would remember the few days we shared in his bass boat when he was kind enough to take a non-fisherman out to enjoy what he enjoyed most. I might even occasionally think back on much earlier days when two boys of 12 and 6 walked through the woods with their grandfather. Two boys who would stop by a spring for a drink or run to a nearby tree with limbs low enough to climb. To some, I knew I would just be one of those old men on the trail; to others I would represent hope for future endeavors, when perhaps they too were old. This hike really wouldn't be about one thing in particular. It would be about a lot of things. Most of all, it would be one man doing something for two, which the one believed the other would have appreciated. After all, we are all mere transients on this planet. Our time is brief, but what time we have we must utilize fully.

So I decided to go for a walk on the Appalachian Trail. Yes, I decided to hike. I knew as I hiked that I would be grateful for having had a strong, courageous, kind, and loving brother to share my life with while he was alive. I also realized that spending time in the woods would keep us connected even after he was gone because my brother Don loved the woods.

To my knowledge Don never went on a backpacking trip. What he did do was hunt. In the pre-dawn hours of many an October morning, my brother could be found sitting in a tree stand awaiting the arrival of what he hoped would be an antlered buck. Hunting was something Don learned from an early age from our father. Don had an eight pointer and a ten pointer mounted on a wall in a room of his home. Other smaller racks were also displayed. For Don, however, hunting was not just about amassing trophies for the wall; it was one of his visceral connections to nature. Many times the kill provided food for the less fortunate. For my brother, it afforded a spiritual relationship as well, since Don was also a man of faith.

My brother Don also loved to fish. Don hunted mainly in the fall and winter; however, he fished year round. And in addition to those mounted racks, four largemouth bass also adorned the walls of his study. Don was more of a tournament fisherman than he was one to collect trophies. He practiced the catch and release philosophy both when fishing with friends as well as when fishing for competition. He cherished the days he could take out his bass boat on an early spring Saturday morning to cast the day away with a good fishing buddy. Fishing was special for Don, especially when he shared the sport with his long time best friend, Steve, or his regular tournament partner, Mike. It was even more special when he fished with Lisa, his wife, or Brent, their son.

Whether in the woods or on a lake, Don embraced all that nature had to offer. He connected with the streams, the trees, the fallen leaves that silently crumbled beneath his boots as he walked. He took pleasure in and celebrated the true fecundity that surrounded him with every opportunity that he had to spend in nature. And Don always appreciated those opportunities. He felt blessed to be able to have and develop this relationship with nature as he fished and hunted.

Nature has something to offer all of us. It provides lakes and rivers to lull the day away in peaceful bliss. It provides forests and woods for hunting or walking or hiking. It provides a sanctuary from the confines of rooms and buildings of this more mundane world. Nature offers a place of refuge for the fisherman, the hunter, and the hiker alike. It provides solace and comfort when the everyday tasks of life overwhelm. I think most of us want to connect in some way with nature. We want to escape from the obligations, the bustle of the world of clocks and schedules. We long to, like Emerson and Thoreau and Whitman, search for tranquility and feel that as we approach the end of this life that we have truly lived.

I knew that when I arrived on Springer in March that I would carry my brother Don's memory with me every step of my hike. On beautiful sunny mornings I expected to greet him just up around the next bend in the trail or just over the next crest of a peak. I figured that I would see him by the lakes I passed. On rainy, cold miserable mornings, he would remind me of this opportunity I have to walk to Maine, this privilege of enjoying all that nature has to offer every day of the journey......and with his encouragement I would continue. I knew that whenever I saw a deer, whenever I crossed over a stream, and yes, if I encountered a hunter in the forests, or saw a fisherman, rod in hand, strolling toward a lake, I would remember Don, my brother, and I would be grateful.

When I began my thru-hike of the Appalachian Trail, I didn't know what would await. Each day would be the same; each day would be different. But most importantly, every day would be a day that I would remember my brother Don and a day I would be thankful for all that we shared on this earth together.

# 2

# A Beginning

In the fall of 2000, a fellow teaching buddy, Alton, decided that he and some of his friends should begin taking some "adventure trips." Since most of us were about to turn 50 or just had, Alton thought that a backpacking trip in the late spring of 2001 was just what we needed. For this first trip he chose as our destination some place up in New England called the White Mountains. I had heard of the Rockies, the Smokies, the Adirondacks, and even the Green Mountains of Vermont, but quite honestly, I didn't know much about the Whites.

For the next several months Alton meticulously outlined details for our excursion. After weeks of reading a variety of informative "what to and how to" literature, he provided each member of the backpacking group with folders containing an itinerary, maps, a list of supplies needed, and a discourse on the much dreaded black fly of New Hampshire. Doc, Reg, Alton and I (the already or about to be 50-year-olds) and Fitts and Lindsey (30 something's) eagerly awaited the end of the school year and our trek up to the northeast.

The flight from Atlanta to Boston and the subsequent van journey to Lincoln, NH proved uneventful. The next morning we set out near Franconia Notch with great enthusiasm. Our first day goal was about a 12 mile hike that would culminate at the Guyout campsite off the A.T. We made it to our destination, but along the way we learned much about backpacking like.....it's not a good idea to bungee gear to your pack, don't plan to camp at a site .7 miles off the trail, taking turns carrying the two 4-man tents does not diminish the weight of the tents, check to find out if fires are allowed before purchasing steaks to pack in to cook over campfires, and lastly, visit a physician before beginning the hike if you're 50, slightly overweight, and have never hiked in the Whites.

Alton and I, who were the only two of the group really in shape, were the first to arrive at the campsite. We were greeted by a young female caretaker who gazed on our appearances with what might have been considered utter amazement that we were still standing. I remember declaring to this young lady that this was our first backpacking trip and that it was about to be the first night I had ever spent in a tent. And I unabashedly added, "And I just turned 50 two weeks ago." She was not impressed. When she asked, "Why did you choose the Whites?" neither of us could think of a good reason.

About two hours later, shortly after dark, the rest of the gang arrived, and they were a pitiful looking bunch. The caretaker graciously offered to boil us some water for our dehydrated meals after telling us that campfires were not permitted. After our meals, we settled in to our tents. Alton, Fitts, and I shared one; Doc, Reg and Lindsey the other. I slept very poorly that "first night in a tent." If I had brought a sleeping bag, it might have been better.

The next morning six very sore hikers (yes, we were hikers now) awoke to near freezing temperatures. To warm up we began that .7 mile trek from the Guyout campsite back to the trail that would take us southbound on the Bondcliff Trail up to South Twin and then down to Galehead Hut. Before reaching the A.T., however, Reg declared that he couldn't make it and actually asked the caretaker if he could be airlifted out. When she informed him that the only type of rescue that was available was for him to be carried out, he opted to accept her suggestion that she carry his 60 pound pack to Galehead for him. Reg smiled broadly sitting atop a rock on South Twin, packless, as the rest of the group arrived. As we continued down what some have called one of the toughest miles on the A.T. from South Twin to Galehead, I prayed feverishly that I wouldn't break a leg and made one of those deals with God that if "He would just get me out of these mountains safely..."

After a night at the 13 Falls campsite, on a trail off the A.T., we finally made it back to Lincoln. For days, every time I closed my eyes I saw giant rocks. This was one adventure that I would never attempt again. I was a runner, not a hiker. I didn't even like camping or sleeping in a tent. This would definitely be my last backpacking trip. But alas, it wasn't.

When you do something poorly the first time, you sometimes want to try it again. As the next school year began I couldn't help but recall how we had been planning our hike in the White Mountains this time last year. Even though the memories of the Whites were still fresh in my mind, I felt this desire, almost need, to get back out there. A former student and athlete, whom I had coached in cross-country, had thru-hiked in 2000. After listening to Cam (trail name, Jeremiah Johnson) talk about the trail to one of my classes, I knew that I had to give the A.T. another try. He spoke of covering the entire 41 mile stretch of Maryland in one day as some sort of challenge. As a distance runner, this seemed like something I could do. After all, I had read that Maryland was the easiest (not a term that really ever applies to the A.T.) state.

So without hesitation I approached my buddies about hiking Maryland as soon as the '01-'02 school year concluded. This time it was I, not Alton, who did most of the planning. For the entire fall I spent time convincing the others that we needed to give hiking one more try. So in late May of 2002, five of us (Fitts' truck broke down before we left GA) set out in two SUV's for Harper's Ferry, WV. I had even arranged for a stay in a real A.T. hostel the night before we were to begin our southbound trek from Pen Mar Park at the PA/Maryland border.

Like the previous year in the Whites, that first day was an ordeal despite the "easier" terrain. After a night at a shelter some 9 miles in, Doc, Reg, and Lindsey decided that hiking definitely was not for them. They hitched a ride back to the vehicle and opted for a tour of Gettysburg. Alton and I trudged on, determined to complete the entire 41 miles, even though we had already decided that this was a three day-hike, not a one or two day one. Our buddies, before deserting us, did offer to carry some of our gear to the Dahlgren campsite, where we planned to set up our tent (yep, still the 4-man one) the second night. We didn't know what slack-packing meant at that time; however, over the years, "slackpacking" has become one my favorite hiking terms.

Day three took us into Harper's Ferry and to the end of that year's hiking adventure. With Maryland complete, Alton and I continued the section-hiking, knocking off a state here and a state there. Fitts even joined us for the section from Springer to Neels Gap during spring break, 2003. None of the sections, however, took longer than two weeks. Over the next twelve years since that first taste of the A.T., I would section-hike over 1000 miles of the trail and now actually own a sleeping bag. So, twelve years later, and with a brother who was dying of ALS, I decided it was time to attempt a thru-hike of the Appalachian Trail.

My primary goal was obviously to reach Katahdin, but along the way I had some other goals I hoped to achieve as well. One of those goals was to write daily, detailing as accurately as possible what it's like out on the trail. Knowing that my brother would be dead before I began, another goal was to share his life with those I met along the way. Deep within my soul, I was just looking for an adventure, and I figured the A.T. just might provide one for me.

# 3

# The Plan Continues

So here I was, planning for not just a couple of weeks, but instead, for maybe up to half a year. Even with the pledge I made to my brother as motivation, the task appeared daunting as I worked on my preparations throughout the winter.

As I planned and prepared for my attempt at a 2013 thru-hike of the Appalachian Trail, I thought often of Alfred, Lord Tennyson's poem, "Ulysses." After having been away from his wife and son for twenty years, the now graybeard Ulysses has finally returned home. Having experienced multiple adventures during those two decades, Ulysses quickly grows restless. He remembers fighting with his comrades on the hills of Troy as well as events that occurred during the return voyage. And as he remembers, he longs for new adventure. Despite being reunited with a faithful wife, Penelope, he realizes that his life can never again be confined to his home of Ithaca. After all, neither his now grown son, Telemachus, nor the citizens of the city he once ruled, really knows him.

Therefore, he urges his fellow mariners to join him on another great adventure. When Ulysses proclaims that it is "not too late to seek a newer world," he is charging all with the responsibility, the duty to continue on the quest to become the persons we were intended to be. He reminds us not to "rust unburnished, but to shine in use." He challenges us "to strive, to seek, to find, and not to yield."

I believe that for all of those "over 60" would-be thru-hikers of the Appalachian Trail that Tennyson's words ring true. Like Ulysses, we are perhaps seeking a "newer world," a world for some free of obligations and stress; for others a world free of loneliness or boredom. The "retired" hiker wants to replace the perhaps daily feeling of "wondering what he is going to do" with wonderment. He wants to breathe deeply from the mountain air; he wants purpose again in his life. And like Ulysses, the older thru-hiker is seeking. He still seeks meaning in a life that may have only a decade or two remaining.

The youthful hiker, however, may be attempting to make some sense of a post college existence. He may be escaping from the rigors of a classroom to a carefree, solitary jaunt through the woods prior to settling into the routines of responsibility. And he hopes that what he learns on this pre full-time employment peregrination will sustain him in the years to come. He may flaunt his youth as he bounces over tough terrain, but simultaneously he will appreciate the less agile footfalls of the aging hiker. And as the miles and days go by, each will view the other with respect and admiration as they walk together toward Katahdin.

The Appalachian Trail can toughen you or break you. It can offer you solace and contentment; it can bring you to your knees with frustration and pain. Ulysses knew frustration as he tried to navigate his way back home, but he also knew solace as he found moments to rest under the stars. Like so many aspects of life, we too are engaged in an odyssey of sorts. We expect to confront obstacles that may force us to take a detour on the road of life. We also hope for a path that will provide us perspective and direction. Whatever the reason for hiking, all are pilgrims together on the Appalachian Trail.

So as I planned I figured that having already hiked over 1000 miles of the Appalachian Trail was a definite advantage for someone planning a thru-hike. Then again, it seemed that having already hiked over 1000 miles of the Appalachian Trail could prove to be a disadvantage for someone planning a thru-hike. Knowing just what awaits around the next bend or up over the next ridge may bring a smile to one's face and a pleasant memory to the mind. Knowing just what awaits around the next bend or up over the next ridge may evoke an emptiness in one's stomach, a soreness in some body part, a reminder of the agony felt at this same place, at another time...on another hike.

But isn't that what life is like. Just when everything is moving along comfortably, we hit a bump in the road. In our memories we constantly revisit the past, sometimes wanting to repeat those wonderful events from long ago. More often than not we forget, or block out the memory of, the less than desirable occurrences that may have come before, or after, or even paralleled the good times. Still, we reminisce, we long for; we might even yearn for bygone days when we were stronger, thinner, more flexible, faster....youth.

And so it goes on the Appalachian Trail. You awaken one morning early in the hike to sunshine. Despite the fatigue in your muscles and the blister on your heel, you break camp with enthusiasm, eagerly anticipating the climb up the next mountain. The walk goes smoothly along the pine straw covered path. Birds chirp; the sunlight filters through the budding hardwoods; the crisp early spring morning is invigorating. You are hiking the A.T. Then the climb begins. The sun gets higher and warmer. Sweat beads up on your forehead. You remember the blister and the soreness in your shoulders returns. You pause and look up to what seems an insurmountable task, reaching the summit of yet another mountain. You realize that you're still in Georgia. There are 13 more states to follow and many mountains to crest. Still you walk. You reach the top; you admire the view; you try to think of a better word than "breathtaking" to describe what you see. You rest, and then you move on until the end of another day, a good day, on the Appalachian Trail.

# 4

# Hitting the Trail in Georgia

My adventure officially began on a beautiful sunny early spring day. A former teaching buddy, Scotty Brooks, took a day off to drive my wife Linda and me up to North Georgia. Lisa, Don's widow, drove herself up and met us in Dahlonega. After a trip to Amicolola Falls State Park, where I signed in as official A.T. thru-hiker number 590, we spent the duration of the afternoon walking around the tourist town, winding up at the Back Porch Oyster House for an evening meal. On the square several vendors were setting up tents in preparation for an Appalachian Trail Fest. I received a favorable weather forecast from a young man who was preparing an exhibit. After I informed the fellow that I was beginning a thru-hike the following day, he stated that he had begun his thru-hike four years ago on March 25. I felt that meeting the A.T. 2000 miler just might be a good omen. He wished me well as I walked on to catch up with Linda and Scotty who had headed into a chocolate shop.

Overall, the day went well. On the day before leaving my wife and the normalcy of life, I felt good about things in general. A touch of anxiety existed; however, I was packed, well rested, well fed, and quite frankly, ready to begin walking north. Several times throughout the afternoon I thought that I'd really rather have gone ahead and started. Then I reminded myself that I needed to be patient. There was going to be plenty of time for hiking over the next few weeks. On my final night before beginning my northward journey, it was important to enjoy special time with family and a good friend.

I thought about Don many times today. Brent called to wish me well. He loved his dad dearly, just as Don loved him. Many people sent text messages; others commented on Facebook; some called. I appreciated all those who reached out to offer support and prayers. I knew I would need them every day as I made my way north. So as the time grew late I knew that I needed to sleep. Morning awaited as did the 2,186 miles of the Appalachian Trail.

## March 23, Springer Mountain to Hawk Mountain Shelter

When the next day did arrive, a feeling of excitement had replaced the anxious one. The journey began with a drive up a series of mountain roads with the destination of Big Stamp Gap, one mile north of Springer Mountain. The trip up the sometimes unmarked forest roads proved to be more of a challenge than much of the white-blazed trail I would confront over the next five months. After Scotty made a wrong turn somewhere along the way, we wound up at Nimblewell Gap, at around the 6 mile mark of the approach trail. It occurred to me that I might be the only thru-hiker ever to begin a hike at Nimblewell Gap. It didn't really matter. I just wanted to get started.

A light drizzle had begun as Linda, Lisa, Scotty and I emerged from the mud-covered black truck. Lisa had prepared two signs for my sendoff. She held one declaring, "We love Don's Brother." Linda clutched the other that stated, "Maine or Bust, August 28, 2013." So there I stood, south of Springer, about to walk away from my wife for the longest period of time that we would be separated in the thirty-seven years of our marriage. It was a bittersweet moment. On a bleak, windy, misty morning, I headed north. Linda walked a few feet up the trail behind me, still clinging to her sign. I turned once to wave and suddenly felt about as alone as I could ever remember. Then I remembered that Don was with me and a smile replaced the quivering lips. I was OK. The adventure had begun.

When I reached the summit of Springer Mountain I spent some reflective time by the plaque. I signed the trail log and took a couple of photos. Just as I was about to depart three hikers approached from the north.

One took my picture by the plaque. I was grateful, but said little to the trio who had hiked up from Big Stamp Gap. I was ready to walk that first mile of the 2,186 that awaited.

Overall, the terrain of the hike that first day was fairly easy, at least by A.T. standards. I thought of Don often. I also met several other hikers along the trail including a family of four from Asheville, two section-hikers from Florida, and a few thru-hikers. Reaching Hawk Mountain Shelter, I decided to pass up the last spot inside and to tent instead. About 25 other hikers milled around the site. Some had already settled into their sleeping bags despite the early hour. Others were in various stages of setting up tents. I found a spot next to a couple of retired army officers who kept me laughing throughout the evening with a variety of stories from their pasts and some interesting planning strategies for the next few days. When their tent became silent and heavier rain began to fall, I gazed at the ceiling of my tent, feeling content and peaceful. I would feel a little different when morning arrived.

## March 24, Hawk Mountain Shelter to Woody Gap

"It was a dark and stormy night." As we had negotiated the forest roads in our search for the start of the A.T. yesterday, I had kidded with Linda, Lisa, and Scotty that at some time during the hike I wanted to begin a post with that famous opening line. I just didn't know it would come so soon. Folks, it deluged my first night on the A.T. As my granddaddy, Harry Andrews would have said, "It came a gullywasher." The thunderstorms commenced around midnight and didn't subside until dawn. They were relentless. Lightning lit up the sky like a bomb exploding. I envisioned that line of dark red on the weather radar. Needless to say, I slept little.

At first light I began to pack up. Water had crept beneath my tent despite my meticulous selection of what I had thought was the ideal camping spot. So after packing a damp sleeping bag, wet clothes, and a partially soaked sleeping pad, I ate breakfast. Then I added a few extra pounds to my pack with a drenched tent.

The hike today was a lot more strenuous than yesterday. Due to the rain, there was a considerable amount of standing water on the trail. The streams were rushing as well, which meant that crossings were also a bit challenging. At one point there was no other choice but to step directly in the water. I thought about changing socks but decided to forgo the stop. In addition, mud was everywhere. I slipped several times; however, fortunately, I was able to stay vertical.

Along the way today I hiked briefly with two firefighters from Winston Salem and also stopped to chat with a southbound section-hiker, Pilot, from the Boston area. I stopped briefly to eat and rest at Gooch Mountain shelter where I shared some info with a young couple from Indiana. After a tiring final 5.3 miles I arrived at Woody Gap in a dense fog. I had only hiked two days and I was beat. It didn't take me long to realize that I would have to come up with a better nutrition plan if I was going to make it to Maine.

Standing on the south side of the highway, I could barely see the picnic tables in the parking lot across the road. A car had just stopped to let out another hiker. Wanting to get to the Hiker Hostel up the road, I approached the couple to ask for a ride. Hitching was something that I had grown accustomed to on my section-hikes, so I boldly inquired if the two were going my way. When the young lady said that she and her husband would be glad to drive me to the hostel, I felt a sense of accomplishment. I also remembered a mother's warning and the first ride I had ever hitched on the A.T. That was nine years earlier near Wingdale, NY.

As a child I remembered hearing stories of my Uncle Dexter who was purported to have hitchhiked all the way from California to his home in south Alabama. A career navy man, with a sailor vocabulary in tow, he would also regularly hitch from his base in Jacksonville, Florida back to his Alabama home. So from an early age I had a fascination with hitchhiking even though I was regularly warned as I reached the driver's license age that I was not to ever pick up a hitchhiker, nor was I to ever engage in the sinister practice myself. On a morning in late May, 2004 I was about to go against my parents' warnings and become an Appalachian Trail hitchhiker.

Alton and I had decided that for our first really long section-hike we would cover the states of Connecticut and Massachusetts. After flying from Atlanta to New York, and taking a taxi to Grand Central, we boarded the Metro North Railroad for Wingdale, NY. Wingdale, the closest town to the New York/Connecticut border, was still over 3 miles from the trail. We knew this because for this hike we had finally purchased A.T. Data books. What we failed to consider was the distance from the Metro North train stop to the center of Wingdale.

So as we stood on the platform, wondering if there were taxis in Wingdale, a young lady pulled up in a rusty red, slightly damaged compact car. Approaching the car reluctantly, we asked if she would be willing to drive us to the Wingdale post office. We explained that we were hikers and planned to hike all the way to Vermont. Looking as if she really doubted what we were telling her, she asked as she opened the passenger door from inside the car, "You're not going to kill me, are you?" We assured her that neither of us had ever entertained the idea of murdering someone. We simply wanted to pick up some supplies in town and head for the trail.

Fortunately the distance was not too far, because within about 10 seconds of entering her automobile, we both realized that she was more likely to die from the cigarette smoke within her vehicle than by the hands of a would-be murderous hiker. She did make a point to mention that after dropping us off, she had to pick up her boyfriend after he got off work. Still we were grateful for the lift and thanked her appreciatively when she dropped us in Wingdale. Now, nine years later I was still hitchin'. Only this time it was as an Appalachian Trail thru-hiker.

When I arrived at the hostel I was greeted by the owners, Josh and Leigh, who had thru-hiked in 2000. In my nutritionally depleted state, I was extremely grateful that Josh offered to take me in to Dahlonega to pick up a meal. He also offered some caloric advice regarding breakfast, the hikers' most important meal of the day. After returning to the hostel and devouring about 1500 calories, I was able to talk to some of the other hikers about Don. All listened with compassion as I told them about my reasons for giving this thru-hike a chance. It would be the first of many times that I would share my brother's story with others. It would always be special when I spoke of how much Don loved the woods.

## March 25, Woody Gap to Neels Gap

The next morning at 7:30 Josh and Leigh served a breakfast of pancakes, eggs, oatmeal, and grits before shuttling all the hikers back to the trail. I sat by Alex, a young man from England, and enjoyed watching him try grits for the first time. After finishing off a bowl, he declared that he liked them. Also at the table were the group of four from Maine, a mom and her two young adult daughters from Ohio, an older fellow from South Africa, and a young lady from Nova Scotia.

Fortunately I was the first in the van to be dropped off. When I began my hike at Woody Gap at about 9:00 the temperature hovered around 28 degrees with flurries just beginning. I hiked in snow and wind all day. Walking through a dusting of snow made for an enjoyable day. I'll take snow over mud any time. Eventually the ground froze as the snow increased. I saw no other hikers for the first few miles, so I just enjoyed the peacefulness.

Climbing Big Cedar Mountain at the beginning of today's hike posed somewhat of a challenge, but since it was early in the day and I had had a hearty breakfast, I made it to the summit without too much difficulty. By the time I started the ascent of Blood Mountain, the wind was howling and the trail had become an icy path. About half way up I caught up with Kristen, who was going to Davenport Gap. We hiked together over the icy rocks to the summit and Blood Mountain shelter, a stone shelter that was off limits to overnight stays due to bear activity. Two young lads were holed up inside without water and carrying less than appropriate gear. I was a little concerned for the two. I felt better when a family out for a day-hike from Neels Gap arrived with extra water and food.

After a short break and adding a layer of clothing, I started the hike down Blood, arguably the toughest mile on the Georgia A.T. The icy rockfaces required a slow, meticulous descent. Still I made good time and managed to complete another day on the trail without a fall.

By mid-afternoon I walked into Walasi-Yi at Mountain Crossings to greet George, Pirate, and some of the other former thru-hikers who work there. George took my picture for their Facebook page and arranged for sleeping accommodations. Since all the bunks were taken at the hostel, I shared a cabin with three young kids, Walmart, Boomerang, and Overalls. I'm already referring to any hikers in their 20's as the "young kids." Not only were the three respectful of the "old man," but they also offered me the upstairs bed. Seeing that I am bordering on being one of the "elderly," I accepted their kindness. Nick, the last to arrive, is hiking in overalls, so when he told me he didn't have a trail name, I dubbed him Overalls. He liked it. Overalls is also hiking with a loaf of bread hanging off his pack.

Today was another good day on the trail. For much of the day I was given the privilege of experiencing the beauty of my snowy surroundings immersed in solitude. I felt my brother Don's presence with me in the powdery woods. It was peaceful and serene. My brother would have enjoyed today as much as I did.

## March 26, Neels Gap to Hogpen Gap

At first daylight I peered out the window on a bleak, cold, windy day. Walmart had been shuffling around downstairs in the dark for some time, trying to get his pack ready. He needed an early departure in order to try and catch a group with whom he had previously been hiking. When I heard him whispering with Overalls, I told them to turn on some lights since I was already awake. A short while later I wished Walmart well as he stepped out into the frigid day.

Boomerang awoke, gathered her gear, and left next. Then Overalls went to meet the group he had been hiking with to determine their plans for the day. At this point I still had about an hour before I needed to start today's hike since I had arranged for Doug of Alpine Taxi to pick me up at Hogpen Gap at 1:00 for a shuttle into Helen. So with the time I had left, I laid my still wet tent out in the sauna-like bathroom to see if I could get it dry. Much to my amazement, it was almost completely dry within an hour.

After packing up myself, I walked up to Walasi-Yi to get some milk before hitting the trail. The outfitters buzzed with at least a score of thru-hikers. Some mingled around within the building while others milled around outside in the flurries. Daypack, from my first night on the trail, was there as was Jacko who had come over to hike the trail from Australia. He recognized me from trail journals and offered to share some doughnuts while we chatted. I only ate two of the Krispy Kremes as somewhat of a dessert to the leftover pizza I had finished a few minutes earlier. I drank half of the pint of milk before securing the remainder of the bottle in my jacket pocket for "on up the trail." In this cold weather milk will stay fresh all day.

When I discovered it was almost 10:00, I quickly said goodbye to George, thanking her for her help. George and her dog Gracie thru-hiked the trail a few years back. She, along with all of those who work at Mountain Crossings, offers an invaluable service to the hikers. I think most, like me, are grateful. As I walked through the arch of Walasi-Yi toward the woods, a blustery wind hit my face. I put the hood of my fleece securely over my head and part of my face before starting the climb upwards. I quickly passed three very slowly moving hikers who carried heavy packs. The frozen snow over the mud actually made for good traction early in the day.

Over the 6.9 miles from Neels Gap to Hogpen Gap, I passed several hikers. I spoke with a German gentleman, Red Specs, and Dundee, a hiker from Oregon. I had another opportunity to talk about Don with Mark who had also lost his brother last year. He was doing a section-hike with his dog Hero, to determine if she is trail worthy. By the way the pooch scampered down the frozen rockfaces, I'd say she is. A little after 11:00 I reached the top of Cowrock Mountain where I finally was treated to some beautiful views. The day continued cold and windy. According to Dundee's thermometer it was 23 degrees as we headed down Cowrock.

The ice on the rocks made for difficult hiking much of the day. During the descent, I slipped on an icy rock and fell. I quickly recovered, however, but decided to wait there to warn Boomerang who was just a little behind me. She handled the area well and hiked on with me until we reached the blue-blazed trail down to Whitley Gap Shelter, where she planned to stay the night. The climb over the mountain just before Hogpen Gap was tough; however, I managed to arrive just before Doug drove up in his SUV. He said that yesterday he had shuttled many who needed to get off of the mountain and into the towns due to the dangerously low temps.

The little Alpine themed town of Helen overflowed with hikers. After checking in at the Best Western, I enjoyed a hearty meal at Wendy's and then returned to the motel. Much of the evening I relaxed in front of a blazing hearth in the company of others who still excitedly talked of a journey that had just begun. I was less than 40 miles from Springer, but my mood remained positive. As the evening waned I thought of those I had already met in such a short while.

One of the nicest aspects about hiking the Appalachian Trail centers around the fellow sojourners you meet along the way. Overalls, who hails from Tulsa, Oklahoma, spent some time working on an oil rig. He came to the trail for his own reasons, determined to reach Katahdin. The time it takes to get there is irrelevant for Overalls, just as it is for many hikers. After beginning his trek lugging a 70 pound pack, he recently decided to lighten his load. One of the items Overalls sent home was his fishing pole. That would definitely have made Don laugh. I think my brother would have really liked Overalls. Like Overalls, Don loved to fish. And also like Overalls, Don loved the woods.

## March 27, Hogpen Gap to Unicoi Gap

The following morning the sun shone brightly. It was still cold out-side, but at least it looked like it was going to be a beautiful day. As I gazed through the sheers from a table in the lobby of the Best Western, a small fire burned in the nearby fireplace. I began my day with a huge breakfast of eggs, sausage, toast, jam, and coffee. Then I patiently waited, enjoying the fire.

Carol Powell, the owner of the motel, graciously shuttled ten hikers back to the trail beginning at 10:00. One other hiker, Cole, from Texas, also was returning to the trail at Hogpen Gap, so we began the day together. Cole attended three semesters at Texas Tech before deciding to take some time off to hike. When we hit the trail just after 11:00, I quickly pulled away, knowing that I'd see Cole again "somewhere up the trail."

The trail today consisted of several ridgelines with views to the east and west. I stopped often to take pictures and just enjoy the vistas. Snow and ice remained in some areas while others had converted back to mud. The abundant level sections afforded some faster miles. I've come to call this my cruise mode. On the climbs I "work hard" much like I did when hill repeats and track intervals were a part of my preparation for getting ready to run a road race a couple of times a month. On the descents I "go slowly" since it's these sections that present the greatest possibility of falling. Then when I hit those level places, I cruise.

Early in today's hike I made really good time. I reached Low Gap shelter at the 4.6 mile mark by 12:45. Even though the path down to the shelter was a quagmire, I wanted to sit at the picnic table and enjoy my lunch. I had decided to "eat fresh" today, having bought a footlong Subway Melt this morning before leaving Helen. I declined "making it a meal," so only had water to drink. When I reached the shelter, a hiker I had talked to on the trail yesterday, Mark, from Chicago, was there with his Jack Russell terrier, Hero. As we chatted Cole walked up.

Shortly after leaving the shelter I met two older hikers hiking SOBO (southbound). Leap and Faith were getting off the trail because one of them has a knee issue. I don't remember who was Leap and who was Faith, but it was the lady who was injured. I wished them well after telling them about my website. Just before reaching the Blue Mountain shelter, I encountered three hikers taking a break. Early yesterday I had passed the trio of Mei Mei, Rosy, and Highlighter, but had not stopped to talk. Today I did. Recognizing that they were tired and cold after spending consecutive nights in the frigid woods, I suggested that they consider a town night. They were mulling over my recommendation as I hiked onward. After separating myself a good distance from the group, I took a brief break to finish off the other half of my sub.

On the downward approach to Unicoi Gap, numerous rocks of varying sizes required a more concentrated descent. Although I slipped a few times, I managed to cover the 14.3 miles today without a fall. Hoping for a hitch at Unicoi Gap, I noticed a white pick-up in the parking lot as the road came within view. Robert, vacationing in Helen with his 12-year-old daughter Victoria, was more than happy to offer a ride. He smiled when I told him he was now an official Appalachian Trail Angel. Robert calls Cape Coral, FL home, but says he loves the mountains. It was a real pleasure riding back into Helen with the two.

After showering I walked down the road to have supper at Wendy's. Just as I was entering, I spotted Mei Mei, Rosy, and Highlighter in line. They had taken my suggestion. They said yes with smiles when I asked if we could dine together. They seemed much happier than they had been a few hours earlier, clean and enjoying town food, ready again to continue their quest of thru-hiking the A.T. I felt their enthusiasm.

Today's hike rewarded me with many special moments. Of them all, however, I think the most special was getting to see Hero again. Don loved dogs. Even though he and Lisa had not owned a dog recently, two neighborhood dogs had taken up dual residency at their home. Don fed, bathed, and provided comfortable pillows for Buster and Chatzee. Don would have really loved Hero. As I hike each day, I continue to be reminded of my brother's kindness. He was a compassionate man in many respects. I could imagine him bending down to pet Hero before walking on up the trail through a place he always felt at home, the woods.

## March 28, Unicoi Gap to Addis Gap

At the end of my sixth day on the trail I found myself back in the woods. Before 7:00 I was already in my tent. It was cold, but not as cold as the past few nights. I wore tights with shorts over them, a short sleeve T-shirt, a long sleeve T-shirt, and a fleece, plus two pairs of socks and a stocking cap. The only time I removed my gloves was to type. Still, I expected to stay warm in my 10 degree down bag.

The day had begun with a shuttle back to Unicoi Gap with Carol. Red Specs was the only other hiker for the ride up. When we arrived at the parking lot, a tent was set up and the smell of grilled burgers filled the morning air. A group from McConnell Baptist Church provides trail magic as a service to the A.T. hikers every year. Jeannette Cole listened intently as I explained to her the purpose of my hike. Others were equally compassionate. Having only finished breakfast a short while earlier, I took a burger for the trail. Another nice lady insisted that I take a brownie as well.

The hike out of Unicoi Gap commenced with a climb up Rocky Mountain of about a mile. Once on the ridge, spectacular views abounded on this sunny, yet still cold, day. Occasional snow and ice patches spotted the perimeter of the trail. I started the hike solo; however, about half way up the mountain Red Specs caught me. Hiking much stronger than I remember from our first meeting, he strode along with me for much of the morning.

At the Cheese Factory site (a campsite where a cheese factory had at one time stood), we stopped for a break. As I sat with my back against a tree, eating my trail magic burger, two hikers stopped as they passed. To my surprise, it was Circuit Rider and Sherlock. I had met them on my section-hike of the Shenandoahs in 2006. That summer they were helping Queen Diva run the Bear's Den Hostel. The two have thru-hiked multiple times and were out for another walk to Maine. They provide Christian ministry to all hikers who will accept it. Circuit Rider equates himself in a manner to John Wesley and the days of the circuit preachers. Sherlock asked to pray with me. So there in the middle of the Appalachian Trail, my family, my hike, Don's life, and I were lifted up in prayer. It was a special moment.

Throughout the remainder of the afternoon I continued to be blessed with gorgeous weather and spectacular views, often in more than one direction. As the day passed, I decided to camp for the night and wait until tomorrow to get to Hiawassee. Some other hikers had mentioned Addis Gap as a desirable site. So when I reached the turn which led to the camping area, I headed down the gravelly road despite the half-mile walk to the tent site. When I arrived, several other hikers that I had previously met were setting up their tents. The Aussies, Jacko, and his son, the Invisible Man, were there as were Wilson and Army Ant. I also was introduced to Mother Teresa and Hikerboy. Hikerboy, who is somewhat of a legend on white-blaze.net, resides on Long Island. After meeting Jacko on Whiteblaze, he decided to quit his job and drive the two Australians from JFK to Georgia. He's hiking part of the trail with them. After we all had supper, it was good to exchange hiking stories around the hiker TV (a campfire on the trail).

I turned in first, but after journaling for a while I left my warm sleeping bag to stand by the fire. Most had already gone to bed by then. It was peaceful listening to the rushing stream cascading over the rocks in the distance. As darkness enveloped the campsite, I watched the dying embers of the fire, while standing next to Mother Teresa.

## March 29, Addis Gap to Hiawassee

It proved to be a restless night. I slept intermittently, awaking about every half-hour until around 4:00. Then I actually dozed without waking until almost 7:30. When I heard WILSON (he prefers his trail name be stated emphatically) and Army Ant retrieving our food bags from the tree where they had hung them last night, I began packing up inside the tent. Within half an hour I was ready to hike.

First, I joined the others around the fire ring for breakfast. They all cooked; I had cheese crackers and a few sips of coke I had bought before leaving Helen yesterday. I followed that with a Baby Ruth. The unofficial candy bar of the A.T. is Snickers; however, I've decided to eat the bar which brings back memories of Lou Gehrig's teammate and baseball. Plus Don and our mother always enjoyed a Baby Ruth.

After filling up my water bottle and treating it with Aqua Mira, I began the half-mile walk back up to the trail. I bid the others farewell, saying as I always do," I hope I'll see you somewhere up the trail." The hike began with another substantial climb which took a lot of stamina. I keep saying that I've got to do a better job with nutrition. I hike very strongly after a large town breakfast but tend to drag in the morning when starting the day with trail food.

Later in the morning I once again encountered trail maintainer Rock-kicker. He advised me to go ahead and call the Blueberry Patch Hostel from the trail since there is rarely reception from Dick's Creek Gap. I had previously spoken to Gary, a former thru-hiker who, along with his wife, Lennie, offers bunks for hikers as a Christian ministry on a donations only basis. When I arrived at the gap there were several hikers waiting for shuttles or taking a break before heading back up the trail. Among them were Walmart and Kristen, a young lady from Montana whom I hiked with up Blood Mountain. Walmart was dressed in all camo, which Don would have liked. Gary drove up soon after, and Kristen also rode with us to the hostel. After a shower and having my laundry done, Gary drove some others and me into Hiawassee. The others returned with him after a brief time in town. I decided to stay in town for a while.

I made my way to Daniel's Steakhouse where I decided to partake of the AYCE (all you can eat) buffet, a favorite of hikers. After my first plate of food I began my writing for the day. Since the restaurant was almost empty in the middle of the afternoon, I lingered for over three hours. With a hospitable waitress who filled my glass with sweet tea each time it measured half-full, I couldn't have been more comfortable. When the evening supper crowd began arriving I deemed it time to return to the hostel.

I walked to the edge of town, confident that I would be able to hitch a ride. That was not to be the case. Under a threatening sky I finally gave up and called Gary. A light rain had begun to fall by the time he pulled into the fast food parking lot to drive me back to his home. On the return trip I felt a need to share some more about Don. Since I knew what a strong Christian the former thru-hiker was, I wanted to talk of Don's faith. And so I did. I don't remember everything I said. What I do remember is what a genuinely compassionate listener Gary was.

A short while later, lying in my bunk in a dark, cold room, among strangers that I already realized I might never see again after tonight, I thought more about my brother. This place, the Blueberry Patch, was the kind of home where Don would have felt comfortable. Don would have appreciated the wood burning stove; he would have petted the goats out back; he would have slept peacefully in this humble, Christian abode, among folks he barely knew if at all. He might have even thought of a Bible verse that would have fit the setting. And before allowing himself the luxury of sleep after a tiring day, Don would have prayed.

My brother Don was a man of faith. Our mother used to say that Don had first found the Lord after attending a camp meeting with our grandmother one summer. For a few consecutive nights, a then elementary school age Don accompanied our Grandmama Andrews to a tent revival, led by some missionary cousin of the family. These "meetings" were held in the woods and could be heard for "miles around" according to those who lived in the vicinity. Apparently Don was saved during one of the altar calls that summer. When he returned home, he asked our mother to buy him a Bible.

As children, Don and I would often walk together to Sunday school at a neighborhood Baptist church about a mile from our home. We departed each Sabbath wearing shiny black, leather shoes that our father had polished for us the night before. In our Bibles we carried envelopes with our offering, usually a dime. Even though I never remember praying with my brother, I'm sure we both did when we were alone.

After reaching adulthood, getting married and starting families, Don and I joined the same United Methodist Church. We also attended the same Sunday school class with our wives. When our mother became a member of our church as well, we proudly claimed a pew of our own in the sanctuary for the 11:00 worship service. Our mother would faithfully arrive early each Sunday to ensure that the third pew from the front, on the right side of the church, was not usurped by some other family.

Don didn't just attend Sunday school and church. He also served. Don and Lisa taught Sunday school classes at different times and also kept the three-year-old nursery for many years. The children loved my brother as much as Don loved them. Whether there were four little ones in the room or fourteen, Don always had an uncanny knack for keeping them interested. With three-year-olds that was no simple task, but for Don it just seemed to come naturally.

In the sanctuary, on days when Don and Lisa weren't keeping the nursery, Don would garner the attention of any youngster who sat in proximity to our pew. Before the service began, Don placated many an unruly toddler with a variety of antics, most notably with his nearly famous, invisible frog. The croaking sound that resonated from Don's clenched hands not only calmed the fidgety child, but quite often piqued the curiosity of unsuspecting adults. On other occasions, Don would draw a funny picture for the disruptive child. Whether Don displayed a seven dwarf lookalike caricature, or moved his hands to imitate a contemplative frog, he always seemed to soothe the child's discomfort and to bring some much needed relief to the somewhat embarrassed parent as well.

About once every two or three months Don would also deliver the children's sermon. In the Methodist church, children in attendance from the ages of 4 to about 10 are invited to come to the altar to hear a brief message prepared specifically for them. The children of our church loved the Sundays that Mr. Don did the children's sermon. Quite often he would relate the Bible message to the outdoors, sometimes bringing in pictures of wildlife or some other part of nature. Don loved Christ and showed the children how Jesus loved them.

After Don was diagnosed with ALS he still attended church with Lisa for as long as he could. At first he walked into the sanctuary gingerly, using a cane. Later Lisa or I wheeled him in, in a wheelchair. Even after he had lost all of his mobility in both legs and the use of his right hand, he managed to maneuver his power chair by using his quickly diminishing left hand. As he sat at the end of our pew, somewhat slumped and in pain, the children would still come by to see Mr. Don. It saddened my brother beyond description when he could no longer draw the funny pictures or produce the croaking frog which had been requested.

On one of the last Sundays that my brother attended church, he brought with him a collection of shiny, new Matchbox cars for a few of the little boys that had grown so fond of him. He let them examine the cars before each was allowed to make a selection. His gift to each of them exemplified a final act of kindness. And my brother Don was among the kindest and gentlest of Christian men.

Before his illness, Don could often be seen striding down the church's corridors, camouflaged-covered Bible in hand. During the worship service Don opened his Bible and followed along with the minister's sermon. After his illness, the same Bible laid open on his lap as he listened to the pastor deliver his message. When his hands no longer worked, Don's eyes and ears still did.

As Don's disease progressed he never lost his faith. Every evening he and Lisa would have a devotional time together. During the last few days of my brother's life, I had the privilege of sharing these special times with them. When our pastors came to visit, Don always appreciated their thoughtful compassion and the prayers they lifted up on his behalf as well as for his family. Throughout those final weeks, he reminded all who came to visit to "Read your Bible and pray."

One day a couple of months before Don's death, I said to him that I thought my faith had increased as a result of his illness. He replied, "I think all of ours has." He was right. Even though we were all losing a man that we so dearly loved, we held to our faith as we knew that he wanted us to.

Don had said to me one day shortly after his diagnosis, "I'm not afraid to die; I just worry about what the dying process will do to those I love."

Even after being told that he had little time to live, Don always thought of others above himself. Losing my brother was difficult, but as he struggled with a horrific disease, I and everyone in our family knew that Don's life was in the hands of God. And what better place can we hope that our lives will be, if we too, live like my brother Don, as a man of faith.

As I closed my eyes on what would be my last night on the trail in Georgia, I prayed. I prayed for guidance and direction, for safety and peace. I prayed for Gary and Lennie and their ministry. And I prayed a prayer of thanksgiving for my brother's life. It had been a good first week on the trail. I felt strong physically and emotionally. More importantly, I felt my brother with me. As I lay in that cold bunk I knew that I would be OK. For the first time I truly felt like a thru-hiker. I would sleep and perhaps dream. I knew that I had to get to Maine, and I knew that with Don's help, I would.

5

# North Carolina and Tennessee—the Smokies and Beyond

**March 30, Hiawassee to Deep Gap**

As I rode in the front seat of Gary's Jeep on the way back to the trail, I thought about how Don loved to be out on his bass boat on beautiful Saturday mornings like this one. A couple of years ago in late March, he very well could have been fishing in a tournament with his good friend Mike.

It had already been a special morning, sharing breakfast in Gary and Lennie's home at the Blueberry Patch hostel with other hikers around the family table. We had held hands while Gary offered up thanksgivings. Now I was about to begin another day on the trail, after pancakes with fresh blueberry syrup, sausage, potatoes, biscuits, orange juice, and coffee. I expected to hike strong.

Today I crossed the border from GA into NC. I took a moment to reflect on leaving my home state for hopefully the next five months. It would be the longest period of time I had been away since moving here as a young child. I had travelled before and often, but never for as long as it would take me to hike the entire Appalachian Trail. The magnitude of the endeavor became even more daunting as I peered at the small wooden sign nailed to the tree. I tried to overlook a brief moment of melancholia on this, the prettiest day I'd had to hike thus far.

The sun shined brightly and inspiring views appeared around every bend of the trail. Along ridge-lines it was easy to see for many miles. On one stop I noticed Blissful sitting by a tree. Like some of the other former thru-hikers, she is just out for a section-hike this year. After a brief break, I hiked up on a couple who had stopped for a rest. Maddy and Whiskers reside in Cambridge. For about a mile I hiked with Maddy, who is from Minnesota, but currently serves as the cross-country ski coach at Harvard. She is hiking the trail before beginning graduate school in the fall.

By mid-afternoon I was ready for a break, so I stopped at Muskrat Creek shelter to prepare myself a snack. Since there were still four hours until sundown, I hiked on. For the first time on the hike I put my earphones on to listen to music on my small clip-on radio. The miles sailed by as I hiked steadily toward the next shelter. I only stopped one time, to talk with Tammy and Tony who were out for a section-hike. They alerted me to the fact that there was going to be some serious trail magic at Deep Gap tomorrow morning. What they didn't know was that the magic had already begun.

As I approached the parking lot at Deep Gap, I knew immediately that I would be tenting there tonight despite the rain in the forecast. After all, I felt my tent needed another rain test. Large tents were set up and a camp fire blazed. I was greeted as I walked in to the gap by some fine folks who showed me where I could use a spit to roast hotdogs. I told them I would be right back after setting up my tent and changing clothes.

I meandered down to the campground and found a desirable spot between Blake and Blair, a weekend camping couple from Charleston, SC, and a family from Blue Ridge, GA. Scott was out for a short section-hike with his 13-year-old son Uriah and his three younger sisters. Uriah, or Where Are You, helped me set up my tent.

The evening was another special one. I sat by the fire for a couple of hours visiting with the other hikers and the folks who were providing the trail magic. One of the "Omelet Angels" that I spoke with was Jeff from Haywood County, NC. As the sun set over the mountains, I talked with

Jeff and his adult son about Don and the reason for my hike. Quickly, I noticed others turning their heads to listen. Jeff, a veteran who flew med-evac helicopters in Desert Storm, showed great compassion as I spoke of my brother's fate.

With the campfire still raging and hikers exchanging their plights of the trail, I called it a night and headed back to my tent. Just as I slipped into my sleeping bag, I heard the raindrops begin to hit the top of the tent. Even though the storms of last Saturday weren't expected, a steady rain all evening was. It had been my longest hiking day thus far, 15.5 miles. As I tried to get comfortable to sleep, I once again gave thanks for the incredible opportunity of hiking the Appalachian Trail.

## March 31, Deep Gap to Long Branch Shelter

Despite another night of heavy rain and a tent with a small bit of water inside, today started on an amazingly positive note. For the past 22 years the "Omelet Angels" have served Easter morning breakfast to thru-hikers at Deep Gap and then moved on up the trail to offer lunch at Rock Gap. Without accepting donations, the group offers up massive omelets prepared as each hiker orders. The only requirement was that we had to fill out a menu form before being served. I selected cheese, ham, and peppers. I also added three strips of bacon, a fresh fruit cup, and a piece of friendship bread. The omelets were so huge that we were told that only four or five hikers had been able to polish off more than one over the years. With what was promised to be over 3000 calories to begin my day, I was sure to hike strong again. And hike strong I did, compiling a 17.1 mile day into Long Branch shelter shortly before 6:00 P.M.

For much of today I hiked in the rain. After a fairly difficult ascent up Standing Indian Mountain, I walked in the clouds with no visible views on this Resurrection Sunday. I saw no other thru-hikers either throughout the morning and early afternoon. When I reached Carter Gap shelter, I stopped for a break. The sandwich that the Omelet Angels had packed for me enabled me to get a second wind for the late afternoon pursuit of the shelter.

As the day wore on, the rain increased. By the time I reached the shelter, rain had soaked my jacket. My trail runners were also a muddy mess. The most challenging part of the entire hike thus far was the climb up Albert Mountain in the rain. The slippery protruding rockfaces presented a painstakingly slow ascent. A couple of times I had to lay my hiking poles on a ledge above my head and use my hands to rock scramble up the precipice. About half way up I noticed another hiker above me. When I reached the apex of the mountain and the Albert Mountain fire tower, I met Danny, a young man from Kentucky who was trying to make it all the way to Wallace Gap and a shuttle to Franklin. Danny hiked at a quick pace, so I slogged through the mud on his foot heels all the way to the blue-blazed trail to the shelter.

As I approached the Long Branch shelter, I greeted the group with, "I hope there's one more spot for an old man." I'm finding my age is an asset around this fine group of young folks I've encountered. Since my tent was wet, I had to have a shelter. Fortunately, there were two places available. I chose the bottom level. The Raisin Bran Kid arrived shortly after I did and got the last spot. After getting my sleeping pad and bag ready I finished my sandwich and chips. Then I chatted with some of the other hikers until sundown when everyone turned in for the night.

My two new friends, Maddy and Whiskers, were already settled in for the night. Several others, who had begun their hikes before I did, became my shelter mates for the night. As I settled into my sleeping bag rain began to fall. Its patter on the tin roof brought back memories of a "side room" on my grandmother's farmhouse, a place where Don and I enjoyed many special family memories. So I ended my Easter Sunday among strangers who had quickly become friends, listening to the patter of raindrops on a tin roof, in a shelter, on the Appalachian Trail.

## April 1, Long Branch Shelter to Franklin, NC

After a fairly good night's sleep in the shelter, I awoke to the sounds of others packing up to get an early start. It was town day. All hikers look forward for the opportunity to leave the rigors of the trail behind for a day with a respite back in civilization. Those at the shelter where I stayed last night were no exception. The Raisin Bran Kid was the first to depart, followed closely by Maddy and Whiskers. I lingered for a while enjoying conversation with Hammy, Storytime, and El Gato. Hammy gave me a hug after I told her about Don. Every time I'm asked about my trail name, my response draws sincere compassion from all.

I finally took off on today's hike around 8:30. The initial terrain was very flat although still extremely muddy. I hiked quickly, passing others throughout the morning. Around 11:00 I walked into Winding Stair Gap to meet Rob who had a cooler full of cold beverages in the back of his pickup to offer to all. Several other hikers were hanging out in the parking lot, either waiting for shuttles or preparing to head up the trail. As I was drinking my ice cold trail magic soft drink, a van pulled up to let out a hiker. I asked the driver of the van, Pam, if she were going back into Franklin. She said that she was and that she would gladly give me a ride. Actually, she is the girlfriend of another thru-hiker, Stupid, who was there to see off his friend. Stupid planned another zero day in Franklin before resuming his hike. When Pam asked my trail name, she said that she had been reading my journal from its beginning. I greatly appreciated the lift that Pam and Stupid gave me to the Microtel in Franklin.

After checking in I spent the rest of the day doing town chores. I did my laundry and spent some time catching up on my writing. Tomorrow I've scheduled my first zero-day for rest. Even though my legs feel great, I promised myself that I'd take a day off about every ten days to two weeks. It's been a very good first ten days. I've covered 109.8 miles and stayed vertical nine out of ten days. Today was also the opening day for Major League Baseball. It is my first opening day without my brother. One passion that we shared has always been baseball. We would have talked often over the past two months about the Atlanta Braves' off-season trades, and tonight we certainly would have exchanged phone calls during the Braves' 7-5 win over the Phillies. I won't watch a game all season without thinking about him.

## April 2, Resting in Franklin

Even after a good night's sleep in a bed, I still awoke somewhat early, a little after 7:00. Needing to get several tasks accomplished today, I made a list and set out about 8:30. The first stop was at Bojangles for breakfast. Even though the motel provided a light fare, I wanted something more substantial. I thought about the time last fall when Linda and I had dined at a Bojangles, while vacationing in the Western Carolina mountains.

After breakfast I walked to a nearby UPS store to mail the old tent, sleeping pad, and a few miscellaneous items to my good buddy, Scotty. I had planned to toss the tent; however, when I asked my friend if he wanted it, he said he did. Perhaps he can figure out a way to make it sleep-worthy again. It served its purpose well for me over the past ten years of section-hiking. Next, I visited the Three Eagles Outfitters to invest in a new sleeping pad and look at their tents. Uncertain still of just what tent to buy, I decided to wait until I got to Nantahala in two more days in order to do some more research. I did purchase a Big Agnes pad with a 2.5 thickness and a 4.1 R value. I should expect more comfortable nights ahead in the shelters. In addition, I decided to buy a camp towel to replace the standard hand towel I was carrying. Camp towels are lighter and dry much more quickly.

When I finished at the outfitters, I stopped by a Kerr Drugs for some more necessary items. Among those were travel size sunscreen and deodorant. I also picked up some whole milk and Don's favorite, Reese's Peanut Butter Cups. Then I headed back to the motel where I visited in the lobby for a while with Jolly, Highlighter, and a few others. Jolly, originally from Northern England, now resides in Westchester County, NY. I also set up a shuttle for the return to the trail the following morning.

## April 3, Franklin to Burningtown Gap

The following morning at 8:30 Bill Van Horn (Dayglow) drove up in front of the Microtel in Franklin to shuttle Jolly, Highlighter, and me back to the trail. When we arrived at Winding Stair Gap, there were three hikers awaiting a shuttle into Franklin. When one introduced himself as

Bass, I knew this was going to be a great day. There wasn't anything my brother Don enjoyed more than bass fishing. I briefly told Bass about Don before beginning the climb out of the gap. I quickly hiked ahead of Jolly and Highlighter, walking across a small bridge over a stream with rushing water cascading down the rocks.

For most of the morning the miles zipped by. On Siler Bald, while I was taking a break, a shirtless Grinch and his buddy Kermit hiked past after briefly stopping to say hello. Both had also passed me just before Deep Gap on Saturday. Stopping for a break at 11:45, I checked my guide to realize I had covered in excess of five miles in a little over two hours. A few minutes later I came across a woman doing trail maintenance. Nancy said she was originally from Eufaula, Alabama, a city Don and I often traveled through, as children, to visit our grandparents in Ozark. Don also spent many hours in his bass boat on Lake Eufaula, one of his favorite places to while away an afternoon.

As the day wore on, I encountered a plethora of thru-hikers. Just before reaching Wayah tower, I ran into Chris from Birmingham (now Slim Jim), and Maddy and Whiskers, my favorite thru-hiking young couple. There were many other day-hikers at the tower as well. With 360 degrees panoramic views, Wayah tower is a popular tourist destination. The area is also accessible by car from a gravel forest road.

While I was eating a sandwich, Jolly, my new British friend, arrived at the tower as well. Asking how much farther I planned to hike, I told him of my reservation at the Aquone hostel. When he called Maggie, the owner and a fellow Brit, she told him that there was one bunk left. So Jolly and I hiked together to Burningtown Gap to complete a 14.6 mile day. Shortly after calling the hostel to let them know we were at the gap, Maggie's husband, Steve, arrived to drive us to the Aquone. For the approximately three mile drive down the mountain, I felt more like I was in a Manhattan taxi. At breakneck speeds, the former British military man exhibited flawless driving skills as he navigated the narrow gravelly road. And as he drove, he and Jolly compared their UK pasts. Steve hails from Manchester. A United fan, he said his family is split between the two clubs who are perennial contenders in the Premier League.

After arriving at the hostel, Steve showed us around and told us that dinner was at 5:30. The building, which Steve completely constructed by himself, is unbelievably beautiful. He also made some of the furniture in the hostel as well. Already there were Maddy (now Rocket) and Whiskers, Puffy, Bojangles, Walker, Captain Dan, Tie Dye, Postman and Oxy. Tie Dye, who currently lives in the Park City, Utah area with her husband, has read my journal. Puffy, a 26-year-old former high school cross-country runner, had heard about my reason for hiking and sincerely offered his admiration for my pursuit.

After dinner we all returned to the common room for some hiker banter and viewing of the weather channel. Since most of us planned to hit the Smokies on Sunday, we were closely watching weather patterns for the next week. Even though cold rain is forecast for tomorrow, the next five days after appear to be great for hiking. When I noticed a scrabble game under the TV and asked if anyone wanted to play, Rocket, Whiskers, and Tie Dye gladly accepted the invitation. Once again I've found myself among the finest of company after a day of exhilarating hiking and spectacular views.

## April 4, Burningtown Gap to the Nantahala Outdoor Center

The following day turned out to be the most challenging thus far, mainly due to a combination of the terrain and weather. After a breakfast of an egg, sausage and cheese quiche, bagel, and coffee, Maggie drove Jolly and me back to the trail at Burningtown Gap. As we departed the truck, a frigid, freezing rain greeted us. Needing to get started quickly to avoid potential hypothermia, we hoisted our packs, put on gloves, and headed up the trail. Within a short while, I had pulled away from my Yorkshire friend, hiking briskly to try to warm up my core temperature.

Out of the gap the trail ascended gradually for the initial two miles before descending down to Tellico Gap. Icicles clung to the rhododendron around every turn, often dangling at face level. On more than one occasion I was slapped in the nose by a weighted-down protruding limb. Visions of Robert Frost's "Birches" came to mind as I strained to hear the icy clinking. Unable to keep my head and eyes anywhere but the ground, for fear of falling on the slippery black mud, I was pummeled by the ice-laden branches often throughout the morning.

When I passed Cold Spring shelter during the first hour, four hikers were still hunkered in their sleeping bags, not wanting to face the chilling day. Stopped for a break was Slim Jim, a young Southern man with whom I've quickly established a rapport. We hike at about the same pace, so for the remainder of the day we trudged through the relentless mud together. We also hiked in the footfalls of Whiskers and Rocket for several miles. At one point Rocket asked about Don, so I shared his story briefly with the couple from Cambridge. It brought back the memory of when Don and I took Brent and Sam to watch the Braves play the Red Sox at Fenway, when they were eleven.

Taking only one break to drop my pack, simply because it was too cold, we made excellent time considering the conditions, arriving at the NOC (Nantahala Outdoor Center) at 2:45. I had covered the 12.9 miles in just over 5 and 1/2 hours. With the last four miles being a tough descent from 4000 to 1746 feet, I was very pleased with the effort despite taking my second fall. Really, I considered it a half-fall since I was able to catch myself on a blown-down tree before hitting the muddy trail.

After arriving at the NOC, I quickly checked into the bunkhouse, showered, and put on clean, dry clothes. By far, it was the best feeling of the entire day. Then I walked to the River's End restaurant for a meal. I dined with Slim Jim. Seated at the next table were four hikers from the group of army veterans who are "walking off the war." One member of the group was Brown Squirrel, a member of the trail journals community whose posts I have been reading for the past few months. I got my second hug of the hike from her.

After a lengthy meal of an onion ring platter appetizer, half-pound burger, tossed salad, and sweet tea, Slim and I visited for a good while before leaving the establishment. Several other hikers were also enjoying town food, including Grinch, Kermit, Whiskers, Rocket, and Tie Dye. When Slim and I walked over to the outfitters, we ran into Jolly who had hiked in a little while after us. I got some change and then headed to the laundry.

I selected one of the vintage 1985 washing machines from the four available and loaded it with all my muddy gear including my Brooks Cascadia trail runners, after I had cleaned most of the mud off outside with paper towels. While the clothes were drying I walked across the street to get a cup of coffee which I enjoyed in the laundromat. Slim also dropped by to chat about our upcoming hiking days. He planned a day off to spend time with his wife. I would not see him again for the remainder of my hike.

Eventually I made my way back to the bunkhouse which I shared with five lads whose collective age was probably not much over 100. Among them was Walmart with whom I had shared a cabin back at Neels Gap over a week ago.

At 5:16 AM I awoke in a miserable state. I had been tossing in my bunk all evening, trying to get some sleep in a room where the temperature had to be hovering in the high 80's. I lay on the outside of my sleeping bag, unable to tolerate the added heat within, yet needing to keep the bag under me due to the absence of bed linens in the facility. I mulled over the idea of going ahead and packing up and sitting outside the River's End restaurant on a bench until it opened at 8:00. With daylight still two hours away, I decided to persevere for a little longer since at least one of my bunk mates appeared to be asleep.

## April 5, NOC to Stecoah Gap

Finally, at 6:45 the alarm sounded. I quickly packed up and walked down to the NOC outfitters. Even though it did not open until 8:00, a nice lady let me come in early to use the ATM. I then sauntered over to the restaurant to wait for it to open. When it did I shared a table with Jolly and enjoyed a large southern breakfast of eggs, sausage, grits, and coffee. After filling my water bottles and purchasing five candy bars, I set out from the NOC for the long climb up with Jolly. Little did I know at 9:30 this morning the difficulty I would face on the 13.4 mile hike.

41

For eight miles, the trail elevates from 1746 feet at the NOC to 5062 feet on Cheowah Bald. It was indeed a challenging morning. According to Captain Dan, "even the downhills were up." I trudged along through thickets still laden with ice at the higher elevations. When the sun appeared around noon, we were periodically pummeled by the falling ice. At one point it almost seemed as if it were raining. At least the mud from the previous day was minimal.

For most of the day Jolly, my UK friend, and I hiked together. At the highest elevation of the day on Cheowah Bald, we took a break to enjoy the views. Then as the afternoon continued, my energy level diminished. Jolly hiked on ahead as I struggled. As the temperature rose I shed a layer of clothes, hoping my pace would increase. It didn't. At times I stopped on the uphill sections to just lean on my poles. Several thru-hikers passed me as the afternoon wore on. Grinch and Kermit, the two young men from Marietta, GA, stopped to briefly chat and encourage me to keep hiking to today's destination. Postman also hiked past, saying he wanted to get to the next shelter ahead of his hiking buddies. His motivation is a motel room tomorrow for the Final Four. I also met two southbound thru-hikers. One, Biggie Small, said he started in August and has taken 45 zero days. He also is hiking in memory of a relative who died of ALS, so we wished each other well as we headed up the trail in opposite directions.

When I got to Locust Cove Gap I saw Blissful resting by a tree. She planned to camp there. So I dropped my pack to visit for a few minutes. She asked about ALS, so I told her a little more about Don. When I started to hike on, she also offered encouragement by saying, "there's only one more climb and then it's all downhill." She only missed her assessment of the climbs by five. Due to my fatigue it was also difficult to hike over numerous large rocks on the descent to Stecoah Gap.

When I reached the gap, Grinch and Kermit were waiting at the picnic tables for a shuttle into Robbinsville. After only a few minutes more, my shuttle, Phil, arrived to take me and two others to his cabins in the woods. I shared a cabin tonight with Jolly, Captain Dan, and Tie Dye. Hopefully, conditions for a good night's sleep will have improved over the previous evening. Whiskers and Rocket are also here in another cabin. We were all invited into Phil and his wife Donna's home for a meal tonight.

Today was probably my most tiring of the 13 days I had hiked thus far. When I arrived at the cabins I was spent. However, after a hot shower, a hearty meal, two ibuprofen, and some good fellowship with hiking friends, I felt much better. Knowing that the Smokies awaited on Sunday, I hoped to get a good night's sleep so that the following day I could complete the 13.9 mile section to Fontana Dam.

## April 6, Stecoah Gap to Fontana Dam Marina

After experiencing my worst day on the trail thus far yesterday, the next was among my best. It's amazing what eight hours of uninterrupted sleep will do for a weary hiker. When I awoke to my alarm at 7:00, Tie Dye and Jolly were already awake. Captain Dan, who had chosen to sleep on the screened-in porch of the cabin, was soon stirring as well. So I prepared my pack and walked with the others up to Phil and Donna's home for breakfast. After another exceptional hiker meal of eggs, bacon, biscuits with honey, and juice, Phil drove me back to Stecoah Gap. Jolly, Tie Dye, and Captain Dan chose to take a zero-day and remain at the cabin. I'll miss my British friend that I've hiked with off and on since Franklin; however, I knew I needed to keep hiking.

I began my day on a positive note, wearing a light daypack with only food, water, and a couple of incidentals inside. The beginning of today's hike consisted of a gentle path of switchbacks leading up the mountain out of Stecoah Gap. Then after about two miles I was greeted with a steep climb without the switchbacks. Fortunately it was the only time all day that I would consider the hike strenuous. On the climb I passed two young hikers, Napalm, who thru-hiked last year and his cousin, John Wayne. Napalm is just doing the first two weeks with "the Duke."

Taking advantage of the slackpack opportunity, I hiked faster today than at any time in the past, covering the 13.9 miles in right at 5 and 1/2 hours. I talked with thru-hiker Wild Willy and section-hiker Walker T at Cable Gap shelter, just after being treated to some trail magic at Yellow

Creek Mountain Rd. Triton, who hiked the trail in 2011, was grilling up some burgers. The "magic" could not have occurred at a more opportune time since I arrived at the road just past noon and was only carrying snacks in my small pack. Then in the early afternoon, while taking a break, I chatted with section-hiking sisters Hiker Nutt and Nutty Buddy from Dalton, GA. When they asked the reason for my thru-hike, I again was given the opportunity to talk about my brother. Both ladies seemed sincerely moved.

All afternoon I hiked at a fast pace, only pausing to drink water a few times. I did very briefly chat with Mud Puddle and Slider, a middle-aged couple from Maine. I continue to meet many hikers who began their hikes a week or longer before I did. After the brief break I charged down the last three miles of the mountain, arriving at Fontana before 2:30. My timing could not have been better. Jeff, of the Hike Inn where I had a reservation, had just arrived to pick up three other hikers. Two were Rocket and Whiskers. As Jeff drove to the inn he congratulated us for making it this far, saying that over one-third of would-be thru-hikers have dropped out by now. Jeff stated that he has been extremely busy over the past few days shuttling those who have chosen to end their hikes to airports.

Nancy, Jeff's wife, drove Rocket, Whiskers, Piddling Around, and me to Robbinsville for a meal and re-supply for the Smokies. I shared a table at a Mexican restaurant with Piddling Around, a retired postal worker from near Wadley, AL. When I was about finished with my meal I experienced a wonderful surprise. Into the restaurant walked PrayerWalker and her husband Nick. PrayerWalker, a member of the trail journals community, and I have been corresponding since late last year. We had discussed where we might meet on the trail, but at an eating establishment outside Stecoah Gap was never a consideration. I think the excitement over finally meeting was mutual.

After arriving back at the inn, I was finally able to watch a Braves game on TV. When the Braves rallied for the walk-off win, I texted Brent and Sam to share in the victory. On so many occasions when the Braves won with ninth inning heroics, Don and I would replay the last inning over the phone. It was a special ending to the day.

Having been on the trail for two weeks, I felt truly blessed by the support I was receiving from so many. Whether family, old friends, new friends, or folks I had never met, I continued to be humbled by the interest shown in my adventure and the genuine compassion for my brother Don. Thinking about the Smokies, I was encouraged by the five day forecast of perfect weather. I felt focused and all was good, because Don loved the woods, and I thought often that he would be enjoying sharing my journey on the Appalachian Trail.

## April 7, Fontana Dam Marina to Spence Field Shelter

Early the next morning Nancy drove Rocket, Whiskers, and me back to the dam. They were starting at the visitor's center; however, since I had ended my hike yesterday at the marina, I had a little over a mile to cover to get to the dam. When I did get there, Piddling Around had just arrived, so we hiked together over the Fontana Dam and into the Great Smokey Mountain National Park, the most visited park in the US and the one with the greatest black bear population. We hiked together for a mile or so, but then I pulled ahead.

Once again, my legs felt fresh all day. Even though the climb up to the ridge ascended over 3000 feet, ample switchbacks afforded a comfortable ascent. I stopped to rest briefly twice, but waited until I found a comfortable blown-down tree to sit on to have my lunch. While I was enjoying a Subway sandwich that I had brought from Robbinsville, I realized that I had a cell signal, so I called Linda. Then I hiked on strongly for the remainder of the afternoon.

Not until after lunch did I see any other hikers. I met a ridgerunner Carl, or Greybeard, who gave me some information on available spots in shelters. While we were talking, I noticed two trail maintainers headed toward me. One said, "Hey, it's Don's Brother." It was Hopeful, a former thru-hiker that I had met my first day on the trail. He seemed genuinely pleased that I had made it this far and offered encouragement.

45

For the remainder of the afternoon I saw no one else until I reached Mollie's Ridge shelter. Walker T was taking a break for lunch. I retrieved some water from a spring behind the shelter before moving on up the trail. When I arrived at the Russell Field shelter, Whiskers and Rocket were there and going to stay the night. I rested for a bit, but then decided to hike on. Kind of like Forrest Gump, I just felt like hiking. A re-broadcast of *The Prairie Home Companion* escorted me to the next shelter where I arrived before 5:00. Garrison Keillor was at the Town Hall on West 43rd St. in Manhattan. The broadcast almost made me want to be in New York.

When I arrived at the Spence Field shelter, Zeus already had a fire blazing. Among several who were there were my two young fellow Georgians, Grinch and Kermit as well as Piddling Around. The final hiker I introduced myself to lay tightly in his sleeping bag on the bottom platform. With his head facing out, he stated his trail name, Molar Man. It was my initial encounter with the 66-year-young retired dentist from Ohio. What I had no way of knowing was that over the next four and one-half months, Molar Man would become not only a hiking companion but a good friend as well. We would hike through parts of TN, VA, MD, PA, NH, and ME together. On that night, however, we barely exchanged greetings. Like myself, I imagine Molar Man just wanted to stay warm and get some rest. Tarps that had been hung across the open side of the shelter flapped in the cold wind. I crawled into the sleeping bag I had wedged between two strangers on the upper level of the stone edifice. Crackling embers from a nearly extinguished fire escorted me quickly to sleep.

## April 8, Spence Field Shelter to Double Springs Shelter

Before the break of day I awoke to a day that would be filled with many ups and downs in more ways than one. While eating my two blueberry pop tarts for breakfast, I couldn't help thinking of an old saying by one of my kinfolks, "if I had any ham, I'd have some ham and eggs, if I had any eggs." Needless to say, a trail breakfast never stacks up to a town one. And as a result of poor nutrition from the onset, I struggled for much of the day.

A climb over Rocky Top awaited shortly after today's hike began. I couldn't help but hum a few bars of the University of Tennessee fight song. The views at the top were among the most spectacular I've experienced up to this point. Looking back toward the west, Fontana Dam was visible in the distance. I only paused for a minute, however, due to the high winds. For the entire day, I hiked solo.

Throughout the morning my energy level quickly dissipated. Within the first two hours I was passed by Rocket, Whiskers, Postman, and Puffy, who had all stayed one shelter back last night. By the time I reached the Derrick Knob shelter, I was definitely struggling. I took a break to eat and try to rehydrate. Apparently, however, the food was not enough. About a mile after hiking on up the trail, I had to stop for another rest. While sitting on a log, drinking water and eating peanut butter, Grinch and Kermit stopped to check on me. Grinch gave me some jelly beans and both hikers refused to move on until I assured them I was OK. I've hiked in the vicinity of these two young men from Marietta, GA for over a week. They are a good representation of how folks on the trail look out for each other. Before hiking on, they encouraged me to make it to the shelter where they were staying.

As I continued up the trail, the uphills were relentless. None were that long; they just never seemed to cease. And every uphill was followed by a downhill which led to another uphill. I walked on flat terrain very little of today's hike. Still, the often panoramic views more than made up for my difficulties. By the time I reached Siler Bald shelter, I was feeling much better. After another short break I hiked on to Double Springs shelter where I met up with Rocket, Whiskers, Grinch, Kermit, and several hikers who I had not seen before. Everyone huddled around a raging campfire as sundown approached.

The Appalachian Trail presents all hikers with a variety of challenges daily. As I hiked slowly at times today, I could imagine my brother offering encouragement with every step. I made it through some difficulty today, but I knew that tomorrow would again provide another day filled with great vistas, fellowship, and opportunity, as most do on the Appalachian Trail.

## April 9, Double Springs Shelter to Newfound Gap

When I heard Piddling Around piddling around at daybreak, I felt it OK to begin packing up even though most of my shelter mates were still asleep. I quickly readied myself for a short 10.8 mile day to Newfound Gap where church friends Bennett and Lynda Massey would be waiting to treat me to a night in a luxurious condo in Sevierville, TN. The thoughts of a hot shower and "real" food inspired me to get on up the trail quickly.

The trail from Double Springs shelter began with a walk through a canopy of evergreen trees. The scent reminded me of Christmas while the scene brought back recollections of the forest in "The Wizard of Oz" where Dorothy and her friends keep repeating, "lions and tigers and bears, oh my." Knowing I didn't have to worry about any lions or tigers, I was still waiting to see my first thru-hike bear.

Within a mile Piddling Around caught up with me, so we hiked together for a large part of the day. I also hiked for a while in the afternoon with Cabo, a hiker about my age that I had met for the first time last night at the shelter. We took turns leading over the icy slush which still did not make negotiating the trail any easier. I fell three times on the ice. That upped my total of falls to five. And in addition to the falls, I also literally skied down one section for about ten yards before coming to a stop still standing. How? I don't know. I suppose there's no harm in ski-blazing. If not for my trekking poles, I'm not sure I would have ever made it down from Clingman's Dome. Since the observation tower was fogged in when we passed, we chose not to climb the half-mile blue-blazed trail to the tallest point in TN. Still, the trail was at over 6500 feet.

After I finally reached an elevation where the trail wasn't quite so icy, I made good time hiking on to Newfound Gap. As had been their custom every day for about the last week, at some time during the day Grinch and Kermit passed me. So with about two miles remaining in today's hike they zipped by. I actually hiked with them for a few minutes before they pulled away.

About 300 yards before reaching Newfound Gap, I looked up rounding a bend and Bennett and Lynda were walking toward me. They were the first familiar faces I had seen since starting the hike over two weeks ago. When we got to their truck in the parking lot, they had a cold soda ready and even stopped for me to get a burger on the way to the condo in Sevierville, TN. It definitely raised my spirits to see old friends. The trail community is unique; however, I was especially grateful for the kindness shown me by the Masseys. Even though I didn't want to admit it, I was starting to get a little homesick. But at the end of a beautiful day in the Smokies, I began to feel like I was going to be OK. People from near and far were taking care of me. After all, I was a thru-hiker, walking up a trail with the memory of a brother whom I kept reminding myself always loved the woods. Life was beginning to feel really special.

## April 10, Newfound Gap to Tri-Corner Knob Shelter

Seventeen years ago today, my dad died, exactly eleven weeks after suffering a massive stroke. My mother and I were at Northside Hospital in Atlanta with him. When his condition had become grave, I called my brother. Don and I consoled each other at a difficult time. So today I thought of my dad and my brother often as I hiked alone for all of the day. Remembering special times a father had shared with his two sons seemed appropriate while walking through a majestic forest with vistas as far as the eye could see.

After dining on a home cooked egg and sausage casserole with toast, juice, and coffee, Bennett and Lynda drove me back to the trail at Newfound Gap. Bennett even walked a couple hundred yards up the trail with me before shaking my hand and wishing me well. I felt truly blessed to have been able to spend time with these good Christian friends. It's definitely the folks who offer their kindness and hospitality that keep the weary hikers moving along.

As I walked away from my friend I immediately noticed the gentle climb out of the gap. Time passed quickly. When I reached the ridgeline I was treated to the best views that the hike has afforded thus far. At about the 3 mile mark I filled my small water bottle from Ice Water Springs. The water was the coldest I've tasted on the trail. Shortly thereafter I arrived at a 0.1 mile trail to Charlie's Bunion. I walked out by myself to admire the views and take photos. Then I retraced my steps back to the A.T.

So for the entire day I hiked without passing anyone, nor was I passed by any other hikers. I did meet three trios of southbound section-hikers. One group was from Cincinnati. They have been making annual visits to the Smokies for 14 years, one said. Another group was from the local area. A sweet lady in the group said she recently lost a good friend to ALS, when I told them about my hike in memory of Don.

As the day wore on I ate and drank often, stopping twice to enjoy the turkey sandwich I had made at the condo kitchen this morning. I also took numerous short breaks just to enjoy the views. Late in the afternoon I had to again deal with ice on the trail, although the trail was not as treacherous as yesterday. There I was hiking in short sleeves and shorts, with temperatures in the high 70's, walking through ice and snow. Many times, however, I was able to walk around the more difficult stretches. Fortunately, I was able to stay vertical all day.

When I finally reached the Tri-Corner Knob shelter, there was only one space remaining. As I looked around at the crowded shelter, I was glad that it was my last night in the Smokies. A crackling campfire beckoned, so I joined the other sojourners for some hiker chat before hunkering into my sleeping bag. Despite the awesome views and the moderate to easy terrain, I needed a change. I also knew that if all went according to plans, I would hike to Davenport Gap, the northern boundary of the Great Smokey Mountain National Park, the next day. I hoped to be in Hot Springs by late Saturday or Sunday. The runner in me was itching to do a 20 miler, and I felt like Friday just might be the day.

## April 11, Tri-Corner Knob Shelter to Davenport Gap

So when the first hint of daylight crept through the skylight of the shelter, I quietly exited my top floor accommodations as rapidly as possible. Piddling Around was having some breakfast before being the first out of camp. I ate two oatmeal pies and drank as much water as I could hold before following Piddling on up the trail. Having perused today's terrain in Awol's *A.T. Guide* last night, I was looking forward to a very comfortable last day in the Smokies.

Like the *Guide* had indicated, today's trail was among the easiest. What I was not expecting, however, was more ice. Although not for any long stretches, on several occasions I had to slow down considerably and navigate around or over very dangerous areas. I fell once when I stepped on what I thought was a safe place that proved otherwise. Still, I quickly recovered, paying even more attention to the terrain. Many times I was able to step on the footfall of a previous hiker, which allowed me to get a good pace going. Hiking strongly, I arrived at the Cosby Knob shelter, where I planned to stop for lunch, at around 11:30. I only stayed briefly, wanting to get to Davenport Gap before 3:00 where one of my old cross-country runners from Shaw was going to pick me up. So after a brief climb of about 800 feet after the shelter, the remainder of today's hike was downhill.

The day could not have been nicer. Then through dappling sunlight I spotted a runner in a gold T-shirt headed up the trail toward me. "Hey, Coach!" my former student athlete and now good friend Brad Dodson shouted. Brad lives outside Waynesville, NC and often runs with friends on the A.T. Today, however, he was combining a run with driving a weary hiker to a room at Lake Junaluska for the night. A very talented potter, Brad has a studio, Muddabbers, just off the parkway and also does a little cross-country and track coaching himself.

As I reached Davenport Gap I could officially say goodbye to the Smokies. The views had been spectacular, and I could not have had better weather for enjoying them. Today was another day when I paused often to think about my brother and just how much enjoyment he too would be getting from these mountains. It was again a day that allowed me hours of solitude for memories and reflection. And it was also yet another day on the Appalachian Trail when I thought again how much I loved my brother and how much Don loved the woods.

## April 12, Davenport Gap to Lemon Gap

It would only seem appropriate that my good running friend, Brad Dodson, would play a major role in my first 20 mile day (21.4, to be exact). After all, during the four years I had the privilege to coach Brad in cross-country and track at Shaw High School, we logged at least a couple of thousand training miles together. So when Brad offered to let me slack-pack today by driving me back to the trail this morning at Davenport Gap and then picking me up in the afternoon at Lemon Gap, I knew from the outset that big miles were on today's agenda.

After a hearty breakfast at Bojangles, we headed up I-40 shortly after 8:00. By a little after 9:00 I was hiking. What I had not anticipated about the early part of today's hike were the water crossings. During the first two miles they occurred often. Since the rushing water required a concerted effort to cross, the beginning of the walk was a bit tedious. Taking my time for fear of slipping on a wet rock or taking a tumble in the chilly streams, I managed to stay upright for each of the crossings; however, I did slightly lose my balance once, which resulted in a wet shoe.

By the time I finally reached the I-40 underpass, I was beginning to move. While walking across the bridge, I noticed a car headed toward me at a very slow pace. Looking through the driver's side window was Piddling Around. All cleaned up after finishing his section-hike from Springer to the northern terminus of the Smokies, he looked excited to be going home to Alabama. It was a pleasure to meet Piddling and hike with him for the past five days. He wished me well as I hiked away in a light rain that would continue all morning.

Just before beginning the climb that would extend for over six miles, with a gain of about 3000 feet of elevation, I met two German hikers, Restless Cowboy and Fresh Coke. I didn't know it then, but I would encounter the brothers numerous times over the next four months. I took a photo with the two before beginning the ascent. On the way up I passed several thru-hikers, including a young lad whose trail name was Chicago. Chicago was wearing a shirt with Wrigley Field pictured on its front. The reference to the "Friendly Confines" immediately brought my brother to mind. Twice Don and I had the opportunity to watch games at Wrigley. On the second occasion we were joined by Don's son, Brent, and my son, Sam. A smile came to my face as I thought about the first of those trips to Wrigley.

Throughout the years I've always liked a good adventure. It's just in the past all my adventures had been much less than five months. In the winter of 1990 I phoned my brother Don one afternoon to discuss my idea for a trip to Chicago that summer. Since both of us had always been avid baseball fans, and since that was the last year for Comiskey Park, I felt we owed it to ourselves to attend a game there before its demolition. And if we were going to Chicago, we might as well see the Cubs at Wrigley as well. As most baseball fans know, however, it's rare that both the White Sox and Cubs are in town at the same time. So after perusing the schedule for the upcoming season, I determined that there was going to be just such an occurrence in mid-August.

When I called Don that afternoon and told him that I was purchasing tickets for an event six months in the future, I must admit that my brother seemed a bit incredulous. Neither of us was in a position to invest a significant amount of revenue for the venture, so my suggestion that we do the trip in only three days, and drive, was met with a mild degree of skepticism. Still, my brother Don, like myself, liked the idea of the "adventure."

So on the morning of August 13, 1990, Don and I set off on our Chicago expedition in my 1989 Ford Tempo. This was before GPS's and MapQuest; therefore, we departed with only the old Rand-McNally road maps in hand. We wouldn't make our first stop until Kentucky, for gas, and would drive until past midnight and Indianapolis before finding a motel to rest. After a short five hours of sleep, we were on the road again.

Without a hotel reservation and not really knowing the location of Wrigley Field, we decided to take what looked like a desirable exit in mid-town Chicago. To our good fortune we were able to locate a Best Western with a parking lot and a James Dean themed McDonald's right across the street. We easily secured a room for one night (yes just one night, because our plan was to hit the road for home as soon as the Cubs game ended the following day). As I remember, the room was comfortable and cost under $100 for the one night. I also recall Don later writing a letter of complaint concerning the construction work that commenced outside our window at six the next morning.

With check-in complete and several hours before the White Sox night game at Comiskey, we journeyed a couple of blocks to a Hard Rock Café for an afternoon meal. En route, Don was approached by one of those sidewalk wholesalers who offered a "great deal" on a Rolex. At times Don loved to feign a sort of "southern ignorance" with vendors of this sort. Today, however, was different. I suppose it might have been that he was just hungry, because Don refrained from any banter as we ambled by.

Shortly after lunch we decided to take the el train for the Southside of Chicago. Arriving well before game time, we rested on a bench in a near-by park, watching neighborhood children playing in a fountain. It was a hot afternoon. A while later we proceeded on to the stadium and found our way to the gate where the visiting team was to arrive. The Sox opponent for the night was the Toronto Blue Jays. I still remember watching a youthful Fred McGriff get off the bus. At the time I had no idea that Don and I would be in attendance when McGriff made his debut as an Atlanta Brave three years later. Even though we were older than most of the players, we enjoyed the moment as if we were kids again.

When the gates opened we were among the first to enter. Not wanting to immediately head to our seats, Don and I secured a spot behind the home team's dugout to watch infield practice. Future Hall of Famer Frank Thomas, a rookie who hailed from our home town, tossed a ball with a teammate only a few feet away. With heightened anticipation, we watched the White Sox warm up for the mid-week game. More importantly, however, we shared this one opportunity to attend a major league baseball game in the last year of an historic park. Unlike the stadiums of the present day, Comiskey exuded the timelessness of the game. It was almost as if Shoeless Joe was still in the lineup.

As the park began to fill, we moved toward the first base side where our seats were located. Still not wanting to sit down, we stood in the first row in short right field absorbing all that the old field had to offer. At some point, a stray baseball bounced into the stands only a few feet from where Don stood. My brother could have easily picked it up, but just as he was about to, he noticed a boy of about ten racing toward it. Don moved his hand aside so that the youngster could retrieve the ball. We both watched the jubilant lad, grin on his face, holding up the Official American League baseball for his family to see. This selfless act exemplified the kind of man Don was, a man who valued the excitement of a boy over a Comiskey Park souvenir to take back to Georgia.

I don't remember much about the game except that the Blue Jays scored quickly and often. Going into the bottom of the ninth inning, the White Sox trailed 12-0. Many of the fans had departed early, but not Don and me. This was our only night at Comiskey; we weren't leaving before the last out.

As the final half-inning began, Toronto brought in Jim Acker, an ex-Brave. 1990 was one year before the Braves would begin their winning ways, so when Acker strode toward the mound, Don commented, "The White Sox still have a chance; a Brave is pitching." Even though we both loved the Braves, we noted the humorous irony of the moment. Here we were in Chicago, watching an Atlanta Braves castoff coming in to finish up the game. And finish the game Acker did, but not before the White Sox had rallied for four runs. Even though the game ended in a 12-4 defeat for the home team, Don and I had relished every moment that we shared that night.

Not wanting to walk to the el station at the late hour, we hailed a cab. As the driver sped along Lakeshore Drive, Don and I replayed parts of the game that we had just witnessed. We both felt so fortunate to have finally watched a game at Comiskey, a park that our father had talked about and even visited himself over four decades earlier. The excitement mounted as we turned our attention toward the Cubs game, which was on tap for the next day.

After a short night's rest and breakfast at the McDonald's across the street from our motel, we walked to the el train station for the ride to fabled Wrigley Field. Again arriving well before the gates opened for the afternoon game, we walked completely around the park, basking in the sights and smells of the neighborhood. We took pictures on Waveland Ave. before moseying through a souvenir store to purchase gifts for Brent, Sam, and Rachel.

When we were finally able to enter the park, we wandered throughout the "friendly confines," soaking in the history of a very special place. First we made our way down the third base line, into the left field corner seats, to watch batting practice. After noticing that a right handed batter could pull a ball into the area where we were located, Don readied himself "just in case." My brother always possessed this uncanny ability to get batting practice baseballs, and that day was no exception. Within a few minutes of positioning himself, a towering fly ball off the bat of Andre Dawson approached. Hurling himself over a couple of rows of seats, Don grasped the ball in one hand as he balanced himself from falling with the other. This time there were no youngsters around, so Don pocketed the Official National League baseball.

As game time grew near, we made our way up to the second level where our seats were located. Even though Don and I were neither Cubs nor White Sox fans, we appreciated with enormity the venues where both teams played. And since the Braves weren't in town that afternoon, we planned to cheer for the hometown Cubs against the Houston Astros. Today, like last night, however, the home team would suffer a loss. I don't remember the score. What I do remember is how quickly the day went by. At the time I think both of us still felt as if we were part of some baseball fantasy, being able to attend two major league games in two historic parks on consecutive days.

When the game ended we again rode the el train back to the station nearest to our motel. Even though we had checked out earlier in the day, we had left the Tempo in the parking lot there with the proprietor's permission. So only a little over 24 hours after arriving in the windy city, we were stepping into the automobile for the journey home.

I remember stopping somewhere in Indiana for supper and again in Nashville for coffee at about 4:00 AM, but we never stopped to sleep. Don may have dozed briefly, but for most of the trip home, we recalled various events of our whirlwind adventure. We had driven to Chicago, watched two baseball games, and driven home. The trip proved to be the topic of conversation at many family events over the years. It was a moment that we shared as brothers that both of us cherished then and that, even after losing my brother, I will continue to cherish. Every time I read or see a reference to the Chicago White Sox or Cubs and Wrigley Field, I'll think of Don, and smile, as I remember those three days in the summer of 1990.

I kept smiling about that trip to Wrigley as the climb continued. When I finally reached the apex of the ascent, the hike became one of the less demanding of the first three weeks. At times I was practically running on the level and mildly downhill portions. Even though I was hiking at a very good pace, I still regularly paused to introduce myself to other thru-hikers that I had not met previously. Among them was Red Knees. Four months later I would see Red Knees for a second time in Stratton, Maine.

Throughout the afternoon I anticipated what I knew would be the highlight of the day, crossing Max Patch, a bald that affords 360 degree vistas. With plentiful sunlight that had arrived in the early afternoon, the views were again.... well, OK, they were breathtaking. I just can't think of a more appropriate adjective right now. With the wind practically blowing me horizontal, I remembered last fall when Linda and I had visited Max Patch by car. It was especially poignant to be hiking up today.

When I finally reached Lemon Gap where Brad was scheduled to pick me up, I was a full hour ahead of when I had expected to arrive. For the half-hour I had to wait, I began journaling in the rather isolated area.

Since I was getting a little cold, it was good to see Brad pull up. Today's hike was indeed special, but not as special as the quality time I was able to share with my old friend on the ride to and from the trail. On the return trip it was especially meaningful to discuss how some of Brad's former high school teammates are doing these days. It seems hard to believe it's been 25 years since I coached them. In fact, I couldn't have asked for a better ending to another beautiful day on the Appalachian Trail.

## April 13, Lemon Gap to Hot Springs

When I've section-hiked on the A.T. with my good friend Alton, we have often talked about the sameness of the trail at times. Alton has said on such occasions, "If you didn't know what state you were in, what state would you say you were in?" Today was one of those days when the trail was a path through the woods of ups and downs with not much variety until the town of Hot Springs first came into view. Still, the sun shone throughout the day, a cool breeze appeared just when it was needed, and the difficulty level of today's 14.4 mile section would probably be classified as a 2 or 3 on the old 1-10 scale, with 10 being the most challenging.

It was tough to say goodbye to my good friend Brad when he dropped me back at Lemon Gap around 8:30. I will be forever grateful for the time we had to spend together. Parting, however, was a little less sad because just as I was embarking from Brad's SUV, who should be hiking up the trail toward us but Rocket and Whiskers. I had not seen my two Cambridge friends since the night before Newfound Gap. They had begun their hike early today from near Max Patch in order to log big miles with a slackpack. The timing could not have been more perfect because Whiskers was able to take a couple of photos of Brad and me.

Brad wished me well as I headed up the trail in the footsteps of the two. Within a mile, however, they began to pull away, hiking at a faster pace than I was able to maintain. So again for the remainder of the day I hiked solo. But unlike yesterday, I saw few thru-hikers throughout the day. For some reason I didn't feel very social today, so I didn't even ask the trail names of the few I did see. I just enjoyed the tranquility of my surroundings and my mind. I'm not sure why, but early in the day's hike I reminisced about viewing Saturday morning television with my brother when we were little. Donald and I would rise early enough to watch Roy Rogers on Western Theater and follow up the cowboys with cartoons. Somewhere in between we would join our parents at the dining room table for a large country breakfast. Then we would head to the backyard for an afternoon of play. Times were so simple then.

As the afternoon waned, I finally spotted Hot Springs from the ridge-line. When towns are first sighted, however, it's usually at least an hour before the trail winds down to the road. Hot Springs is the first trail town where the trail actually goes down Main St., or in the case of Hot Springs, Bridge St. Walking into town, I headed straight to Elmer's Sunnybank Inn. Built in 1840, the house is the oldest in town, according to Elmer. A thru-hiker back in 1976, Elmer returned to Hot Springs in 1978. A B &B of sorts, the inn caters to thru-hikers. Elmer even offers work for stay options.

In the early evening Rocket and Whiskers joined me for a meal at the Smokey Mountain Diner, an eclectic establishment located across the road from Elmer's. We talked about our first three weeks on the trail, teaching, and my brother. The two represent all that is good among young folks today. With their futures on hold, the twenty-somethings seem in harmony with their surroundings. Each displays a countenance of contentment. They possess pleasant smiles and a love of the outdoors. In many ways they remind me of my son and daughter. Dealing with a tad of melancholia, I was grateful for their friendship and for the opportunity to share. While walking back to Elmer's, I suddenly realized that my home had become the Appalachian Trail.

## April 14, Hot Springs to Log Cabin Rd.

The trail out of Hot Springs took an immediate right after crossing the French Broad River. For about half a mile the trail ran parallel to the river before heading back up the mountain toward Lovers Leap Rock. I saw no lovers as I passed the outcrop. The trail leveled briefly before becoming a roller coaster for much of the day. None of the climbs were particularly difficult; however, every uphill preceded a downhill with the scenario continuing for many miles. Rarely did I walk on level ground.

At some time in the late morning I passed a pond. I don't know if there were any fish dwelling there, but a pond on the trail also brought Don to mind. He would not only have been able to tell if there were fish, but he also would have speculated on what breed. Since there was also a bench by the pond, I dropped my pack for a brief rest. While I was sitting on the bench, Rocket and Whiskers passed by. I shared with Rocket, a native of Minnesota, that I was listening to last night's re-broadcast of *A Prairie Home Companion*. Just like last Sunday, the folks of Lake Wobegon accompanied me up the trail. So with my radio as my only companion, I again hiked alone throughout the day.

Having seen very few hikers all day, I finally passed some late in the afternoon. One was Bulldog from Dawsonville, GA. Bulldog had a fire going at his stealth campsite. I saw two other hikers tenting alone but didn't stop to chat. I merely said hello and kept walking. It seemed like there were more single tent sites today than at any other time since I started.

When I reached Log Cabin Rd., I left the trail to walk about a mile down a gravel road to Hemlock Hollow Inn. Both a cafe and hostel with a quite comfortable bunkhouse, the establishment has become a popular destination for hikers between Hot Springs and Erwin. After registering with Hattie, I walked through the cafe to see Rocket, Whiskers, and Say What, a hiker who had been at the last shelter I stayed at in the Smokies. After settling in and showering, I returned to the cafe for a chef salad and grilled cheese sandwich. The last one in the cafe, I sat and chatted for a while with Hattie, who owns the property and business with her husband. She filled me in on the history of the place. I always enjoy talking with the locals.

## April 15, Log Cabin Rd. to Devil Fork Gap

The following morning I literally walked in a fog, at times so thick that I could only see a few feet in front of me. For the first two hours or so I saw no other thru-hikers. I did meet a group of southbound section-hikers from Florida, including Mayor who sported a top hat. Then I came across a hiker I had seen yesterday but not met. Pigpen is another 20-something hiker also from GA. He proved to be an asset on two occasions today. First, he happened along when I was staring down about a ten foot rockface, trying to figure out how I was going to get down it. Pigpen managed easily and then held my poles as I followed the path he had taken. Later in the day he topped off my nearly empty water bottle with his Sawyer squeeze filter, which saved me a trip down a path to a spring. There are some really fine young folks hiking the trail.

The highlight of the day was a climb up an exposed section of trail to Big Firescald Knob. The sun had come out by the time I reached this section of trail, which made for some more spectacular views. This is one section that even offers a blue-blazed alternative trail for bad weather or for those uncomfortable with exposed ridges (where there are severe drop-offs on both sides). The 360 degree views along the ridge definitely made the challenging navigation of the rocks worthwhile. At the best vantage point for views, I came upon Nick, another young hiker who was taking a break on a ledge. Before leaving the rocky area, I had lunch on a rock outcrop.

Later in the afternoon I again stopped briefly at Flint Mountain Shelter where a large group of hikers that I had not met before were taking a break. I introduced myself to the group and told them about Don and the reason for my hike. Again my words were met with compassion by all. Then when I reached Devil Fork Gap I ended the day's hike at 18.7 miles. I had arranged for Hattie's son to shuttle me into Erwin where I planned to take a day off before shuttling back to hike into Erwin.

When I got to Erwin I checked into the Super 8 Motel. After a hot shower, I walked approximately a mile to the Country Scrub Board Laundry where I enjoyed chatting with Judy, the proprietor, and her friend Melissa, as my clothes washed and dried. Judy commented that many hikers had stopped by the past few weeks. So I told the ladies about my hike and shared my website with them. After leaving the laundry I stopped by

McDonald's, one of only two restaurants nearby, before ending my day back at the motel.

## April 16, Resting in Erwin

Even though I didn't go to bed until around midnight, I awoke at 6:00. When I remembered that a rest day was planned, however, I went back to sleep until 9:00. At that time I got on the phone to set up a shuttle back to the trail for tomorrow. My first try was the legendary Miss Janet, a wonderful lady who has been helping out hikers for many years in the Erwin area. Even though she was booked for the early morning, she said she could drive me at around 11:00. Wanting to do another 20 plus mile day, I took her advice and called Tom "10-K" Bradford instead. Tom said that he would be more than happy to pick me up at 7:00 the following morning for the shuttle back to Devil Fork Gap.

With my shuttle set, I walked back to McDonald's for a hotcakes, sausage, and coffee breakfast. Then I meandered up the Main Street of Erwin to a Dollar Store and Food Lion. Since I planned to do some slackpacking over the next two or three days, I decided to invest $3.00 in a very light daypack. Actually it was more of a cheap, kids' book bag. Still, it looked like it would suffice.

As I walked up the road after leaving the store, a gentleman in a pickup stopped to ask if I needed a ride anywhere. I took advantage and accepted his offer of a lift back to the motel. In the brief span of five minutes I quickly discovered much about trail angel, Robin. Originally from Detroit, the baseball fan rattled off the starting line-up for the Tigers of the late 60's just as easily as if he had been doing play by play. When I told him I had seen my very first major league game at Detroit's old Briggs stadium, we immediately established a rapport.

But then as Robin pulled into the Super 8 parking lot something else happened. Before departing his truck, I told Robin about Don. When I mentioned ALS, Robin removed his sunglasses, revealing the beginning of a tear in his eye. Almost choking up, Robin stated, "My mother died of ALS." So for another ten minutes or so Robin shared how he had taken care of his mom after she was diagnosed at the age of 68. Here was a man who truly understood the horrendous conditions of the disease. Robin gave me his cell number, offering to help me in any way he could while I was in the Erwin area. As my new friend drove away, I sensed that each of us had helped the other in a small way. We never know what person might appear in our lives that brings with him some degree of understanding and comfort.

## April 17, Devil Fork Gap to Spivey Gap

Booming thunder awakened me at 5:30. When I looked out the window of my motel room, rain glistened on the pavement at the pre-dawn hour. I lay in bed until my phone alarm announced that 6:00 had arrived. When I walked into the lobby to have breakfast, other hikers were surveying the weather, trying to decide whether to hike or not to hike. I called 10K to get his take on the forecast. Tom said that he was "hard core," and therefore, would hike. Taking the local's advice, I asked him to go ahead and pick me up at 7:00. Several others said they were going back to bed.

By the time I arrived at the trail, the rain was coming down pretty good. Still, since I would only be carrying water and food in my slackpack today, I figured I could hike the planned 21.9 miles despite the weather. Before Tom drove away at Devil Fork Gap, however, I asked him to be on the alert to come get me at Sam's Gap if the weather proved too much. He agreed.

So off I walked into a steady rain, not seeing a soul for the first couple of hours. Then just as the sun made a feeble effort to peek through the clouds, I came upon Oaks and Sweet Pea who were sitting in front of their tent having some breakfast. In fact, I passed several tents throughout the morning with their occupants still inside I presumed. At some point I noticed the Germans, Restless Cowboy and Fresh Coke, taking down their tent.

"Hey, Don's Brother!" Restless Cowboy greeted me.

I only paused briefly and then headed on up the trail. A little later I spotted Nick, the young man from Washington state whose picture I had taken on the exposed ridgeline on Monday. We hiked together for a while before he pulled away. Later I passed Nick when he was taking a break and I didn't see him again after that. I also passed Bulldog just before Big Bald.

The rain returned at around noon and was relentless for about three hours. Even though I was wearing rain gear, I was soaked. I also fell on muddy sections twice. Both were quite comical. I could hear my brother shouting, "safe," as I went down in a position that resembled a hook slide. The other time I literally hydroplaned for several yards before crashing into some small trees. If anyone had gotten that trick on video, he would have had a YouTube sensation. That fall occurred as I hiked down from Big Bald, another open area with I'm sure great views. Today, of course, all I saw was fog. At times the wind and rain almost knocked me over. As the rain pelted me mercilessly, I hiked with one pole, trying to use my other hand to keep my rain jacket hood on.

Then just as suddenly as the downpour had begun, it ceased. By the time I reached High Rock, it was clear enough to enjoy a view and take some photos. Realizing that I had fifty minutes to cover the last two miles, I began the final descent to Spivey Gap, arriving just a few minutes after Tom. It felt good to know that once again I had accomplished big miles, but that I also had a hot shower and bed waiting. Before he drove away from the motel parking lot, good ole 10K made arrangements to shuttle me back to the trail the following morning. Having two more days of slackpacking planned with Erwin as my base, I concluded the day as a happy hiker.

## April 18, Spivey Gap to Erwin, TN

During the six months leading up to my departure for the A.T., I regularly read other hikers' preparatory entries at trail journals. So when Tom picked me up this morning at 7:30, and informed me that he had to stop by Uncle Johnny's for another hiker who was also going to Spivey Gap, I had no idea what surprise was in store for me. The other hiker turned out to be Susquehanna Slim, someone whose journal I had been reading, but had never met. We exchanged stories about our hikes and listened to Tom's advice along the way.

After arriving at Spivey Gap, Slim and I parted ways since he was headed south today to cover part of the section that I had completed yesterday. So with a slackpack on for the second consecutive day, I meandered up today's rather mundane trail. Other than the views coming into Erwin, it was just an up and down path through the woods with leaves, rocks, minimal mud, and an occasional water crossing. With an easy trail, just about perfect weather, and a short mileage day, I walked the 10.7 miles in just a few minutes over four hours.

Throughout today's trek, I only saw three other thru-hikers, Bulldog, Danno from Hawaii, and Tracy McG, who hails from Wisconsin. I had talked with each one before today. At one point I did see two runners from Johnson City, who were out for a marathon distance training run. When I mentioned Don to Andy and Joel, Joel said that he had lost a friend to ALS who was only 38. I continue to be amazed at the number of people that I am meeting who know or knew someone with Lou Gehrig's Disease.

As I walked throughout the morning my mind wandered incessantly. Today would have been my dad's 87th birthday, so I naturally thought a lot about things he did with Don and me while we were growing up. I remembered the summer afternoons, when he would take us to King's Pond fishing, after he had gotten home from work and we had had supper. My dad taught us how to bait a hook with a wiggler. We would fish for bream from the bank. Since most were too small to keep, my brother and I would compete to see who could throw a fish the farthest back into the lake. Don had a good arm, even at five.

In addition to thoughts of my dad and brother, my mind travelled elsewhere. At one time I silently recited the opening lines of Eliot's "The Love Song of J. Alfred Prufrock." Then I thought about James Joyce as my stream of consciousness transported me away from the innocuous trail for lengthy periods of time. I wrote the first page of a James Michener-like novel, thought of people I had met over the past week that Flannery

65

O'Conner could have used in a short story, and remembered my childhood friend Eddie Shaw when I heard the whistle of a locomotive in the distance. A quite adept photographer, Eddie always sends Christmas cards with trains he has photographed on them. So today I hiked and thought and remembered.

After coming in from the woods at the Nolichucky River, I ambled over to Uncle Johnny's hostel and outfitter, where I met the proprietor, Uncle Johnny himself. When I asked him about a shuttle into town (3.8 miles), he said it would cost me $5. What he didn't say, until he rang it up, was that there was sales tax. First shuttle I've used that charged tax. Still, I found no reason to quibble over the $5.49 fee. Bulldog, who had also arrived, needed a ride as well, so we both rode in with former thru-hiker, Grim. Bulldog had been in the woods five consecutive nights, so he was in great need of a shower and real food. About an hour before leaving the trail, Bulldog had told me that he was going to buy a dozen cheeseburgers when he got to town. When I saw him headed back toward the motel later in the afternoon, he had the leftovers in a bag in one hand and what appeared to be a 12 pack of Mountain Dew in the other.

The following day called for more rain. Still I planned to do another 20-plus mile day and then spend one more night in Erwin before resuming my full-pack hiking. Throughout the day and into the evening I thought often of a man I loved very much, my dad. Johnnie James Stephens–April 18, 1926-April 10, 1996. He loved his family, baseball, and fishing. The world is a better place because he was here.

## April 19, Erwin, TN to Iron Mountain Gap

So much for $3.00 dollar store, drawstring, nylon, (made for elementary school kids) daypacks. What was supposed to be another slackpack day turned out to be a no pack day for the final 19 miles of today's 20.6 mile hike. The undoing occurred when I tried to overstuff the sack with my rain gear. Then I spent at least ten minutes trying to re-thread the strings before giving up. At first I attempted carrying the bag, by alternating hands and awkwardly balancing my trekking poles. Finally, however, I arrived at the perfect makeshift solution. First I put all my food, including two burgers I had bought at McDonald's last night, in one of my jacket pockets. I also put a water bottle in my shorts pocket and another in my other jacket pocket. Then I unfastened the hood of the jacket and placed the ziplock bag containing dry gloves, socks, and shirt in it. Finally, I pinned the hood to the back of my jacket. So off I went, with no pack, but a very heavy jacket.

Up until Beauty Spot, the trail continued to be rather non-descript. All morning the cloudy sky had threatened rain, but none came. Then at about 1:00, to use another colloquialism, the bottom fell out. The rain quickly turned the trail into a river. And with the deluge came dropping temperatures. As I hiked through the downpour, I felt increasingly colder. Wading through water, dodging slick roots, and trying my best to sidestep unending black mud, the trail challenged me for three hours. On a clear day this section would have been cruise city.

As the uncomfortable afternoon continued, I met several thru-hikers who were slackpacking south today. Among them were Hobo and Trouble. Hobo immediately asked about my cap with the black slash mark through the red, encircled ALS. When I told him about Don and the purpose of my hike, he responded like so many others by telling me that he had lost a good friend to ALS. Before we headed in opposite directions, Hobo thanked me for telling him about my brother.

By the time I reached the Cherry Gap Shelter, the rain had temporarily subsided. One lone hiker had built a fire and was trying to divert water away from his tent site. For just a brief moment I thought that I might like to be staying in the shelter by the fire. Then I remembered the words, "hot shower," and thought, "not tonight." As I walked on I did see a couple with two German Shepherds and a single older man who said he was hiking on to the next hostel.

When I reached Iron Mountain Gap at 4:15 Tom was waiting. I couldn't have been happier to see that silver truck. Since I was completely drenched and cold, Tom turned on the heater for a few minutes to warm me up. When we arrived back at the motel, I had to say goodbye to 10K, a fellow runner and hiker who, quite frankly, reminded me a little of myself. Tom had certainly provided me with invaluable information about the trail in his area as well as reliable transportation for the past four days. At the time I didn't know that my extended slackpack idea would eventually gain a reputation. All I knew was that I needed to avoid the shelters around Erwin due to the norovirus. Since I wasn't carrying a tent, beds became my only other option. I wasn't complaining. I liked my strategy. Eventually, however, I knew that I'd have to spend another night in the woods.

That night, however, I was still in Erwin, a town I stayed in so long that I did my laundry twice. So when Molar Man's wife, Diane, offered to drive me to the Country Scrub Board, I graciously accepted. While my filthy clothes became clean again, I sat down to chat with Judy. Spending so much time in towns has its advantages. One of them is the opportunity to connect with the locals. Even though I had only met Judy earlier in the week, she seemed like an old friend. I kind of hated to say goodbye. As I did, I thought of how my life continued to be enriched by all the wonderful hikers and townspeople alike that I was meeting as I journeyed northward. A sad sort of happiness enveloped me as I walked back to the motel in darkness.

## April 20, Iron Mountain Gap to Carvers Gap

When I met Molar Man back in the Smokies, I didn't know if I would ever see him again. When he re-introduced himself to me over breakfast at the Super 8 in Erwin, I both appreciated his offer of a ride back to the trail and looked forward to having a hiking companion for a few days. So under a cool, sunny, picture-perfect day, Molar Man and I embarked on the first of what would eventually be many days on the trail together. On the first part of the hike up from Iron Mountain Gap we shared the trail with Pete, a weekender who was packing in a steak to cook over an evening campfire. Familiar with the area, Pete pointed out patches of ramps, a type of wild onion that grew along the trail. Having hiked this part of the A.T. many times before, Pete identified mountains in the distance and offered information on other aspects of the trail between Iron and Roan Mountains.

The beautiful weather continued to accompany Molar Man and me as we hiked briskly throughout the morning. Just about the time we reached Little Rock Knob, Risscuit, a young lady from NY, and Salad Days from Maine, passed by. Salad Days sported the same trail runners that I'm hiking in, Brooks Cascadia, so I took a picture of our shoes as we stood side by side. Risscuit hiked with Molar Man and me for a while, leading the way while we momentarily picked up our pace.

After a little trail magic at Hughes Gap, we tackled the 2000 foot climb up Roan Mountain enthusiastically, expecting to be rewarded with gorgeous views. The A.T. did not disappoint. Since switchbacks were plentiful and Molar Man and I were tandem hiking, the first of the two climbs did not prove to be too difficult. With a couple of rest stops, we made good time reaching the top of the 6194 foot mountain. At the higher elevation ice crystals hung from trees. The Fraser Firs seemed Christmas-like. Somehow we failed to notice a sign indicating Roan Mountain Shelter, the highest shelter on the entire A.T.

As we descended Roan, we met three section-hikers from Lexington, NC. Graham, Randy, and Michael listened compassionately as I told them about Don. Michael said he regularly followed thru-hikers as they headed north and vowed to make my journal one that he read. After walking away from the three, Molar Man and I had to deal with an extremely rocky descent going down Roan Mountain. Still, we made good time, arriving at Carvers Gap around 3:00. It had been a good day. I felt fortunate indeed to be walking with the retired dentist from Ohio. What I didn't know on this crisp, early spring afternoon in North Carolina was that my newfound friend would still be by my side on the ascent of another mountain up the trail a bit in Maine.

## April 21, Carvers Gap to Buck Mountain Rd.

Don loved to hunt. So when a deer crossed the road as Diane drove Molar Man and me back to the trail at Carvers Gap this morning, I thought of my brother. And like all the other days I've hiked, his memory remained fresh on my mind throughout the day. With what at times seemed to be unending, indescribable views from three balds, I took more pictures than I had on any other day. It seemed truly impossible to put into words the majestic vistas I experienced on Jane Bald, Little Hump, and Hump Mountain.

Even though the sun shone brightly as Molar Man and I began today's 18.3 miles, it was cold! I don't mean chilly. It was cold! My ears and hands were especially susceptible to the frigid conditions while going over Jane Bald. My hands felt frozen even though I was wearing gloves. My ears ached due to the harsh winds, until I stopped to affix the hood of my rain jacket. The wind chill had to have been in the teens. I can't remember this severe a wind chill on any of my winter long runs. Despite the cold conditions, the views, which never ceased all morning, were mesmerizing. We walked downhill for about four miles, passing Stan Murray Shelter and a blue-blazed trail leading to Overmountain Shelter, a converted barn that sleeps 20. The trail then climbed about 800 feet, culminating with an ascent of Little Hump Mountain which afforded a view back to the Ovemountain Shelter.

Molar Man and I hiked strong all day. A mile descent followed Little Hump before we began the climb up Hump Mountain. The ascent challenged us, but the 360 degree views more than made up for our efforts. The *A.T. Guide*, which warns of several false summits, was accurate. About three-fourths of the way up, Molar Man and I took refuge behind a large rock to enjoy some lunch. While we were stopped, two northbounders, Paisley and Mr. Gigglefits, paused to say hello. I took an immediate liking to the young couple from Maine that we would see many times throughout the day.

After the summit of Hump Mountain, the trail gradually descended for the next five miles. At one point a section of medium to large boulders made for some treacherous maneuvering. We also crossed the NC/TN border for the last time. Since the Smokies, the trail has zigzagged between the two states. Until Virginia, the trail now will remain in Tennessee.

When Molar Man and I reached the road, Diane was waiting with snacks. She was also providing trail magic for Paisley and Mr. Gigglefits. After a brief respite we headed on across the road to begin the final 3.3 miles of the day's hike. Shortly after, a bizarre event occurred. Out of nowhere a white and black spaniel-looking dog appeared. He raced past us, did an abrupt U-turn, zoomed past in the opposite direction, and sat down in a large mud puddle. After wallowing briefly, he charged away in the direction from which he had originally come. The dog never barked, nor did he slow down. Don would have liked the mystery dog.

So for the final short section the trail again seemed rather nondescript. We did pass a cemetery just before reaching Buck Mountain Rd. where Diane was waiting to take us to Elizabethton for the night. After checking in at the motel, I walked a little ways up the highway to a Lone Star Steakhouse, where I ordered a sirloin. No one said a thru-hike had to be drudgery. Life continued to be good as I strolled along the busy highway back to my room at dusk.

## April 22, Buck Mountain Rd. to Dennis Cove Rd.

Lucky Lucy, a very young-looking great-grandmother from Pennsylvania, proudly stated that she had been section-hiking the A.T. for several years. She introduced herself before describing her passion for the trail during breakfast. It is hikers like Lucy who crave all that the mountains have to offer, even though others, including their families, may not understand. They repeat hikes over favorite sections for pure enjoyment. Roan Mountain was Lucy's destination on the crisp, early spring morning. The excitement of a looming adventure resonated in her voice. She was eager to hit the trail once again.

So after a calorie-filled early morning meal, Molar Man and I returned to the trail at Buck Mountain Rd. With plans for Molar Man's first 20 mile day, we set off a little after 7:00. Early in the hike we walked parallel to the Elk River for a while. I imagined Don standing on the bank, casting into the slowly moving waters. It would seem a certainty that fish aplenty swam beneath the surface. Without really understanding how, at some point Molar Man and I found ourselves on the opposite side of the narrow river. Apparently we had crossed at a small inlet. With numerous water crossings of varying length and difficulty, it sometimes becomes uncertain just where you are in relationship to the bodies of water.

At Cascade Falls we stopped to take in the beauty of the spot. A little later in the morning we came to a bench with a picturesque view. Molar Man and I both reclined briefly to soak in the view and rest our feet. A little later we passed the 400 mile mark, a benchmark I had hoped to hit before I had hiked a full month. Since the following day would mark exactly a month since I left Springer, I had achieved that goal.

As the afternoon continued, Molar Man and I took a few short breaks since both of us were getting a little tired late in the day. Approaching the end of the day's hike, we passed an old log barn that looked as if it had been abandoned for over a century. No remains of a house were evident. Next to the barn, however, was a small pond. I walked to the edge of the water to observe the large number of tadpoles. Again I thought of my brother. The pond reminded me of one where Don and I took Brent and Sam to fish, on property owned by my Aunt Gladys. I still have pictures of the two five-year-olds holding up fish.

When Molar Man and I finally reached Dennis Cove Rd., Diane was waiting as usual. Before we drove away, two cars pulled up with young folks who appeared to be headed to a scenic area adjacent to the trail, just past the parking lot. We had a snack, rested briefly, and then headed back to Elizabethton. The drive down the winding, mountain road went quickly. From meeting Lucky Lucy to sharing another hike with Molar Man, all was going well in Tennessee.

## April 23, Dennis Cove Rd. to Wilbur Dam Rd.

On the one month anniversary of the beginning of my thru-hike, Molar Man and I hit the trail a little after 7:00. From the outset, many large rocks, including several rock stair steps, forced us to be careful and hike a little more slowly. The cascading waters of Laurel Falls highlighted the early morning. The rocky trail literally almost touched the fast moving stream. The sounds of the falls could be heard far up the trail. Past the falls the trail began to ascend. We hiked steadily upward for over two miles with an elevation gain of over 1700 feet.

The ascent was followed by a descent all the way to US 321 where Diane was waiting with Molar Man's lunch and a cold drink for me. The park adjacent to the Shook Branch Recreation Area still revealed signs of recent flooding. Partially submerged picnic tables dotted the area. Signs had been posted indicating a 0.3 mile detour since water covered portions of the trail around Lake Watauga. I wondered what fish might be in the beautifully blue lake as I thought about my brother. Don would have liked Lake Watauga.

After making our way around the lake, Molar Man and I hiked on to where a dam crossed the water. The trail followed a paved road for almost half a mile. When we finally returned to the woods, the terrain was relatively flat for the remainder of the hike. Due to the shorter distance, we finished today's walk at around 2:00. We had seen only three other hikers all day. Two were out for the day, and the other was a southbound section-hiker. It seemed rather odd that we had seen so few hikers the past three days.

When we arrived at Wilbur Dam Rd., Diane was waiting. They offered to drive me to the Appalachian Folk School, where I planned to stay the next two nights. Warren Doyle, an author and the record holder for the most thru-hikes of the Appalachian Trail, welcomes hikers into his home on a work for stay basis only. When Molar Man, Diane, and I arrived, we found a note on his back door indicating that he was out for a short hike, but that I could make myself at home and look around the house. After a brief walk-through, my two friends of a week drove away, leaving me a solo hiker once again.

In our phone conversation yesterday Warren had told me that I could pick up sticks in his yard, so I went ahead and began. About an hour later Warren returned and gave me a tour of the premises. In addition to his residence, the Old Donnely House, there are cabins, the school, a dance pavilion, and a red barn. Warren also showed me where his new dance facility is being erected. After the tour I spent about another hour and a half moving some lumber. The hike and the manual labor made for a tiring day. Still I was grateful to be spending the night in a bed.

## April 24, Wilbur Dam Rd. to Low Gap

My day began behind the wheel of Warren Doyle's back-up automobile, an older model, faded red, Ford Escort station-wagon, with a stick shift. The odometer is frozen at 316,370 miles. So at just after daylight I followed the taillights on Warren's other compact into Damascus. Our stop was Cowboy's, a local eating establishment often frequented by hikers. At the early hour no 2013 thru-hikers were there. The hiker that was there, however, was Warren Doyle, the man who is to the Appalachian Trail what Jack Nicklaus is to the PGA, a major record holder. Warren has thru-hiked the entire A.T. a record 16 times. For the duration of our meal I had the honor and privilege of conversing with a legend.

Today Warren was headed to Hot Springs to meet friends for a day-hike, so his idea was to place the Escort at Low Gap, the finish of a planned 22.6 mile jaunt. After we made that stop, Warren shuttled me over to Wilbur Dam Rd. With another light pack, I started today's walk at 8:35. Even though the trail ascended over the first four miles, numerous switchbacks made for comfortable hiking.

Throughout the morning views of the Watauga River and rich farm land were present. At the Nick Grindstaff Monument, a small bench had been placed in front of a marker identifying the final resting place for someone's uncle. The trail continued to be gently rolling for several miles. Near TN 91, a cooler filled with cold drinks had been positioned near the trail. I took a Pepsi and silently thanked the members of the church group who had provided not only the beverage but prayers to go along with it.

Just across the road the A.T. crossed a cow pasture. The cows ate the grass indifferently. They did let out a chorus of moos when the rain commenced just about the time I exited their confines. At first it was a cold, blowing rain and then just a steady drizzle. I ducked under an eave at the final shelter of the day to gulp down some water. Six hikers were already in the shelter for the night. After the brief respite I hiked on hurriedly due to the cold rain, covering the final 3.5 miles quickly. The trail continued to be forgiving except for some minor patches of mud. At Low Gap, US 421, the reliable Escort was waiting. After changing into a dry shirt, I navigated my way down the winding highway like a pro, never once coming close to running over the side of the mountain.

A little over half an hour later the home of Warren Doyle appeared. After a shower and starting my laundry, I drove into Mountain City for supper and a little shopping. Since Warren had requested that I finish moving lumber as my "work for stay," I resumed the task early the following morning. After my work responsibility was complete, I also phoned Susie at the Montgomery Homestead Inn in Damascus to reserve a room for the next two nights.

## April 25, Low Gap to Damascus

Because Warren wasn't able to drive me back to Low Gap until late morning, it was after noon before I headed up the trail. A climb greeted me from the outset, but I still made good time, reaching the crest quickly. Then for the remainder of the afternoon the trail continued relatively flat with minimal ups and downs. Within the first two hours I saw Mr. Gigglefits and Paisley taking a break. Throughout the day we would leapfrog one another. A chuckling Gigglefits was often heard before he was sighted.

When I arrived at the Tennessee/Virginia border, thru-hiker In Progress took my picture by the sign. I returned the favor for her and her husband, Outfitter. Reaching my fourth state was special. Virginia comprises about one-fourth of the entire trail; therefore, it will be about a month before the next state line. Even though schedules don't mean much on the A.T., I've made it to Virginia about two days before I had expected. With my light pack in tow, I optimistically hoped to continue averaging over 15 miles a day.

Shortly after crossing into Virginia, Moses passed me for the second time today and quickly disappeared into the distance. When the town of

Damascus came into view from the ridgeline, I called to let the innkeeper know that I was nearby. Coming into Damascus, the A.T. passes through a park before heading up the center of town. Couples walked holding hands while young mothers strolled their children on the comfortable afternoon. While in the park I struck up a conversation with a man walking his two dogs. Trace had thru-hiked in 2003, met his wife on the trail, and later moved with her to Damascus. We walked together until I reached the street where my inn was located. At the inn Hester gave me a tour and showed me my room.

After settling in and showering I walked about a block toward the Blue Blaze Cafe. Approaching the restaurant, I spotted Whiskers and Rocket walking toward me. We all began smiling simultaneously. I had not seen the affable couple since Hot Springs.

"Would you like to dine with me?" I asked.

Rocket regretfully replied, "I'm sorry. We just ate."

Knowing that our paths would undoubtedly cross the following day, I sadly smiled before walking into the Blue Blaze alone. While waiting for my food, I thought about my brother. He would have found the Blue Blaze a bit loud. Intoxicated laughter emanated from an adjoining room. Several thru-hikers celebrated their entrance into Virginia with beer and music. For them it was a great time to be alive. They displayed an unbridled, youthful exuberance, one that Don had embraced not too long ago. Looking at my brother's cell number, still in my phone under contacts, I thought about how much I would have liked to tell him about my hike. But then again, I think he knows.

"Hey Donald," I whispered in the booth, choking back a tear. "We've made it to Virginia."

# 6

# Southern Virginia

## April 26, Damascus to US 58

Today's hike was as much about people as it was about the trail. It began with seeing Walker, whom I had not seen in over three hundred miles, to being rescued by Snowball's family, Anne and Eddie Blevins. In between the cast just kept increasing. Every day events occur that I never expect when the day begins. Today was no exception.

I walked out of the front door of the Montgomery Homestead Inn at 7:00 directly onto the trail which runs down Laurel St. Stopping at Cowboy's for a hearty breakfast, I met for the first time Trucker and Z-Man. While we talked over breakfast, in strode Walker, a hiker from Atlanta that I had first met at the Aquone Hostel. A member of his family had commented at my website, so I was happy again to see the fellow Georgian. Trucker seemed interested in my journal, so the three of us talked about Don.

Lingering too long over my eggs and pancakes, it was a little after 8:00 before I continued the hike out of Damascus. Just as I returned to the trail Whiskers and Rocket were also starting, so I hiked along with them for part of the morning. After an early climb, the trail today resembled many other days of a walk through the woods. There were numerous water crossings; however, none proved difficult. Some required rock skipping while others had footbridges. The sound of the rushing waters was a constant companion for over an hour.

With a mild sunny day and gentle terrain, the miles zipped by. When I reached HWY 58, where I intended to end my hike today,

Whiskers and Rocket were waiting by the road. They too had decided to return to Damascus. Having been told by someone in town that this was an easy hitch, I had not arranged for a shuttle. After trying for about half an hour, I realized that the info had not been accurate. Finally, I suggested that if I walked farther up the road perhaps the two of them could get a ride. It would be the final time I would see the two on the trail.

This is where the rescue commenced. When I finally came upon a rural home, two dogs greeted me at the roadside. Seeing their owners in the yard, I asked to use a phone to call a shuttle. After that option failed I asked if I could pay the folks to drive me to Damascus. They were kind enough to agree as long as I didn't mind sharing the backseat with Snowball, a part border collie with about as pleasing a personality as I have ever encountered in a dog. He provided good company as did Anne and Eddie on the ride into town. The conversation moved from their Christmas tree farm to a rental property to Eddie's fishing. When I showed Eddie the picture of Don and the big bass, he seemed impressed. My brother and Eddie would have hit it off immediately, and Don would definitely have taken a liking to Snowball. The trail angel couple adamantly refused to take any money for the ride.

After arriving back at the inn I tried to call Whiskers. Since his phone went to voice mail, a safe assumption seemed to be that he and Rocket had decided to camp. After my call, another people moment occurred. While I was sitting in the parlor looking over possible itineraries for tomorrow, another hiker arrived. She introduced herself as Journey, thru-hiker from 2003 and friend to my friend, Switchback.

My final people encounter of the day occurred during supper at the Blue Blaze Cafe. While dining, Journey asked if I knew a hiker who was seated behind me. When I turned around, to my surprise it was The Raisin Bran Kid. I hadn't seen him since the day before Franklin. The postal worker from Ohio came over to explain that he was dealing with an injury. Kid expressed frustration over having to curtail his miles. With a definite time frame for completion, his slower than expected progress had put a damper on his hike. I was sorry to hear of his problems, but it was still great to see the Kid again.

## April 27, US 58 to Massie Gap

The day began with my third and final breakfast at Cowboy's before leaving Damascus. The Raisin Bran Kid joined me. While we were discussing the Kid's injury, Orange Peel, who was at the next table, joined the discussion. He, like so many other thru-hikers, expressed frustration with a similar injury of his own. Many hikers are dealing with some kind of shin or knee issue. A very discouraged Kid is trying to decide whether to hike fewer miles or return home for a couple of weeks of rest. It's almost impossible to console an injured A.T. thru-hiker.

Just about the time I finished my blueberry pancakes and bacon, Journey pulled up in her rental car. Her offering to drive me back to the trail in trail angel capacity saved the cost of a shuttle again. It was good to share a pleasant conversation with Journey over the winding roads. She lamented that the abundant mountain laurel and rhododendron were not yet in bloom. She also encouraged me to spend an occasional night in the woods. I assured her that I would soon.

Today's hike included a climb of 2000 feet over four miles which culminated with the ascent of Whitetop Mountain at 5190 feet. Expansive panoramic views appeared at the crest. Even though the sky was partly overcast, seven mountain ranges were visible in the distance. After Whitetop the trail became a mass of gnarled roots. At one point my foot got caught between two roots which resulted in a fall.

At HWY 601 the trail entered the Grayson Highlands. Only a few yards beyond the highway, I encountered my first wild pony. The gentle fellow walked right up to me, nudging my back in what appeared to be an attempt to get into my pack. Hikers are discouraged from feeding the ponies, so I adhered to the park's policy, saving my apple for myself. Despite not getting a treat, the pony was kind enough to pose for a close-up. Unfortunately he was the only pony I would see for the remainder of the day.

Since I was trying to reach Massie Gap by 3:30, I didn't take a side half-mile trail up Mt. Rogers, the highest elevation in Virginia. When I discovered the difficulty of hiking over the large rockfaces in the Highlands, I was glad of that decision. The tactical hiking delayed my arrival at Massie Gap by about half an hour. During the last mile I hiked briefly with five young ladies from Davidson College. When I commented on the challenging rocks, one assured me that she had first aide and was Red Cross certified. The agile co-eds quickly left me in their wake. Thankfully, I didn't need their medical assistance.

A gentle rain began falling just as I reached the parking lot at Massie Gap which had to be at least a half-mile off the trail. Mary Riggins from the Troutdale Baptist Church Hostel was scheduled to pick me up. Not seeing her, I waited about half an hour and then walked to the road to try to get cell service. Finally a car pulled up at the stop sign. The kind folks inside took the Riggins' number and promised they would call when they got service. A short while later the couple returned to tell me there were two parking lots and Mary was in the other one. It was a relief when she came into sight.

On the ride to the hostel, Mary answered questions about her church and its congregation. Already there were Titan and Tugboat. The hostel is actually two bunkhouses with four bunks in each, so I had one to myself and the two young guys shared the other. They did come over to my side for supper and some hiker banter. It was good to converse with the two throughout the evening. I didn't know it at the time; however, I would hike near Tugboat for much of northern Virginia and later see him in New York. A deep orange sunset preceded a steady drizzle which lulled me to sleep in the stillness of the rural setting.

## April 28, Resting in Troutdale

Howling winds and heavy rain awoke me at dawn. Realizing that I was in a warm, clean, dry bunkhouse, and wasn't going to hike today, I quickly decided to sleep for a little longer. My tired body thanked me. Then when I did get up, I walked to the shower house to get ready for church. Since the rain was still steadily falling, I donned my rain gear for the walk of about 200 yards to the Troutdale Baptist Church. The small red brick structure sits at the base of a hill across the road from the former church, a white wooden building.

Ken Riggins, the pastor, taught the Sunday School lesson from the book of Leviticus. He also correlated scripture from other books in the old and new testaments. Then at 11:00 Ken delivered an impassioned sermon centered on the book of 1st Peter. Molar Man and Diane sat on the pew with me, and Titan also attended. At the conclusion of the service, Ken said a special prayer for me as well as for all the other hikers on the trail. Ken's sermon truly enriched my hike. It was also special meeting and talking with members of the small congregation.

After church Titan and I walked back to the bunkhouse. Ken had told us that he would drive up to take us back to his home for lunch in about half an hour. Rain still fell as we drove the quarter mile to the Riggins' home where we were treated to a wonderful Sunday dinner. Mary had prepared baked spaghetti, chicken, baked sweet potatoes, green beans, and homemade biscuits. There was also a chocolate bread pudding for dessert. Great fellowship and conversation accompanied the meal and continued for an hour or so afterwards. The Riggins were especially interested in Don's life and illness. We also discussed his strong faith while he was sick.

After Ken drove us back to the bunkhouse, he picked up two other hikers at Dickey Gap, Taz and Owl. A little later in the afternoon Sun Duk arrived on his bicycle. The native South Korean recently completed his Master's degree at the University of North Carolina at Chapel Hill. He is on the fifth day of a cross-country bike ride by himself. After the ride he hopes to reside in California. Titan and I enjoyed comparing hiking logistics to cycling logistics with Sun. Simple relaxation dominated the remainder of the afternoon and evening.

## April 29, Massie Gap to Dickey Gap

Rich pulled over his small tan pickup truck in front of the Troutdale Baptist Church at daylight. I had walked down the hill from the hostel to a spot where Ken and Mary said I shouldn't have a problem getting a ride. When Rich asked my destination, he said he would be happy to drive me to the log store about ten miles up the road and near the entrance to Grayson Highlands State Park.

"I'm hoping to find someone who will drive me to Massie Gap for $20," I told Rich.

"For $20, I will." Rich replied.

As we drove I learned much about the man who was raised in the western Virginia mountains, moved away and raised his own family, but needed to come home after his children were grown. A true "salt of the earth" individual, Rich was on his way to a site where he was building a log cabin when he stopped to offer me a ride. After pointing out the cabin as we drove, the conversation turned to fishing. A trout fishing enthusiast, Rich tried to give me two of the mess he had on ice in the back of his truck. I thought about my brother as I listened to the excitement in Rich's voice while he talked trout. Don would have surely relished talking fishing with Rich.

When we reached the parking lot at Massie Gap, I gratefully thanked Rich, insisting that he take the twenty, even though he was reluctant to do so. Then I had to hike probably a mile on an A.T. blue-blazed spur trail back to the white-blazed A.T. With an overcast sky and a gentle trail ahead, I hoped to hike the 18.3 miles to Dickey Gap by 4:00. Other than some light rain, all went well throughout the day.

I arrived at the Wise Shelter, the 500 mile mark on the trail, and took a brief break. Another thru-hiker, Long Gone, was packing up to leave. I tried to hike with him, but within about three minutes Long Gone was long gone. The Raisin Bran Kid, who has decided to do some shorter days to allow his injury to heel, crossed my path as well.

At the Old Orchard Shelter I took another short break. Matt, a section-hiker from Atlanta, was the only one there. A little later at Fox Creek, Not Yet and Sunshine, a couple from the DC area, rested. From Fox Creek the trail ascended about 800 feet over two miles; however, the climb involved many switchbacks. Hiking solo throughout the day proved peaceful and afforded me plenty of solitude.

The day passed quickly. I made it to Dickey Gap a little before 4:00. Not Yet and Sunshine sat by the road, hoping to hitch a ride to the hostel. The three of us tried unsuccessfully for about fifteen minutes before I decided to just walk the 2.6 miles. Not Yet and Sunshine were among others who later arrived. Not having eaten well all day, I broached the subject with the others about trying to get a ride to the log cabin restaurant. Only Not Yet and Sunshine were interested. As fate would have it, about that time a small car drove up toward the hostel. Joss and Jess happily offered us the ride. Both personable young folks sported colorful tattoos. As we drove they spoke enthusiastically about the beauty of the western Virginia mountains. With smiling faces, the trail angels said they would return in about an hour to take us back to the hostel.

After an outstanding supper and the ride back to the hostel, I spent the rest of the evening chatting with all the others. I especially enjoyed being around Coy, Disciple's dog. Another very well-behaved canine, he seemed to like everyone. Don would really like all these great trail dogs I'm meeting. As darkness arrived I envisioned my brother sitting on the wooden porch petting the pooch. In so many ways, Don would have appreciated and enjoyed the company of a dog and the springtime splendor of rural western Virginia.

## April 30, Dickey Gap to VA 16, Mt. Rogers Visitor Center

Over the past three days I received several text messages, emails, and comments wondering why I hadn't posted to my journal. Since so many expressed concern, I thought I'd pose a multiple choice question for the answer. Don's Brother writes every day; however, he has been unable to post his entries over the past few days because he (a) had his pack stolen by a bear (b) fell off a mountain (c) had no cell phone service (d) decided to leave the trail and fly to Argentina (e) was kidnapped by mountain people who refused to release him until he learned to pluck the banjo. "e" should be the first to be eliminated. All the mountain folks I have met have been both kind and helpful. "a" is highly unlikely since there are rarely bear encounters on the A.T. I have considered "d" a couple of times;

however I'm traveling without my passport. That leaves "b" and "c." Almost every day I hike near the edge of a mountain, but falls are also rare. Plus, if that had happened, it would have probably been on the news. So if you answered "c" you are correct. I have been in one of the most rural, remote areas of the entire trail the past three days.

Since Mary had offered to drive any hikers to the trailhead who were waiting by the church at 7:20, I made sure I was ready at the designated time. Not Yet and Sunshine joined me by the road. We said our goodbyes and thank yous to Mary before she drove away at Dickey Gap. I hiked away from the other two who had decided to have something to eat before beginning. Like yesterday, the gentle trail made for fast hiking. After a short climb, the trail descended for about seven miles.

At VA 672 trail magic in the form of a variety of snacks and soft drinks had been provided by the Valley View Baptist Church youth of Sugar Grove, VA. The church is located less than a mile down the gravel road near where the magic was left. I took an oatmeal pie and fig bar, but chose not to take one of the canned soft drinks. The churches in this area of Virginia support the hikers to the fullest. You have to admire young folks who take on projects like this. It appeared that it was an ongoing endeavor on their part.

Throughout much of the day I hiked to music. One aspect of what appears to be the most popular country music station in the area is a fifteen minute devotional every weekday at noon. It seemed a bit unusual to be getting an inspirational message from the Bible between songs by Blake Sheldon and Carrie Underwood. The communities appear to revolve around the churches in this neck of the woods.

At the Partnership shelter, one of the nicest on the entire A.T., I took a brief rest even though the Mt. Rogers Visitors Center was located just around the next bend. Matt and Scarecrow were the only two there, but it was early afternoon. This 16-person shelter, which has running water and a shower, is favored by A.T. hikers because pizza can be delivered. Still I needed to go into Marion since I hadn't done laundry in a week and was almost out of food.

After walking across the road from the Visitors Center, I quickly got a ride from a gentleman in a work truck. Unfortunately, he could only take me to the edge of town which meant another road walk of about 3 miles. With my full pack and under a hot sun, I trudged the distance to an Econo Lodge. En route I stopped for a KFC meal and updated my journal after eating. Later in the afternoon I decided to embark on the mile walk to the laundromat. Upon leaving my room, I spotted the white Volvo in the parking lot. Molar Man and Diane were here as well. Surprised to see me, Diane quickly volunteered to take me to do my laundry. After the chore, I made a stop at Walgreen's and McDonald's before returning to the room.

I arrived just in time to turn on the TV to see Atlanta pitcher Tim Hudson hit a home run. Thinking about my brother, I sent Brent and Sam text messages. Don always loved watching and discussing the Braves' games with Brent and with me. I couldn't think of a better ending to another great day of hiking than being able to watch Tim Hudson's 200th victory. Having graduated from the same high school as my brother, Tim showed kindness and compassion to Don when he was sick. I miss my brother greatly, but I continue to carry many memories with me. Smiling, I remembered Tim and Brent's standing behind Don's power chair before a Turner Field game last spring. Thinking about Tim's milestone, Don would have been smiling tonight. I smiled with him as I rested alone.

## May 1, VA 16 to VA 683, Atkins, VA

The town of Marion provides a shuttle bus "up the mountain" three times a day for the meager fee of 50 cents. So Not Yet, Sunshine, and I were waiting outside the Econo Lodge for the ride back to the trail at 9:00. At the Mt. Rogers Visitor Center several hikers who had stayed at the Partnership Shelter last night boarded for town. Some didn't have their packs, expecting to simply re-supply and then return to the trail. Outfitter, In Progress, and Bubblegum were among them. These would be the only hikers I would see for the remainder of the day.

The hike began with several minor ups and downs before leveling off at the crest of Glade Mountain. This spot provided by far the best scenery of the day. Otherwise, the hike bordered on the mundane side until the final few miles. About three miles before VA 683, a marker stated, "1890 Farm." I took the side trail for about one hundred yards to a well-preserved farm from the late 19th century. As I walked around the old homestead I thought about how much my brother would have liked this site. It reminded me in many ways of the home of our grandparents in rural Dale County, AL. Don would have really been impressed with the old farm equipment which included a plow like our granddaddy used when we were kids.

After walking the side trail back to the A.T., I moved quickly once again to reach the road a little after 2:00. Just before VA 729, I passed by an old one-room schoolhouse. The words "Lindamood School 1894" were etched in the weathered wood above the door. History on the trail continues to fascinate me. For a couple of minutes I paused to think of how it must have been in the area almost 120 years ago. Children from the farm had probably attended the school. Their descendants might still live in the community.

The trail then wound through a grassy field for most of the final two miles to VA 683, US 11, I-81 in Atkins, VA. At the road one solitary hiker appeared. PePaw was headed to the Relax Inn after a meal at the Farm. Many hikers stay at the small local motel just a few feet off the trail. Within minutes Molar Man and Diane drove up to give me a ride back to Marion. After a hot shower I walked down to the KFC and joined Bubblegum as he literally devoured the buffet. An older Southern fellow like me, Bubblegum returned to refill his plate multiple times. When he hit double figures in chicken, I stopped counting.

The mind goes everywhere during five hours of solitary walking. How often in the real world do we have the opportunity to spend this much uninterrupted time with ourselves? At times throughout the day I sang silently my favorite Bee Gees tune, "The First of May," in recognition of the new month. A smile came to my lips as I replayed some of those carefree days of childhood. Thinking of old friends, playtimes, and Christmas trees, and in a way embracing a brief tinge of melancholia, I marched happily onward on this, the first day of May.

## May 2, Atkins, VA to Chestnut Knob Shelter

I'm a little tired. As I write this journal entry I'm in my sleeping bag at Chestnut Knob Shelter after a personal best 23.0 mile day. This shelter is made of cinder blocks, and has four sides and a door. It's my first shelter since the Smokies. Officially I've passed the 25% mark of the trail. The section-hiker to my right is already snoring and it's still light outside. I'm comfortable despite the howling wind. Fortunately, my 10 degree bag will keep me warm. I hope to stay awake at least until dark which will give me a better chance of sleeping through the night.

Today's hike began with a short walk under Interstate 81 near Atkins, VA. After leaving the road, the trail followed a grassy path before moving back into the woods. Like many recent days, no other hikers appeared throughout the morning. Two local ladies out for the day asked about my thru-hike. I also met Dustin, the supervisor of a road crew that was re-marking a nearby road. He had walked up the trail during his lunch break.

The trail today again crossed a few cow pastures. Stiles were plentiful. One served as a chair as I ate my lunch. Several water crossings, some with footbridges, dotted the trail. A couple of creeks offered opportunities for reflection. Each time I paused to look for fish, thinking about my brother. None appeared. Don would definitely have liked all the potential fishing holes.

At the Knot Maul Branch Shelter I stopped for another break. Smiles, a young man from England, who hiked with the Union Jack on his pack, was taking a break. Not feeling great, he had decided to stay the night even though it was only 1:45. I briefly thought about it myself, having already hiked 13.9 miles. After about thirty minutes, however, I hiked on, relishing the idea of putting myself in position to hit Bland and another room the following day.

During the next portion of trail, I met a few section-hikers including Pat and the Virginia Creepers. They stopped to camp at Lick Creek right before the final five mile climb up Chestnut Knob. Also tenting by the creek was Tonto, a former Chicago resident who had coached cross-country and track. Section-hiking southbound from Waynesboro to Damascus, the shirtless Tonto appreciated the jelly beans I shared with him.

After beginning the final and most challenging climb of the day, my energy level began to decline. So I continued eating jelly beans and kept drinking as I hiked. The most beautiful views of the day appeared at the open, grassy field on Chestnut Knob. Needing to get to the shelter before it got too late, I only hesitated briefly to enjoy the late afternoon splendor. Upon my arrival at the shelter, only one space remained. Several hikers had already settled in for the night. Among them was All the Way, a retired soldier whom I would later hike with in New Hampshire and Maine. A little later young Nick came in and claimed floor space. I hadn't seen him in about a week.

As darkness arrived, others settled in to sleep. For me, a little music awaited. It had been another very satisfying day. I had hiked big miles, had eaten well, met some more good folks, and like every other day, had been treated to some of the most beautiful scenery that the world has to offer. It even felt good to be sleeping in the woods again, among fellow sojourners, who like me, anticipated more challenges as the thru-hike continued on the Appalachian Trail.

## May 3, Chestnut Knob Shelter to US 52, Bland, VA

Emotional and physical ups and downs superseded the ups and downs of the trail today. From the outset my nutritional imbalance was evident. Without the good "town food" breakfast, I quickly noticed a diminished energy level. My exceedingly slow pace could most certainly be attributed to both the long, hard day yesterday and to the lack of nutrients. Still I plodded along, early in the company of 20-something Nick (Shrek) and 66-year-young All the Way. We hiked off and on together until just past the first road crossing. After that they pulled away.

Maybe it simply was due to my nutrition, but emotionally I just wasn't into hiking today. Even with some nice nearly level stretches, the hike was more drudgery than it was enjoyable. There was no gittyup in my stride. Approaching the low point of the day emotionally, I spotted a southbound hiker walking toward me, toting a bucket.

"I've never seen a hiker carrying a bucket," I commented.

"Well, you have now," replied Animal.

A 2012 thru-hiker, Animal said he had carried the same bucket every step of his hike last year. He stated that it contained hiking supplies. When I told him I was dragging today, he gave me some advice based on his experience.

"Listen to your body," Animal advised. "It will tell you what to do."

After a 23.0 mile day yesterday and a 21.7 today, both with full packs, I think it's trying to tell me something.

Within five minutes of meeting Animal, another southbound hiker came into view. Pulling out a small spiral notebook and pen, seemingly before he even stopped, the older gentleman immediately asked my trail name. He wore a T-shirt with a large letter "B" over the word "Wrestling." Identifying himself as the Coach of Pennsylvania, Randy quickly rattled off a brief history of his collegiate wrestling background as well as of his coaching accomplishments. He hikes a portion of the A.T. every year just to, in his words, "offer motivation" to the would-be thru-hikers. Was his timing ever accurate for my day! Before I finally broke away to hike on up the trail, the coach drew a symbol in the dirt, explaining how the hike and life revolve around joy and hope. I almost choked up as I told Randy about my Hike of Hope. The coach was certainly at the right place, at the right time today.

After our chat I seemed to have more enthusiasm even though my pace still lagged. At one point during the final two miles, I walked into a large, overhanging tree limb which about knocked me down. Stunned from the unsuspected collision, I just stood and stared in the opposite direction for a couple of minutes. It wasn't the first, and probably won't be the last time, I walk into a limb. Then within the next few minutes I heard rustling just to the left of me. As I looked down the side of the mountain a young black bear scampered away. When he paused to stare back in my direction, I tried to zoom in for a picture, but he blended in too well with the trees. It took me almost 600 miles to see my first bear of the thru-hike.

The last one-half mile of today's hike travelled a gravel road down to US 52 near Bland, VA. At the highway I phoned a local shuttler, Bubba, for a ride to a motel just off an I-77 exit. After checking in and showering, I walked across the road to a Dairy Queen for some much needed food. It's amazing how much better the body and soul will feel after some hot food, even if it is fast food.

The day was a difficult one on the trail. At times I asked myself if I would rather be working in the real world. Remembering that restaurants are plentiful in that other world, I almost said yes. While contemplating the differences, I began singing the Rolling Stones' "You Can't Always Get What You Want." I didn't have the best of hiking days today, but maybe this was the kind of day I needed. I walked on and I learned. And through it all I thought about my brother. He walked with me today in a profound spiritual sense. I needed Don today. But more importantly I needed to remember that above all, in good times and not so good, I was in the place that my brother loved, the woods.

## May 4, Bland, VA to VA 606

Remembering Animal's advice from the previous day, I listened to my body. It recommended a slackpack and another bed. So with that in mind I made arrangements with Bubba to pick me up at VA 606 at the end of the day's hike. It proved to be a smart decision. With a cool, partly sunny day and gently level to downhill hiking for most of the trail, I cruised. In seven hours, which included two breaks of thirty minutes total, I covered 18.6 miles and felt great! The key to the day was a pancake, bacon, and coffee breakfast. A footlong sub also made its way up the trail with me. Food by far played a significantly positive role in today's hike. With plenty of calories, unlike yesterday, nutrition was not an issue.

The hike commenced with a 0.9 mile road walk, including an over-pass of I-77. With a fairly easy trail, at least by A.T. standards, I hiked steadily for two hours, before stopping to eat my first lunch. Later in the afternoon, at Lickskillet Hollow, I partook of a second lunch at the base of a small footbridge. Just before taking out my sandwich, I noticed a group of northbound hikers walking toward me. The group included Hammer,

Torch, Rango, and Half & Half. Later in the afternoon I would pass Rango and Half & Half. Both carried large heavy packs.

After the second break I continued at a quick pace. The highlight of my day was not a view; it was a call from my daughter, Rachel. We chatted for a few minutes as I walked on up the trail. I'm not sure if it was the call or the terrain, or maybe a combination of both, but I made great time for the last five miles of the day. At Kimberling Creek, just before VA 606, I paused to talk with Hammer and Torch, who were going to camp by the creek. When I commented that there had to be fish in the slow moving stream, Hammer got out fishing line to attach to his hiking pole. As I walked over the suspension bridge thinking about my brother, Hammer was preparing to try to catch some supper.

Reaching the road, I walked the half mile to Trent's Grocery, where Bubba was scheduled to pick me up. Shrek was there doing some re-supply, so we dropped him off at the trailhead before driving back to Bland. While travelling down the winding roads, Bubba talked about relocating to the area five years earlier. He also offered some information regarding copperheads.

"If you smell cucumbers," Bubba stated, "copperheads are nearby."

I would recall Bubba's warning weeks later when Speck would say, "I smell cucumbers."

Hiking, like life, comes with its good days and bad days. Oftentimes, however, it's not what occurs that matters as much as what we learn from our circumstances. With the ability and opportunity to get up each day and simply walk, there should never be any reason for complaint. I hiked well today and I was grateful. But more importantly I am thankful for all those who send up a prayer each day to help me along my way. The folks who are praying for me now are the same ones who prayed for Don during those final difficult fifteen months of his life. For them I am thankful just as I am thankful for each day I can continue the journey along the Appalachian Trail.

## May 5, VA 606 to Sugar Run Rd.

Woods Hole, an 1880's chestnut-log cabin, located half a mile off the trail down Sugar Run Rd., has welcomed hikers since 1986. The hostel was originally opened by Roy and Tillie Wood. Their granddaughter Neville and her husband Michael are now the hostel's proprietors. As I walked toward the cabin, a light mist dampened my jacket. I was thankful that the threatening skies had not opened up earlier. On the front porch Neville greeted me with a smile. Upstairs she became the consummate salesperson, convincing me that I needed the largest and only private room.

After I somewhat reluctantly agreed, she then asked, "Would you like a blueberry milkshake?"

When I said, "Yes," she continued to smile, saying, "They're $6."

She quickly returned with the pint mason jar-filled treat. When the hard rain arrived later in the afternoon, I was grateful for my cozy accommodations.

Earlier that morning my now friend, Bubba, had shuttled me back to the trail. He had been kind enough to drop me by Subway first so that I could have breakfast while he drove two other hikers, Not Yet and Sunshine, to the trailhead at US 52. By the time he returned I was ready for a planned short 13.9 mile day. On this overcast, cool morning, I smiled as I read a comment at my website.

"We're comin' after you, Don's Brother. You're smokin' us."

Kermit and Grinch, my young Georgia buddies from the Smokies, were after me.

Within a few minutes of beginning the hike, I heard rustling leaves to my left. Two white-tail deer peered in my direction. Pausing to take a picture, I thought of Don and the many deer that had walked onto his property. He often set a motion activated camera to catch their actions. For a minute or so, the deer and I stared at each other until I finally turned my attention to the trail.

Like so many other days, today's hike started with a climb. This ascent led to a side trail to Dismal Falls. Wanting to arrive at the hostel as early as possible, I chose to forgo the falls. From there the trail leveled off over the next six miles. For a while it paralleled a stream, necessitating several water crossings. Some required rock skipping while others had footbridges. There were no less than six stream crossings during a one-mile stretch. Still I managed to stay dry and vertical.

At the Wapiti Shelter I stopped for lunch and signed the register. From there the trail ascended over the next three miles, culminating with a beautiful view to the east. During the climb I felt a little sluggish; however, overall I made good time throughout the day. Just after Big Horse Gap, signs of a recent controlled burn altered the landscape. For about a one mile segment, charred remains of foliage and trees were visible. The burning smell still filled the air. Up until late afternoon I had seen only two female southbound hikers. Then about a half-mile before my turn, Torch passed by at a brisk pace. At Sugar Run Rd. I took the turn toward the hostel.

Tonight was another special one. I enjoyed a communal meal of homemade pizza, bread, grilled cheese, and tomato soup, all prepared by Neville. Other hikers dining with me were Rainbow Braid, Sugar Bomb, Finder, and Novi. I would later see Finder often from Pennsylvania through New Hampshire. With close-cropped light brown hair and sparkling eyes, Finder displayed a somewhat mysterious, mesmerizing countenance.

Before we ate, Neville asked that we join hands, tell our trail names, and share something for which we were thankful. Thinking of my brother, I said I was grateful for the ability to walk and for my family. Each day I give thanks for both on this solitary walk toward Maine.

## May 6, Sugar Run Rd. to Pearisburg, VA

Rain, rain, rain, rain! For the better part of the day I slogged through a steady drizzle of varying degrees. A continuous, somewhat cold wind added to my discomfort. With only a short 10.4 mile hike scheduled, and a motel room waiting at its conclusion, I persevered and managed to "remain vertical" throughout the day. Considering the extremely muddy downhill section descending into Pearisburg, that in itself was quite an accomplishment.

The day began nicely around the breakfast table at the Woods Hole Hostel. Like last night, Neville requested that we join hands and state that for which we are thankful. I said that I was thankful for my brother Don's life. The same group of hikers, plus Owl and Zag, were served scrambled eggs with sausage and kale, cantaloupe, peach crisp with homemade yogurt, and fresh baked bread. A special coffee blend was also available. So much for trail food. I'll take this kind of breakfast on any day.

Several chose to forgo hiking today due to the poor weather conditions. In fact, when I walked away from the hostel, in a light sprinkle, no one else had left the building. The half-mile walk up the gravel road leading to the trail set the mood for the entire day. I was wet before I stepped foot on the A.T. Still the ascent from Sugar Run Rd. didn't pose any serious obstacles despite numerous slippery rock slabs. Nevertheless I made good time even in the rain. And like yesterday, I saw two white-tail deer in the first mile. It was disappointing, however, that all the views listed in my *A.T. Guide* were fogged in. I missed the view to the west at Angel's Rest. For consolation I reminded myself of the spectacular vistas I had already been fortunate to have good weather days to enjoy.

With about four miles left in the hike I came across Snailmail, a section-hiker from north Georgia who had stopped for a break. A little while later he caught me, so we hiked together into Pearisburg. Snailmail had been out for a 100 mile section-hike which ended today. A postman in Chattanooga for thirty years, he has been using vacation time to hike the A.T. for a while, getting all the way from Springer to Pearisburg. A seminary graduate as well, Snailmail shared his faith with me as we hiked. I, in turn, talked about Don's. Finishing the day in such fashion minimized the discomfort from the relentless rain.

When we reached the outskirts of town, we made a tactical error by not conferring with our guides. Not realizing that he had parked his truck just down Lane St., we continued the hike over the New River. Only then did we realize that we were walking away from Pearisburg. Backtracking across the river, we located Snailmail's truck in a grassy lot just up the road from the trail. My new friend then drove me to my motel before beginning his homeward journey.

So tonight I'm in the Plaza Motel, not to be confused with a hotel by the same name at Central Park South and 5th Ave. in Manhattan. The amenities may not be the same, but hey, it's an Appalachian Trail town. And considering the six hour walk in the rain, I couldn't be more comfortable. I'm dry, I've had a meal, I'll probably have another a little later, and the Braves are on TV tonight. Even on a wet day, all is good along the Appalachian Trail.

## May 7, Pearisburg, VA to VA 635

My good buddy Kevin and I have a phrase that we apply to days like today when we go for a run in a park near my home: "Just me and the ducks." I can't think of many creatures more suited for a day like today. For hiking it was dismal. In fact, I thought about using the same opening paragraph that I began with yesterday. Again, the rain never ceased until the final two miles of a 21.7 mile day. At times it was downright annoying.

Despite the rain, my day got off to a great start over breakfast at Hardee's. Nearing the end of my meal, I heard a voice from a nearby booth say, "Not very good hiking weather lately." That brief comment led to a fifteen minute conversation with Fred Austin and his son, Steve. After sharing with the gentlemen about my hike in memory of my brother and his faith, Fred asked about our church. When I told him that our family was Methodist, he revealed that he had been a Methodist minister for 38 years. The final portion of that tenure had been as a superintendent. Before our chat ended he had shown me a picture of his red-headed great-granddaughter. The retired minister exuded a sense of pride and kindness. His generosity became even more evident when he drove me to the trailhead about a mile up the road. My good fortune to keep meeting fine local folks continued. Before the reverend drove away, I let him know that he was now an official trail angel.

Walking into the woods, I felt a little irritated that I had to re-walk about three-quarters of a mile that Snailmail and I had hiked yesterday. Still within half an hour I had again crossed the New River Bridge and was headed back up a mountain. Shortly after beginning the climb, the first turtle of my journey sat in the middle of the trail. After the tortoise sighting, the rain began. And I mean rain. For the next eight hours I would hike in a steady drizzle. A dense fog added to the discomfort since the trail was only visible a few feet ahead.

Getting to a slick, rocky section, I noticed a safari-type hat lying in the center of one of the flat slabs. Recognizing it as belonging to Jungle Juice, I picked it up and placed it in the mesh pocket on the back of my pack. I had met the young hiker last night in Food Lion. He was re-supplying to return to the trail even though it was almost dark and getting to the Rice Field shelter would require a 6.8 mile hike. I was a little concerned for him as he headed back to the trail.

Retrieving the hat, I was counting on Jungle Juice still being at the shelter. I was right. When I walked up Jungle Juice was in his sleeping bag, alone on this wet, cold morning. Very grateful for the return of his hat, which he said he lost in the dark trying to prevent a fall, Jungle Juice said he planned to stay at the shelter and take a zero today.

"I'll see you up the trail," I told him, before hiking back into the thick fog.

For about the next four miles I hiked on relentlessly, trying to maintain a fast pace just to keep warm. Like yesterday, I lamented not having the opportunity to enjoy the views. Suddenly in the distance I noticed an approaching hiker wearing a green poncho. I said something like, "I don't believe it....another hiker!" The lady paused to ask if I were Mike. Don, the shuttle driver, had dropped her off where he was scheduled to pick me up in the afternoon. He had also told her that she might meet a hiker named Mike on the trail. Speck, who said she was on day two of a section-hike to Waynesboro, was slackpacking south today.

With rain dripping from the hood of her poncho, Speck asked my trail name.

I replied, "Don's Brother."

"No way!" She almost disbelievingly exclaimed.

Speck had been reading my journal regularly before beginning her hike. So in a steady downpour we talked about sharing a shuttle the following day. Finally realizing that we had better get moving before a chill set in, we parted ways.

And so on I slogged, only seeing three other hikers all day. Two northbound thru-hikers, also slackpacking south today, only paused long enough to tell me that plan. Then toward the end of my hike I met southbound thru-hiker Crazy Horse, a young man wearing a Washington Nationals baseball cap. He had begun his hike in August, taken the winter off, and was now continuing to Springer.

With about five miles to go, I called Don to tell him I was about an hour and a half ahead of schedule. He said he could be at VA 635 shortly after 4:30. I was getting colder as the incessant rain continued. A short while later a couple of flooded stream crossings would pose significant challenges. Stepping stone rocks were under water at the first stream. Since my shoes and socks had been wet all day, I simply stepped on the submerged rocks and crossed. At the next crossing, however, things would be different. Had it not been for an overhanging limb to use for balance, I'm not sure I could have made it. As I stepped on the first underwater rock, I felt the rushing water pulling on my shoe. Fortunately I maintained my balance as I carefully made my way across.

At about the same time I navigated the final stream, the sun peeked out for the first time in three days. After a quick stop at the Pine Swamp Branch Shelter, I steadily hiked to the road, crossing by wooden bridge over the raging Stoney Creek. Within ten minutes Don drove up to shuttle me back to Pearisburg. After a very wet, occasionally challenging, and a bit lonely day, it definitely felt good to be in a town tonight. With more rain in the forecast, tomorrow could pose difficult as well. Still, when tomorrow's hike concludes, I'll be just that much farther north on my way to Maine along the Appalachian Trail.

## May 8, VA 635 to Rocky Gap

For the third consecutive day, I got wet. Really wet! I was again soaked at the end of a modest 13.1 mile day. My pack is wet, my rain gear is wet, all my clothes are wet.....I suppose it's clear by now that I'm not a happy hiker. Well, actually I couldn't be more content. I've covered 45.2 miles over those last three days, and somehow I've managed to stay afoot while doing it. Plus, the forecast for tomorrow is sunny with a high of 75, which hopefully will help dry out the, saturated beyond recognition in places, trail.

Another reason that I'm feeling so good is that for the first time since I moved on up the trail from Molar Man, I had a steady hiking partner all day. Speck, a cardiology RN from Atlanta, shared the shuttle back to the trailhead with me this morning. Speck hikes about my pace. Our styles seemed to complement each other well over the sloppy terrain. Also a runner and mountain biker, Speck has section-hiked the A.T. from Springer up to where we concluded our hike today. Her plans are to hike four days with her youngest son's fiancée beginning on Friday and then to finish up this section in Waynesboro in a couple of weeks.

Today's hike began with a climb of about 1000 feet to Bailey Gap Shelter. Several rocky areas necessitated focused walking for a couple of miles. Just like the past two days, no views were visible. At times the trail transformed into a stream of moving water. Keeping shoes and socks dry proved impossible. I've just come to accept the inevitability of uncomfortable conditions when they occur.

Unlike yesterday, only one water crossing presented a bit of an unnerving situation. Speck handled the walk across a log bridge easily. I, however, inched my way across, trying not to look at the raging waters underneath. Every time I heard rushing waters in the distance, I feared a raging stream without a bridge. It's doubtful that the water will subside over the next twenty-four hours, so I could have more obstacles to deal with tomorrow. There was no point, however, worrying about the inevitable.

After passing Lone Pine Peak, the trail descended almost 2000 feet. With a quagmire to deal with, the downward hike required some slow, tedious maneuvering. When Speck and I reached the War Spur Shelter, we took a short break. Two hikers were sitting out the rain. Then just past the footbridge over Johns Creek, the trail again began to ascend. With more wet rock slabs to handle, we slowed slightly on our way to Rocky Gap where Don was waiting to transport us back to Pearisburg. An extremely affable gentleman, Don insisted on stopping first at Wendy's so that we could get a late lunch.

For the first time in several days I've gotten in a good hike, showered, had a meal, and written my journal entry before 5:00. I'm about to go do a little shopping and then have dinner at a Mexican restaurant across the street. And as I look outside I notice that it has stopped raining. Despite the rain and messy trail conditions, good company and thoughts of my brother made for another joyous day on the Appalachian Trail.

## May 9, Rocky Gap to Craig Creek Rd.

Blue skies and bright sunshine prevailed on a perfect day for hiking. Even with a couple of precarious stream crossings on slanted wet rocks, nothing could spoil the picture-like views or detract from the pleasant company. From pasture crossings to rock hopping, the trail offered great variety throughout the morning and the afternoon alike. The 16.8 mile day raced by, leaving me happily tired with my feet in a stream at its end.

Like the last two mornings, my day began at the Pearisburg Hardee's. For the third time I had the pleasure of chatting with Fred Austin and his son Steve. Since the post office had already closed when I needed to buy stamps yesterday, I asked Fred if he would mail some cards for me. He graciously agreed. I felt honored to have made the acquaintance of these two gentlemen while in Pearisburg.

Right on schedule, shuttler Don arrived at 7:00 to drive Speck and me back to the trail. We were immediately greeted with a straight-up climb from Rocky Gap. Then the trail leveled to Kelly Knob which afforded us our first view in what seems like a week. After passing the Laurel Creek Shelter, we encountered the first of two challenging stream crossings over wet rocks. The still swollen creeks were not as high as yesterday; however, rocks were still submerged. After watching Speck cross the first stream with relative ease, I chose a different approach which led to a wet shoe.

We then made our way over a pasture which provided beautiful views in all directions. Puffy white clouds dotted one of the bluest skies I have ever seen. A footbridge at Sinking Creek was a welcome sight. Then a little over a mile later we arrived at the Keiffer Oak. The largest oak tree on the A.T. in the south, it is estimated to be over 300 years old. Carpenter and Little Seed, two northbound hikers that we had seen yesterday, were stopped for photos. We alternated taking each other's pictures. After they had moved on, Speck and I took off our packs for a rest.

When we headed on up the trail, a section of rocky, slanted slabs awaited us. Fortunately, the sun was out and the slabs were dry. Skipping, hopping, and climbing from one slab to the next made for a somewhat unnerving, yet fun segment of trail. Breathtaking views to the east enhanced the hike. At one time Speck commented that the rocks were exhilarating. I agreed. Beginning to feel more like a seasoned hiker, it was all exciting.

After passing the Niday Shelter and walking across one final stream for the day, Speck and I arrived at Craig Creek Rd. Speck's son's fiancée, Jodi, had not gotten there yet. So while we waited, Speck and I took off our shoes and soaked our feet in the ice-cold water. When Jodi was over an hour late, I decided to walk up the road in hopes of finding a home with a phone since there was no cell service in the area. Because a ferocious-sounding dog guarded the first house I saw, I kept walking. A few minutes later, a friendly man in a pickup stopped to ask if I needed help. He owned the home with the dog and had seen me walk by. Again a trail angel had come to the rescue. Jeff not only let me use his phone to call Jodi, but he also drove me back to where Speck was waiting. Shortly thereafter Jodi drove up and we were on our way to Daleville. The ladies dropped me by my motel before heading to theirs.

After getting cleaned up, I joined Speck and Jodi for dinner at a Cracker Barrel. When the subject of trail names came up, I suggested Lost Girl for Jodi. We all laughed. She plans to join Speck for a four day section-hike, her first on the A.T., beginning tomorrow. For me, it will be back to the woods alone to deal with Dragon's Tooth and perhaps a thunder shower as I keep heading north with renewed enthusiasm yet also with a little fear.

## May 10, Craig Creek Rd. to Newport Rd.

Like many other times, I used a shuttle to get back to the trail for a 15.4 mile day. Actually Speck arranged for Homer to drive us. A trail and shelter maintainer in the Daleville area, Homer exemplifies all that is good about the Appalachian Trail. Along with his wife and two youngest children, Homer thru-hiked the A.T. a few years back. When I asked him about the difficulty of the section around Dragon's Tooth, he said he had come down it carrying a chain saw. At 71, Homer takes a very active role in maintaining the trail. When he picked me up that afternoon, Homer told me that he had cut grass near the trail and run five miles earlier in the day. In the evening he was playing bridge.

After returning to the trail at Craig Creek Rd., I hiked on ahead of Speck and Jodi since they were planning a shorter day. Not arriving at the trail until 11:30, I hoped to hike quickly so that I could get to Dragon's Tooth before the predicted afternoon thunderstorms arrived. After the initial ascent up Brush Mountain, the trail very slightly descended for four miles to Trout Creek. During the descent, a short blue-blazed trail led to the Audie Murphy Monument. The monument was erected near the site where Murphy died in a plane crash. Since two wooden benches were available, I relaxed on one to eat a sandwich. Scarecrow, an ex-marine from Pennsylvania, occupied the other.

For much of the day the trail was friendly. Then came Cove Mountain and a variety of rock structures to climb over. None proved especially challenging; however, a certain degree of anxiety seemed to encompass me as a feared descent loomed in the immediate future. Having stressed all day over a section of the trail that is significantly technical, I feared that I would have to tackle the narrow ledges alone. Then just around a bend on the climb up the southern side, there sat a bespectacled, curly-haired young man who exuded what might be classified as a sort of shy intelligence.

After I told him that he was a Godsend, Howdyman introduced himself and informed me, "I hike slowly and like to talk."

Happy to have a partner to accompany me down from Dragon's Tooth, I replied, "Go ahead; just stay close by."

"I always want to know why people are thru-hiking the trail," my new buddy stated.

So I told him a little about my hike and my brother. Howdyman paused a few times, looked over his shoulder to make eye contact, and listened. For a lad of only twenty-two, he exhibited thoughtful compassion. After I had explained about my hike, I asked Howdyman about his.

Although exceedingly young for such, Howdyman said, "I have kind of a bucket list."

He went on to say that initially he considered eliminating the thru-hike goal, thinking he would never find the time.

"At first I didn't know when I would get around to a thru-hike." "Then I just decided, why not now?"

He had put life on hold for a while to walk the Appalachian Trail. Even though he has a degree in Mechanical Engineering in hand, Howdyman said he has always wanted to be a policeman. The Barney Fife want-to-be talked of small town departments where he might like to work, as I concentrated on getting off the ledges without a slip. For such a young fellow, he appeared to have a firm grasp on his future. On this overcast, suddenly breezy late afternoon, I was glad. Howdyman continued by telling me about getting his trail name and some of his rather unorthodox hiking strategies. For one, he carries a very light tarp which he only uses if it's raining. On most nights Howdyman said he cowboy camps, sleeping under the stars.

After stopping briefly to admire the monolithic Dragon's Tooth, Howdyman and I quickly returned to the trail. With dark clouds overhead and a thunderstorm approaching, I hoped that my new hiking buddy would pick up his pace. He didn't. Still, I figured hiking over the dangerous stretch with another hiker nearby outweighed passing Howdyman to descend Dragon's Tooth alone. Still we needed to get down the potentially dangerous rocky section of trail before the imminent rainstorm arrived. Then out of nowhere, a swarm of some kind of black fly decided to harass me. Swatting flies while going over the rocky trail was not what I had expected. But neither was the trail. I had become so concerned with the difficulty of the rock ledge section that I had failed to appreciate a couple of beautiful views.

So as Howdyman led the way, I followed, swatting flies with one hand and balancing myself with the other. Howdyman just kept smiling and talking. All was good. Each time I thought we had finally come to the end of the treacherous section, another portion requiring the use of hands appeared. Howdyman thought it was great fun, and as matter of fact, after the initial adjustment to hiking without poles, so did I. Howdyman's companionship for the descent allowed me to fully enjoy a section of the trail I had been dreading. Even though I handled the rock scrambling segment well, I was still glad Howdyman was around. Although I didn't really need his help, he stood beneath me on some of the more difficult parts, just in case I slipped.

When we finally did reach level ground, I hiked on behind Howdyman until the rain started. Noticing that he had picked up his pace a little, I assumed Howdyman would hike with me to the road and walk to a nearby store to dry out. That was not to be the case.

When the raindrops got bigger Howdyman suddenly stated, "That looks like a good spot," as he ducked under a tree to pitch his tarp.

It didn't look like that good of a spot to me, but then, I wasn't the one pitching the tarp. I yelled goodbye before moving on.

I hiked on at a faster pace, hoping that Homer would be there early. As I got within a few minutes of the road, headlights could be seen glaring from the parked car. Harder rain began to fall just as I entered the blue compact, happy to be driving back to a dry room and a bed for the night. I hoped that Howdyman stayed equally dry under his tarp.

Three days later I would again see Howdyman on the trail. He asked me if I had tried his "cowboy camping" yet. I told him that I had not. I never did, but occasionally I did think of Howdyman as I looked up at the stars. For a person so young, Howdyman resembles many on the Appalachian Trail. He simply walks one day at a time from where he is to where he thinks will be a good place to spend the night. Life can be rather simple when all one has to do is awaken each day to follow the white blazes toward Maine, and the northern terminus of the Appalachian Trail.

## May 11, Resting in Daleville

After having completed one-third of the trail, I spent some time reflecting while taking a day off in Daleville. When this adventure began exactly 50 days ago, I set some short-term goals. I wanted to first get to Neels Gap, then to the Smokies followed by Hot Springs, Erwin, and Damascus. I kept telling myself, "Get to Virginia, and you'll be OK." So now that I'm over 200 miles north of Damascus, I feel pretty good mentally. At this moment I'm about as positive as I've ever been that I can accomplish my goal and finish this thru-hike of the Appalachian Trail.

So after a solid eight hours of sleep, when I don't think I moved all night, I felt physically fresh again. The threatening skies outside my motel room window couldn't alter my mood. And speaking of towns and rooms, it appears that quite a few other hikers are becoming aware of my strategy. I made it no secret from the start that I would utilize every bed and restaurant I could find. Every thru-hiker has a method. For me it's trying to sleep in the woods as seldom as possible. For some it's the exact opposite. Still, many others are also fully utilizing the shuttles. Some shuttle drivers are virtually busy all day.

Recently in Pearisburg, I told Mr. Gigglefits and Paisley (two of my favorite young people on the trail....folks need to hear him laugh and see her smile) that I had finally spent another night in the woods at the Chestnut Knob Shelter.

Paisley said, "You can't count that. It's a fully enclosed shelter with a door."

If that's the case, I haven't slept in the woods since the Smokies, but I've walked past every white blaze. The phrase "Hike Your Own Hike" is one that is often heard on the A.T. I'm definitely hiking mine.

So today, like so many over the past 50 days, was a good day. It was a good day to rest, a good day to write, a good day to catch up on emails and texts with friends, and a good day to watch baseball. I think my brother's smiling. Tomorrow the pursuit continues on the spectacularly beautiful Appalachian Trail.

## May 12, VA 624, Newport Rd. to Daleville, VA

My now good buddy Homer and his lovely wife Teresa dropped me back at the trailhead off VA 624 a little before 7:00. An early start was needed to knock out the planned 25.7 miles. After a short ascent, the trail crossed more pasture land with numerous stiles. Other than a few patches of mud, it was a comfortable trail on an equally comfortable, cool sunny morning. I made really good time, reaching the large parking lot at VA 311 to Catawba in a little over two hours. Lots of day-hikers had parked there for their climb up to McAfee Knob.

At the beginning of this segment of trail, I met four such day-hikers from Blacksburg. A little later I passed a large group including a lady carrying a baby in one of those harness-like apparatuses. On such a gorgeous weekend day, many were in pursuit of the spectacular views that McAfee has to offer. This section of the A.T. is one of the most visited on the entire trail. Easily accessible from VA 311, many will hike the "just short of four miles trail," up and back.

Reaching the Johns Spring Shelter, I paused to reminisce about my snake incident there on a section-hike. Half & Half and Rango, two young hikers I had met about a week ago, were packing up to leave. They scooted by me a few minutes later; however, when I got to McAfee Knob they were both there along with Torch. The three asked if I would take their picture. I took several of the three friends, and Half & Half likewise took a couple of me. Also on the knob was former thru-hiker Low Gear and his dog Tonka. This proved to be a banner day for dogs, and I know my brother would have liked them all.

As advertised, the views from McAfee were beyond spectacular. A more perfect weather day could not have been had. After just soaking it all in for about ten minutes, I headed on up the trail toward Tinker Cliffs, a half-mile cliff walk with a continuous view to the west. From Tinker Cliffs I passed several other vistas over the next four hours. Toward the end of to-day's hike, the trail alternated between rocks of varying sizes and soft pine straw. Rock hopping was again required on the occasional boulders. Before reaching Daleville, the trail also passed under power lines five times. At one of these spots with a view, a lady and two children had walked up to enjoy the scenery. On a picture-perfect day, I could easily understand why.

About 200 yards before the trail reached the highway in Daleville, Jungle Juice had set up his tent. I had last seen him on Tuesday in his sleeping bag at the fogged-in Rice Field Shelter. An easily likable young man, he seldom goes into towns except to re-supply. That's the case with a lot of the young folks on the trail.

After reaching the road I walked on across to where the trail begins to climb again. Then I stopped, turned around, and headed back to my room and a hot shower. A little later I joined Speck, Lost Girl, and Lit-tle Seed for a meal at a Mexican restaurant. Dining with the three ladies was a delightful way to conclude my day. When Lost Girl couldn't finish her fajitas, Speck suggested we take Jungle Juice some town food. So I ventured back up the 200 yards of the trail and presented JJ with the gift from the ladies. He was most appreciative.

Throughout today's hike I thought often of my mother. This was the first Mother's Day in my entire life that I had not spent some time with her. I did call her twice. Since it was her first Mother's Day without her other son, I knew that Donald was on her mind throughout the day. On my first call I also got to speak with Linda and wish her a Happy Mother's Day as well. It felt good to know that my wife was spending the special day with my mother. The views on today's hike were special, but no view is as special as the two most important mothers in my life.

## May 13, Daleville, VA to Harvey's Knob Overlook

There is a section of the Appalachian Trail in northern Virginia that is referred to as the "roller coaster." In a way every day on the A.T. can metaphorically qualify as a roller coaster. From the physical unending ups and downs to the emotional ebbs and flows, each day comes with its set of challenges. On some days I awake and think, "Do I have to hike again today?" Then when I take that first step on the trail, all is well with my world. On other days I wake up raring to go, only to suffer a case of the doldrums within the first couple of miles. Like in life, there is no certainty to how a day will turn out on the trail. I sometimes find myself identifying with Gulliver in Brobdingnag while at others I seem to be Odysseus looking for Ithaca.

Today I got the opportunity to again hike with Speck, along with Lost Girl and Little Seed. We departed from Daleville at 7:30 with a planned 16.1 mile day, which would take us to Harvey's Knob Overlook. Faced with a rather mundane trail, no views were evident until around the first of three crossings of the Blue Ridge Parkway. Such crossings occur regularly through the Shenandoahs. Other than a couple of stiles and four or five short stream crossings over rocks, nothing really stood out.

We did meet two hikers from New Jersey who said they had section-hiked over 1700 miles. El Gato and Calves related some of their hike to us during one of our breaks. I at first thought Calves had said his trail name was Cabs even though he was pointing to his lower leg when he explained. Nevertheless, it took me a while to understand what the man from Jersey was saying. Both seemed like great guys.

When the three ladies and I reached the Wilson Creek Shelter we took a lunch break. A couple of day-hikers were there with their dog. The pooch didn't seem very friendly, so I failed to get his name. As we relaxed, El Gato and Calves stopped by. They were headed to the next shelter for the night. Also passing by was Howdyman. It was good to see my young friend from Dragon's Tooth again. With a somewhat cold breeze beginning to make us a little uncomfortable, we finished our lunch and then resumed the hike.

At the second crossing of the BRP two folks had set up chairs and were providing some trail magic. Footnote, a former thru-hiker, and his wife Pat had quite the spread. From fruit and vegetables to cookies, pound cake, and milk, it was all good. The popcorn, however, seemed to be the favorite. Footnote also told us about his recent completion of a hike of the entire Blue Ridge Parkway.

When our group reached Harvey's Knob Overlook, Homer was waiting for one final shuttle back to Daleville. Very tired from the hike and poor sleep last night, I briefly dozed on the ride back into town.

With plans to stay in the woods the following two nights, I later walked down to Kroger for some groceries. Spotting the Raisin Bran Kid in line at a checkout, I sauntered over to say hello. The Kid continues to plod northward despite his injury. Without knowing it at the moment, this would be the final time our paths would cross. Bidding the Kid goodbye, I walked back to the Super 8 along a busy highway, all of a sudden cognizant of a slight ache in my right Achilles tendon. As darkness approached I replaced the fear of an Achilles issue with thoughts of Don. My brother could not walk the last eight months of his life. Surely a little ache in my ankle wouldn't keep me from continuing my journey on the morn.

## May 14, Harvey's Knob to Jennings Creek

The best laid plans......maybe it was the 25 mile day on Sunday; maybe it was the cumulative miles; maybe it was too many hills.....or probably it was the new shoes. Whatever it was, I had to cut today's hike short with a very sore right Achilles tendon. From the outset I quickly realized that an adjustment in miles would be necessary before the day ended. I had hiked relatively injury-free for 53 days. Now my hope was that the setback would be brief. Having had tendinitis on many occasions over my years as a runner, I knew how to treat the ailment. More significantly, I knew that the most important component of recovery was rest.

A cool, pleasant sunny morning greeted Speck, Little Seed, and me as we headed up the reasonably level trail from Harvey's Knob. After less than a mile, however, I became aware that the day would be a challenging one. Not due to the terrain, but instead due to an Achilles that began talking to me in a language that I unfortunately had heard before. It repeatedly asked me to give it a rest until I finally realized that I needed to slow down. So I gingerly attempted to hike without a limp throughout the morning. Finally, I gave up and limped. Relying heavily on my poles, I somehow still got in 12.1 miles.

My hiking companions were nice enough to stop at the first crossing of the Blue Ridge Parkway to allow me to catch up. It was then that I told the two ladies to hike on and not worry about me. Surprisingly, for a couple of miles I stayed with them as the soreness temporarily subsided. Then just as quickly, it returned with a vengeance. I hobbled the next few miles, finally reaching the Cove Mountain Shelter where my two buddies were having lunch. Also at the shelter were the two Jersey boys we had met yesterday, Calves and El Gato. They had been joined by three other section-hiking friends.

As I dejectedly ate two peanut butter and jelly sandwiches, Speck finally asked me what I was going to do. Reluctantly, I told her I felt like my best option was to try to get to VA 614, Jennings Creek, and go back to town. The other option was to hike on to the planned shelter and face a more challenging day tomorrow. I think I made the only sane decision. All the others commiserated with me until I tried to alter the gloom with laughter. It hurt, but I knew that saying goodbye to my friends of only a few days was really all I could do.

Watching Speck walk into the distance and eventually disappear over the horizon was one of my lowest moments on the trail. We had become good friends in a short period of time. I would miss her. As I continued to very slowly make my way toward the road, I called Linda. She too felt for me. After a brief emotional moment I knew I had to walk on up the trail....for now to a road where old reliable Homer would be waiting, but in a few days back to the same spot to continue north. Again, there really wasn't any other choice.

When I finally reached the road, Homer too showed remorse over my situation. On the drive back to Daleville I outlined my rehab plan to him, mainly so that I could hear it aloud rather than just in my thoughts. Part one was to call my good buddy John Teeples. John agreed to overnight a new pair of Brooks Cascadia trail runners, one-half size bigger, along with some other items that should help with the injury. But for the rest of the night and the next few days, a regimen of ice, anti-inflammatories, and rest was needed.

Assessing the situation, I became even more determined to stay positive. After all, I was over a week ahead of schedule with 15 mile days. I could still take ten days off and finish on the day I planned, and even if I needed to finish a little later, Baxter State Park usually remains open until mid-October. So I'd had a little setback. At least it hadn't come earlier, and hopefully it wouldn't be that serious.

My brother would have said, "Rest, get better, and get going."

Listening to Don, I knew that in just a little while I would be walking again on the Appalachian Trail.

## May 15, 16, 17, and 18, Resting the Achilles

When I started planning this hike back last fall, I prepared a tentative timeline up to New Hampshire. As I regularly perused the schedule, I noted where I should be on my birthday. It wasn't in a motel room in Daleville, VA. Then again, we never really know where we may be on any given day. When he turned 53 in July, 2010, my brother didn't know that less than a year later he would be facing an ALS diagnosis. So while I couldn't help but lament my injury, I was reminded of just how insignificant it was in the big realm of things. In fact, compared to Don's plight, it was like comparing a penny to a billion dollars. Come to think of it, that's not even a wide enough margin.

So as I continued to rest and hopefully heal, I also reminded myself of the virtue of patience. When we are generally healthy, time is the healer. When someone has a terminal illness, however, time is merely that space between life and death. But aren't we all living somewhere along that indefinite line? No one knows exactly how much time he has left on this earth. What we do know is that every minute of every day is precious. We can't waste even one second of the time we have been given.

So sitting in a McDonald's enjoying a second cup of coffee, I tried to dwell on the positive rather than the negative. My family loved me and was supportive of this adventure; my friends had showered me with good wishes for success from the beginning; I was generally in excellent health, and the Achilles would heal. I knew how to rehab the injury, which I was doing. I also knew that rest was important. So despite the setback, the trail awaited.

With time on my hands, I thought often about my brother. I greatly missed his birthday call. Many times over the years Don had treated me to a Braves game to celebrate. I'll never attend another game at Turner Field without remembering those special moments. Things happen for a reason. We don't know why, but we accept. So I accepted this minor setback with patience.

As I planned this hiking adventure throughout the fall and winter, I wrote about my reasons for referring to the endeavor as my "Hike of Hope." One objective was to raise awareness of the multitude of challenges a person with ALS faces. I wanted people following my walk to understand that a thru-hike of the Appalachian Trail, be it difficult in its own way, pales in comparison to those challenges a victim of Lou Gehrig's disease must confront. Hikers of the A.T. have the use of their arms and legs to navigate both strenuous as well as less difficult sections of trail. Most ALS patients eventually can't use any of their extremities. Their minds remain the same; their bodies just stop working.

So each day I continued to remind myself of just how active my brother had been before his diagnosis and just how quickly he had lost all ability to be active. He knew there was no cure, and he knew that he would never get any better. Still with a strong faith and surrounded by so many who loved him, he persevered. Sometimes, I don't know how. Watching his transformation from an avid bass fisherman, hunter, and excellent softball player to a man forced to sit in a power-chair and have others do everything for him was excruciating for all Don's family and friends to endure. For him it must have been beyond any agony the mind can conceive. So as I waited to return to the hike I thought of my brother. I reminded myself often that Don was a man of faith who loved his family, but I also kept remembering how much Don loved the woods.

## May 19, Back on the Trail

Awakening to a cool, drizzly day, I couldn't have been more anxious to get back to the trail. After spending what seemed more like a month than a week in Daleville/Troutville, I needed to hike. As much as I liked rooms and the conveniences that came with towns, I was actually looking forward to spending the night in a shelter. Anyone who had met me on the trail would probably have doubted the remark, but finally with the opportunity to hike, I stated it with sincerity.

Shortly after noon Homer's son Bennett arrived to shuttle me back to the trail at Jennings Creek. Riding and chatting with the former thru-hiker, and now Virginia Tech sophomore, reinforced my faith in the youth of today. At nineteen Bennett seemed mature beyond his age. But then what should one expect of a young man who had thru-hiked the A.T. with his parents and eleven-year-old sister when he was eight?

So as I stepped foot on the trail for the first time since Tuesday, the rain commenced. Fortunately it never got harder than a steady sprinkle as an uphill section tested my Achilles from the outset. Very slowly I began to re-acclimate myself with the nuances of the trail. All appeared fine at the beginning. After the initial climb I faced a downhill section of about the same distance. Gaining confidence with each step, I reminded myself often that I needed to remain patient. And that's exactly what I did.

At the Bryant Ridge Shelter, I picked out a good spot to place my mat and sleeping bag and then hung my damp clothes on pegs in hopes that they would dry overnight. Sleeping 20, Bryant Ridge is regarded as somewhat of a "penthouse." One entry in the shelter log stated, "I could live here." Just when everything was organized, husband and wife Spider and ET walked up. They were on a lengthy section-hike which they planned to end in Waynesboro. Already having completed the Pacific Crest Trail in sections, the couple from the San Francisco area proved to be great company. Spider and I talked about the Pacific Coast Highway and Pebble Beach as he readied his space in the shelter.

So I was finally back in the woods. It was the perfect way to continue the hike. I walked pain-free for 3.8 miles over both uphill and downhill terrain. A luxury shelter (as shelters go) afforded me good accommodations on a night when more rain was in the forecast. My fellow shelter-mates were congenial and about my age. I had burgers in the food bag for supper and my cozy sleeping bag ready when darkness came. I was a very contented hiker at the moment. It had indeed been a good day for hiking again on the Appalachian Trail.

## May 20, Bryant Ridge Shelter to Thunder Hill Shelter

A hard rain awakened me at midnight. It felt peaceful and secure under the tin roof as the rain pelted it. Quickly returning to sleep, I may have slept better than on any other night I had stayed in a shelter. One thing was for sure; it was the first night's sleep I hadn't had to pay for in over two weeks. My plans were to repeat the night in the woods. It seems unfortunate that all shelters can't be as nice as Bryant Ridge.

With only a 10.2 mile day scheduled, I lingered at the shelter until 8:25. Spider and ET headed out earlier. They informed me last night that they always hike about an hour and then take a break for breakfast. When I did start to hike, a tough climb immediately greeted me. The initial ascent was followed by two more of about the same length which culminated at the crest of Floyd Mountain. After passing Spider and ET while they were having their breakfast, I saw no other hikers all day.

Later in the morning, just as I was thinking that I hadn't seen a deer in a couple of weeks, a white tail flashed across the trail right in front of me. Don must have been hearing my thoughts. The large deer paused for a minute to stare in my direction. I also saw two large red-headed woodpeckers. Birds of varying species are plentiful on the A.T. Hawks can be seen soaring through the sky almost every day. I've yet to see an owl, however.

Even though I hiked slower than usual throughout the day, I still reached the Thunder Hill Shelter before 2:00. Unlike Bryant Ridge, Thunder Hill was a bit of a dump. After claiming a sleeping spot for the night, I walked back to a crossing of the BRP in an attempt to get cell service. None was to be found. Back at the shelter I swatted flies until bedtime. The pests made journaling as well as eating a challenge.

A while later Temp, Stumbles, and Onyx, hikers I had met in Troutville, arrived. They immediately began debating whether to stay or continue on for an additional 14.6 miles to Glasgow and a shower. When asked my (parental) advice, I stayed clear of the discussion. Finally after cooking and eating a meal, they set out at 5:35, fully expecting to do at least a couple of hours of night hiking. I admire the enthusiasm of the young. After their 30-plus mile day, I doubted that I would see them again. I didn't.

While the debate was underway, David, a hiker out for a few days to get ready for a southbound thru-hike he hopes to begin on June 1, showed up as did Spider and ET. Just before dark, War Cry also arrived to claim a spot in the shelter. After the trio departed the rest of us sat around the picnic table chatting over our meals. War Cry, like me, has no stove. She too said she just wasn't using it, so she sent it home.

As dusk approached I made one of my fundamental shelter errors. I got into my sleeping bag (mainly to avoid the flies) and fell asleep before dark. Then at a little past 11:00 I awoke to remain so for over two hours. When I go to sleep that early my body thinks it's a nap. So until after 1:30 I rolled from side to side numerous times before finally getting back to sleep. It proved to be a restless night, but all in all the day couldn't have been more important because the heel feels fine and once again my hike appears to be going well.

## May 21, Thunder Hill Shelter to US 501

One good thing about my restless night's sleep was that I awoke at dawn ready to hike. Not wanting to disturb my four shelter-mates, I remained in my sleeping bag until around 5:20 when I also heard War Cry rustling around. With her first movement, I began my "getting out of camp" routine. As quietly as possible I moved all my belongings to the picnic table in front of the shelter before deflating my sleeping mat. Knowing the sound would likely awaken everyone else, I saved that task for last.

After packing up and drinking as much as I could stomach of my Carnation Instant Breakfast concoction, I was on my way. A little quicker to pack up, War Cry beat me out of camp. With gentle terrain and a heel that felt much better, I anticipated hiking the 14.6 miles to US 501 by 1:00. At the Thunder Ridge Overlook, Bill, an A.T. maintainer, was shooting some early morning photos of the clouds below the mountains.

When I reached Petites Gap, War Cry was sitting on a rock taking a break. I likewise stopped briefly. She started up the trail ahead of me; however, I would see her again later in the afternoon. When I got to Marble Spring I walked the 100 yards to fill my water bottles. Then at the Gunter Ridge Trail crossing I took another break to call shuttle driver Ken to let him know that I would be at 501 by 1:00. From there I hiked toward the next shelter on what was becoming a very hot afternoon.

Matt's Creek Shelter is the only shelter that I've seen with a flash flood warning sign attached to its front. Having to hop over wet rocks across the creek to the shelter reinforced my confidence in the stability of my heel. War Cry was taking a break and asked about my shuttle. Having a little knee issue herself, she decided to hike the final 2.2 of the day with me and also ride to Buena Vista. A Wake Forest graduate with two degrees, War Cry has been hiking big miles, having begun on April 6. It was the first time I had hiked with anyone for some time. I enjoyed our conversation as the trail paralleled the James River. The last 0.2 mile was across the longest foot-use only bridge on the A.T.

When we got to US 501 Ken had not arrived. After unsuccessfully trying to reach him, War Cry and I were offered a ride to Buena Vista by Tom Davis, a gentleman from Florida who was on his way to Wisconsin to visit relatives. A retired accountant, Tom and auditor War Cry had a common thread for conversation. Tom was more than happy to become our trail angel for the day as he first dropped War Cry at a hostel before taking me to my motel.

The highlight of my day, however, occurred after I arrived in Buena Vista. Deidra Johnson Dryden, a former Shaw student athlete that I coached in cross-country, had invited me to supper at her home. Meeting her children, Jack, Will, Sophie, and Sadie, made the evening even more special. The outstanding home cooked meal more than made up for my meager diet over the past two nights in shelters. Visiting with Deidra and her family brought to a conclusion another wonderful day filled with good health and happiness.

## May 22, US 501, James River to Blue Ridge Parkway Mile 51.7

Deidra Johnson Dryden excelled as a student and as an athlete at Shaw High School in Columbus, GA in the mid-1980's. From the first time I saw Deidra run, her competitive nature was evident. Now three decades later, she serves as an administrator, mathematics instructor, and coach at Southern Virginia University. She also still competes at various distances including the marathon. Deidra and her dentist husband Brent are raising five children in a beautiful home in small town, America. As we wound our way back up the mountain on the warm morning, the conversation quickly turned to running.

Before hitting the trail I took a few minutes to meet and talk with Spirit, a lady who is driving a small RV up the roads along the trail to support her husband Steady. Our paths would continue to cross over the next one thousand miles. On this day we would not see each other again.

With an already hot day developing by 8:30, the climb from the James River up to Little Rocky Row followed by Big Rocky Row presented a challenge. I stopped often for water and Gatorade. After the two Rocky Rows the trail leveled comfortably for a little over two miles. During the level stretch I came up on Sleeping Beauty with whom I hiked until the Punchbowl Shelter. Sleeping Beauty, with his fiery red beard and bandana to match, set a pace that seemed just right for me today. I continue to find it interesting how trail names are often not gender specific. Sleeping Beauty had been hiking sporadically with Etch-a-Sketch, a twenty-something young lady. As the three of us hiked together I discovered that Sleeping Beauty had left Springer one day after me and that Etch-a-Sketch had begun her hike one day after Sleeping Beauty. Today, however, was the first that I had seen either of them.

The final climb of my hiking day had me going up Bluff Mountain. From the beginning of today's hike the trail had ascended over 2700 feet. Thankfully, much of the climb involved switchbacks. At the summit of Bluff a monument has been erected in memory of Ottie Cline Powell. According to the inscription, little Ottie's body had been found at the spot in 1891, after he had wandered away from his school some seven miles away. The poor little guy was not quite five.

Sleeping Beauty continued to lead me up the trail from Bluff Mountain toward the road where I would end today's walk. Both he and Etch-a-Sketch took the side trail to the Punchbowl Shelter to have lunch and re-fill their water supply. I said goodbye and headed on toward the Blue Ridge Parkway mile marker 51.7, only 0.3 of a mile away. When I arrived at the road, Ken was already waiting for my ride back to Buena Vista. Since it was only 1:00 I had ample time to ice my Achilles, do laundry, and rest. So as I thought about the 10.8 mile day, I reminded myself that once again all was good on the Appalachian Trail.

## May 23, Buena Vista, VA

Zambian Squirrel, Weasel, and Skunk Foot departed from Springer together in early March. Today I met the trio from Vermont for the first time. They were doing a southbound slackpack when our paths crossed on the south side of Rice Mountain. Since the three were carrying little, I thought at first that they were day-hikers. But after I introduced myself as a thru-hiker, they in turn stated that they were as well.

The day had begun at the Blue Ridge Parkway mile marker 51.7, a short drive from Buena Vista. Like yesterday, Deidra played trail angel by driving me back to the A.T. Today's hike actually started out pretty level until a brief climb of only about one hundred feet. For the remainder of the day the trail alternated from nearly level to slightly downhill. I easily covered the short distance in 4 hours and 15 minutes. Other than several stream crossings, nothing really stood out.

One of those crossings, however, proved to be my undoing. Not paying attention to where the trail continued on the other side of the stream,

I attempted to cross at the wrong place. Placing my right foot on a small slippery rock, I fell directly onto my backside. Fortunately the outcome was only a slight bruise on the palm of my left hand. Ironically I had just been thinking that I had not fallen in the past two weeks.

In addition to the Vermonters, I also met thru-hikers Pattycakes, from Michigan and Puddin', from Mississippi. They hiked right behind me for about a mile before stopping at Brown Mountain Creek Shelter. Once again I had the good fortune to meet a personable young couple who seem to be thoroughly enjoying the thru-hiking experience.

When I arrived at US 60, Spider and ET were waiting for a shuttle. About twenty minutes later Ken arrived to drive the three of us to Buena Vista. Before we drove away, Pattycakes and Puddin' crossed the road to where we had been waiting. They were able to secure a ride from a lady who was dropping two other hikers off at the trailhead. Within fifteen minutes I was back at the good old Budget Inn.

After a hot shower, I walked downtown for lunch at the Bluedogart Cafe, an establishment that is known for its hospitality to hikers. My waiter offered a sharpie so that I could sign the "hiker door." While waiting for my meal, Howard, a motorcyclist from Ontario, asked about my hike. I answered his questions and also asked him some about his trip. He and a friend, after having biked on the Blue Ridge Parkway, were on their way to DC. I continue to enjoy all the non-hiking people I'm meeting.

When I finished my lunch I headed toward a barber shop, figuring it was time for a haircut and shave. It was closed. So I stopped by the Family Dollar for scissors, shaving cream, and razors. Even though I cut much of the beard with scissors before shaving, it still took seven razors to become a clean shaven man again. It was just getting too hot and uncomfortable. After the shave I also gave myself a haircut, something I can't remember doing in a long time.

The day again concluded with supper at Deidra's home. It was good to get the "with beard" and "without beard" photos. There are so many special moments on the trail. During my hike there have been just as many special moments off the trail. Being able to share two meals with Deidra and her family ranks right up there at the top. So tomorrow I have to say goodbye to Deidra and her town. Like Helen, Hiawassee, Hot Springs, Erwin, Troutdale, Pearisburg, and all the other small towns along the A.T., Buena Vista has been special. I'll miss the faces of those I only met a couple of days ago. But the trail awaits. Tomorrow I'm back to a full pack and a longer day, but I'm ready to see what lies in store next on the hike north.

## May 24, US 60 to Spy Rock Rd.

Solitude dominated the better part of an unseasonably cold, windy day. I never shed my rain jacket, my only warm article of clothing since I mailed my fleece home two weeks ago. The wind chill hovered in the 40's in the morning. In fact, the wind continued strong throughout the day. At times I had to use my poles to maintain my balance for fear that the wind would blow me over. Still the views atop Cold Mountain and Tar Jacket Ridge more than made up for the uncomfortable weather conditions.

The hike today began with a fairly steep climb up to Bald Knob. Even the switchbacks were steep. On the ascent I passed Etch-a-Sketch and shortly afterwards saw Boo Boo taking a rest. Within a few minutes I was passed by Puddin' and Pattycakes. For the remainder of the day I saw no other northbounders. I did encounter a few southbound section and day-hikers including Freed Bird and his dog Colby. Having completed a thru-hike in '06, Freed Bird was out on a section-hike of about 300 miles. Colby, decked out with blue saddlebags, cooperated for a photo. Don would have really liked Colby.

As I hiked the trail of rocks, roots, leaves, and mud in the cold afternoon wind, I thought of my long deceased granddaddy Harry Andrews. At about the age of ten, I received a Monopoly game for Christmas. After playing the game with me for some time, he declared the game should have been called Monotonous. The same word could have been used for the trail this afternoon. When I finally reached Spy Rock Rd., I had to walk down a rocky blue-blazed road for about a mile before being picked up by Earl for the ride to the Dutch Haus B&B, a hiker-friendly establishment near Montebello.

The evening consisted of a delicious dinner prepared by Earl's wife Lois, followed by coffee and conversation. Chrome Dome had completed a section-hike yesterday. Ranger, who resides in the DC area, is working on a section-hike. Recently retired from the Forestry Service, Ranger talked of trips he and his family had taken in National Parks. Eventually, overall fatigue took its toll. Trying not to think about the over 1300 miles remaining, I allowed my tired body to quickly pass into unconsciousness.

## May 25, Spy Rock Rd. to Three Ridges Overlook

Apparently everyone who owns a backpack in central Virginia decided to go for a hike on the A.T. today. If I had counted the southbound weekenders and day-hikers beginning early this morning, the number would have easily exceeded one hundred. From Boy Scout troop 1893 out of Richmond, to Carter and his dad on Carter's first hike to celebrate his 13th birthday, to "the Shack," a group of five from DC, I had the opportunity to introduce my brother to many. My spirits were lifted by all the smiling faces.

The day began with one of the top five breakfasts I've enjoyed over the past two months. Lois served pancakes with strawberries, an omelet, sausage, juice, and coffee to Ranger, Julie, Chrome Dome and me. After breakfast Earl drove me back up a portion of Spy Rock Rd. where he had to drop me off short of the trail. The remaining approximately one mile uphill walk over rocks of various sizes equaled anything I experienced on the A.T. today in the way of difficulty. It was a relief to finally make the left turn onto the trail.

The first challenge today was a climb up the Priest, with an elevation gain of 700 feet. A descent of over 3000 feet to the Tye River followed. From there the trail again ascended 2500 feet to Three Ridges Mountain. That climb was by far the most taxing of the day. Several beautiful views, however, helped to minimize the toughness of the uphill. Along the way I met another scout troop, 1932 from Williamsburg. For a while I thought a dog had adopted me when the troop's collie mix followed me up the trail. Banzai, a thru-hiker I had met earlier in the day, and I both tried to discourage the dog from trailing us. Finally Banzai asked a southbound hiker if he would leash the dog and hike with him back toward the scouts.

A little later in the afternoon, the most spectacular view of the day occurred at the Hanging Rock Overlook. Banzai had also stopped to admire the vista. Needing a night out of the woods, he decided to shuttle with me back to the Dutch Haus. We hiked briefly together before he pulled away on a downhill section, telling me that he would wait at the road.

Over the final three miles of my 20.3 mile day, I met Pattycakes and Puddin' who were slackpacking a 30 mile day southbound. Several other day-hikers were climbing up to the overlook. From the Blue Ridge Crossing adjacent to the Three Ridges Overlook, Banzai and I hiked the final 0.5 mile together. When we reached the road, Earl was waiting. Before heading to the B & B he drove back to the Tye River to pick up Regina, a ridgerunner in the area.

After arriving back at the Dutch Haus, I discovered that Cyclops, a hiker from Orlando that I had met last weekend in Troutville, was sharing a room with me. While we were getting re-acquainted, a familiar looking young man stepped into the room.

"Don't you know who I am?"

I stared at the young man, trying desperately to recall where on the trail we had met.

"I'm Brandon."

Brandon had been introduced to me by a mutual acquaintance who knew that both of us were planning thru-hikes. We had done one training hike together back in early March. Now smiling at the hiker I had been looking for since my hike began, I apologized for not recognizing him. Brandon was now Betterman. He and his wife, Smothers, left Springer three days before me. Today was the first time that our paths had crossed. Neither of us knew it at the time, but it would also be the last.

## May 26, Rockfish Gap, Waynesboro, VA

One aspect of the A.T. which continues to both fascinate and strengthen me is the uncertainty of what may occur on the trail on any given day.

When Earl dropped Banzai and me back at the Three Ridges Overlook, a lone hiker was crossing the road headed north. He and Banzai exchanged greetings. It would be later in the morning before I introduced myself to Brass Rat. It would be even later in the afternoon before I realized how significant my meeting the MIT grad would be. He helped make the last eight miles of my 18.8 mile day pleasantly endurable, when I had little left in the tank.

The morning had begun with a bit of a downer when Cyclops confirmed what he had said last night. He is leaving the trail to return to Orlando. Betterman tried his best to get him to change his mind, but Cyclops had already booked a flight out of Lynchburg. The two who had hiked many miles together said their goodbyes after breakfast at the Dutch Haus B & B. So as Betterman and Smothers returned to the trail, Cyclops was getting a lift to the airport from Ranger and Julie. I too wished him well on his return to what Betterman calls it, the "regular world."

Before returning Banzai and me to our A.T. point on the Blue Ridge Parkway, Earl dropped our other passenger, ridgerunner Regina, at Reeds Gap. From the outset today, I used caution, planning to pamper the Achilles for a few more days. Expecting to hike slowly, I told Banzai and the hiker I would later learn was Brass Rat to go ahead. The strong, young man quickly disappeared into the distance. It would be New York before the enigmatic Banzai appeared again.

About seven miles into the hike, I heard the sound of poles on rocks behind me. A short while later I was overtaken by a day-hiker, Brad, who was on his way to an overlook with his wife Libby and friend Tracy. Tracy's black lab Dobie had also made the trek. Brad asked about my hike, so I told him about Don. He said that Libby's father had also died from ALS. When we reached the overlook, which afforded beautiful views of ski slopes, I paused for a long break to visit with the three and enjoy the view. The long break didn't bother me since the group revealed such genuine concern when I talked about my brother. I also took Dobie's photo, letting them know how much Don loved dogs.

Feeling somewhat undernourished and dehydrated, I rested often. During one such break I was caught by Brass Rat. We had seen each other several times throughout the day, yet had not said much. That changed when I took a break in the mid-afternoon. After we both stated that we were feeling somewhat depleted, we hiked in tandem for the remainder of the day. With company again, I hiked faster and with more enthusiasm. My new friend also happened to be my brother's age. We shared a lot over the course of a few hours. I was especially interested in his trail name. He explained that it was based on the MIT class ring.

So all the way to Rockfish Gap we maintained a steady, comfortable pace and conversation. Other than a rest stop at Paul C. Wolfe Shelter, we just walked and talked. Since Brass Rat had pre-arranged for a shuttle back to his car near Buena Vista, he offered me a ride to a motel in Waynesboro. When we arrived at Rockfish Gap, we only had to wait about ten minutes.

Even though I only met the section-hiker Brass Rat today, I felt like I had known him longer. Time tends to move slowly on the A.T. As I said goodbye, he promised to read my website and follow me the rest of the way. Section-hiking requires a great commitment. Brass Rat will one day get it all done. Thus a day that could have left me feeling a little down was transformed into another positive experience. Thank you, my friend, for making today another memorable one on my journey north along the Appalachian Trail.

# 7

# Shenandoah National Park and Northern Virginia

### May 27, Rockfish Gap to Black Rock Gap

Welcome to the Shenandoah National Park. Today marked the beginning of an approximately 100 mile stroll through one of the least challenging sections of the entire Appalachian Trail. From Rockfish Gap the trail crosses a bridge over I-64 before re-entering the woods. After being dropped off by local shuttle volunteers Jim and Cindy, Caboose and I briefly started the day together. After signing in at the required registration station near the trailhead, I wouldn't see him again. This time, however, it was because I hiked at a faster clip throughout the day.

With a gentle trail and a Cracker Barrel breakfast under my belt, there was no holding me back. Throughout the park, the trail crosses Skyline Drive several times every day. On today's hike there were eight such crossings. Some had overlooks; some didn't. Some had parking lots; others didn't. Oftentimes cars of day-hikers filled the parking spots. Before some of the crossings the trail ran parallel to the road so closely that cars were clearly visible.

At one crossing I took a break to have some lunch with fellow thru-hiker Steady. We had met about a week ago at the James River but had not hiked together before today. Steady is Spirit's husband and has quite the hiking resume. Unlike most A.T. thru-hikers, Steady began his quest in Key West. After kayaking 700 miles, he road-walked most of the rest of the way to Springer. When he gets to Katahdin, Steady plans to continue on to Halifax, which will make his entire adventure over 4000 miles. Already having completed the Pacific Crest Trail and Continental Divide Trail, the A.T. will also complete his triple crown.

Late in the afternoon I passed two section-hikers from Newnan, GA. Quicksilver and Peach plan to conclude this section at Harper's Ferry. After a brief chat, I moved on up the trail to Riprap parking area off Skyline Drive, where I had originally planned to end today's hike. Getting there, however, I decided to hike an additional 2.8 miles to Black Rock Gap. It was there that Jim picked me up for a shuttle back to Waynesboro and a final night at the Super 8. My motto, "Light pack, big miles, and beds," continues to work.

Although the park is beautiful, views have thus far been limited. Other than from a power line area, there really wasn't anything of significance. All in all, the time passed quickly. I managed to hike a comfortable 19.1 miles with good company and fresh legs. The Achilles felt fine, and everything considered, life is good.

## May 28, Blackrock Gap to Pinefield Hut

"Don's Brother PALS in Site A17 Love to see you" read the sign tied to a tree on the trail. It's common for A.T. thru-hikers to leave messages for those that may be hiking behind them. It was the first, however, that had been left for me. With both excitement and nervousness I walked up the short trail leading to the campsite. When a camper came into view, a dog barked.

A lady who appeared in the doorway asked, "Are you Don's Brother?"

"Yes, I am," I replied.

The lady introduced herself as Chris. As Chris calmed Lucky, a gentleman with a broad smile emerged from the camper. I shook Bob Anderson's hand and then gave him an emotional hug. The ALS patient never stopped smiling during my visit. Even though his speech had diminished radically, Bob still walked and enjoyed camping with his wife and dog. We took several pictures and discussed Don a little. Within a minute Lucky was also my friend. I imagined how much my brother would have loved petting the former pound puppy. Wishing I could stay longer, I explained that I needed to move on to reach my destination for the day.

Before seeing my sign and meeting Bob, Chris, and Lucky, I fully expected that the highlight of the day would be two bear sightings. As Jim (Mr. Gizmo) Wilson drove me back up Skyline Drive to Blackrock Gap, twice we stopped to observe bears. The first, a yearling, stood in the middle of the highway. Only after we crept very close did he move to the side of the road. The second was an older bear who paid no attention to us when Jim came to a stop so that I could take a picture. He nonchalantly kept grazing even as we drove away.

With what was supposed to be another big mileage day over gentle terrain, I started the hike at a quick pace. The views also returned. Atop Loft Mountain I dropped my pack to sit on a rock and just relax for a while. Then after the visit with the Andersons, I walked down the Frazier Discovery Trail to the Loft Mountain Wayside, one of several that offer short order foods in the Shenandoahs. Even though the blue-blazed trail required an additional 0.6 mile hilly hike each way, the burger was well worth it. Also at the wayside were Quicksilver and Peach, Pacemaker and Runner-up, and Tugboat and Liferaft. I hadn't seen Tugboat since we shared the bunkhouse at the Troutdale Baptist Church Hostel. The long leisurely lunch may have been my downfall. Hiking sluggishly for the remainder of the afternoon, I eventually stopped at the Pinefield Hut after only a 13.9 mile day.

Several others were already there including Christian and Annalena, a brother and sister from Germany. Christian is an exchange student at Virginia Tech. Two female section-hikers from France, Maz and Chef, were brewing up some tea. Tugboat and Liferaft stopped for a short nap before moving on up the trail. A little later Quicksilver and Peach also arrived. Pinefield Hut looked like a pretty nice shelter. Most of my fellow hikers tented. Only the two Parisian ladies shared the shelter with me.

At the beginning of each day there is no way of knowing what will unexpectedly occur on the trail. Today I had the honor and privilege of meeting Bob and Chris Anderson and Lucky. Bob's smile will remain with me throughout my hike. As I walked away from Bob, I thought about my brother. Don had a beautiful smile too. And today I think he was also smiling as his brother continued walking north on the Appalachian Trail.

## May 29, Pinefield Hut to Lewis Mountain Campground

Last night I probably slept as well as I ever have in a shelter. My day began at 6:20. After packing up and having breakfast, I followed Quicksilver and Peach out of camp. In less than a mile I passed them, never to see another hiker for the remainder of the morning. Once again, it was just me and the trail. Other than an occasional squirrel and one deer, nothing was seen or heard on a still, very warm morning.

My plan for the day was to get to Swift Run Gap, near Elkton, and try to hitch a ride to town for lunch and trail food. When I reached the intersection where Skyline Drive intersects with US 33, I put out my thumb. Under the noonday heat the task was anything but fun. After about twenty minutes I changed my location; however, very few cars appeared. Eventually I decided to call the Country View Motel, located about three miles down the road, and check on a room. Bob, the owner, said he would come and get me.

When today's trail angel pulled up in his small pickup, he was accompanied by Shadow, his dog. On the drive to the motel, with Shadow perched between Bob and me, I thought about how much my brother would have enjoyed the ride. It's beginning to seem like every day I meet a new dog that Don would have immediately befriended. Shadow ranks right up there with the "best" that I've encountered on the hike.

Since it was only a little after 12:00 and I had only hiked 11.6 miles, I asked Bob if he would slackpack me a few more miles. He agreed. First we drove into Elkton where I bought a bag of burgers. Then when we got back to the trail, I found a shady spot near the trailhead to have lunch before embarking on the afternoon portion of the hike. Walking at a quick pace, I covered 8.3 additional miles in a little over three hours. I saw another small bear at a distance and a second deer practically standing on the trail. Only one lone southbound hiker crossed my path.

On what was becoming a brutally hot afternoon, I drank almost continuously to stay hydrated. Even so I felt depleted by the time I reached the Lewis Mountain campground. Staggering through the parking lot, I was directed to the camp store by a lady at one of the RV spots. Having arrived over thirty minutes before the scheduled shuttle, I bought a soft drink and sat on a bench outside. A young man who said his name was Clifton sat beside me as his wife shopped. He asked about my hike, so I enlightened him somewhat on the A.T. Finally Bob and Shadow arrived for the trip back to Elkton. On the drive Bob shared some of his personal story. A Rhode Island native, he moved to Virginia a few years back, bought a farm as well as the Country View Motel. A widower, Bob seemed to appreciate the company of Shadow.

After a shower, a nap, and a meal, I sat outside under a gazebo chatting with Quicksilver and Peach. Bob, who had recently celebrated his 62$^{nd}$ birthday, brought us each a piece of his cake. With Bob's permission, I shared some of mine with Shadow. As fatigue began to set in, I retired to my room, alone but not lonely. Steadily moving through the Shenandoahs, I felt a sense of accomplishment and expectation. Don might have reminded me, "You've still got more than half of the trail remaining." If only he could have done so by phone.

## May 30, Lewis Mountain Campground to Skyland

Walking through the woods this morning under an already blistering sun, I found myself singing a variation on an old Lovin' Spoonful 60's hit, "Summer in the City." We weren't in the city; we were on the A.T. Nevertheless, it was hot! To divert my attention from the heat, I catalogued all hikers that I had hiked with for any length of time. There was Slim Jim from Hiawassee to the NOC, Jolly from Franklin to the Smokies, Piddlin' Around in the Smokies, Molar Man from north of Erwin to Iron Mountain, and Speck from Pearisburg to Jennings Creek. I also spent considerable time with Kermit and Grinch in the Smokies and Whiskers and Rocket from Deep Gap, NC to Damascus. Today I hiked alone.

Before heading back to the trail, Quicksilver and I walked down to a country store for some breakfast sandwiches and coffee. Then we sat around the gazebo with Peach, enjoying the early morning fellowship over breakfast. Bob, along with Shadow and Cookie (his cat), also visited. At around 7:30 Bob drove me back to the Lewis Mountain Campground. After bidding Bob and Shadow farewell, I walked down a side trail for about fifty yards to the A.T. Even though I had only been around Bob for less than twenty-four hours, it felt like I was saying goodbye to an old friend.

Time passed quickly throughout the morning. Around noon I walked up a gravel road to Skyline Drive which led to the Big Meadows Wayside. Paul with Bunions, a 2010 thru-hiker who was working on another complete trail in sections, occupied one of the picnic tables outside. Most of the interior clientele, however, consisted of Morty Seinfeld lookalikes accompanied by their white-haired wives. A few biker types mingled around as well. The Virginia ham and Swiss sandwich and salad were worth the extra mile of walking.

After lunch I returned to the trail by the same route. Even with several rests, I still hiked more sluggishly in the afternoon. Drinking both water and electrolytes in large amounts, I hoped to prevent the depleted feeling I had experienced yesterday. Views were more plentiful which in a small way offset the heat. At one time thunder rumbled in the distance, but it never rained. Like other recent days, hikers were scarce. I met a few southbound section-hikers and was passed by one shirtless northbound hiker who said he had begun his hike today. Walking at a brisk pace, he disappeared in seconds. Just wanting to get the miles done, I only stopped to chat briefly with a day-hiker looking for Hawksbill Mountain. Having passed it within the last few minutes, I offered directions to the young lady who introduced herself as Susan from Atlanta.

By the time Skyland came into sight, I was ready for a room, a shower, and a meal. After a little negotiation I was able to get a hiker rate at the rustic resort, even though this was by far my most expensive bed. But there was a restaurant a stone's throw from my room, which also meant a hearty breakfast in the morning.

After checking in I ventured down to the tap room for some supper. Also dining were Blister and his two adult children, Bison and Barking Spider. The Texas folks are section-hiking from Waynesboro to Harper's Ferry. I had seen them on the trail late this afternoon and shared with them my affinity for indoor accommodations. After finishing my meal I felt obliged to apologize for disrupting their life in the woods with the suggestion of a room. All seemed to actually be a bit appreciative. After all, they could return to the rigors of tents and shelters tomorrow. As for me, I had plans for another scenic day in the woods followed hopefully by a restful night in a bed.

## May 31, Skyland to Elkwallow Gap

As another month came to an end, I celebrated my 70th day on the Appalachian Trail. In many ways it felt like 70 weeks. Sometimes I find myself trying to remember various aspects of my home. Strangely, the longer I'm away the more vague things back home become. Homesickness has already forced some off the trail. He always seems to be lurking around the next hard climb or within a casual conversation. She can tantalize the weaker hiker at the most opportune moment.

This morning the trail offered up several panoramic views between Skyland and the Pinnacle. Early in the day I came across a group of trail maintainers from the Potomac Appalachian Club.

"What's your trail name?" asked a worker who identified himself as Sisu.

"Don's Brother."

"Don's Brother!" Sisu exclaimed. "I've been following your journal."

Sisu also asked me to tell the others about Don. They all ceased their work as I briefly talked about my brother.

A little later I met a lovely couple from London. John and Rose said they were out for a walk, not a hike. Just a short while later I had my second Blissful sighting in the past week. Having first met the former thru-hiker in Georgia, she had let me know then that she planned to do some work as a ridgerunner in the summer. After meeting her on Monday just north of Waynesboro, today I saw her again. I wouldn't see another hiker until very late in the day.

When I reached Thornton's Gap I walked down to the restroom area to fill my water bottles. The cool cement under the shady edifice offered a much-needed reprieve from the sweltering sun. Bison and Barking Spider were going through a re-supply box the size of a small stove, trying to decide what to keep and what to leave for other hikers. They had way too much to carry. As they rummaged through the box, I ate my ham sandwich and peanut butter cups. They were still sorting items when I wished them well and headed back to the trail.

Hiking strong throughout the afternoon, I had the trail to myself until about two miles before Elkwallow Gap. Daydreaming while navigating the flat path, I suddenly came to an abrupt halt when a distinct rattling sound interrupted my reverie. For the first time on any hike, I came face to face with about a five foot long rattlesnake. After snapping a couple of pictures, I then had to figure out how to continue up the trail. Not really knowing the proper protocol, I first tossed a rock in its direction. Nothing happened. So I tossed another which hit the snake. Still he didn't move. My next idea was to try to bushwhack around the reptile. When he began to coil and rattle again, I nixed that idea. So there I was in a standoff with a rattlesnake. Fortunately he finally decided to slither back into the underbrush. Imagining that Mr. Rattler was smugly thinking, "I won this stand-off," I gingerly walked past the varmint and then quickly picked up my pace.

The rattlesnake, however, was not the only "first" today. Within about a half mile of the gap, I heard a loud noise just off the trail. When I looked to my right, a large turkey was strutting back and forth, obviously irritated about my proximity to his spot. Realizing that trying to get close enough for a photo was not a good idea, I moved on as he continued to display his distress. Oddly enough, this was almost the same place I had seen a mama bear and her two cubs when I section-hiked the Shenandoahs in 2006.

When I finally reached the Elkwallow Wayside, a little unnerved, I ran into the first thru-hikers I had seen in the past two days. Pacemaker and Runner-up, the young German couple who speak excellent English, were resting at a picnic table. We chatted until Mike Evans, the owner of the Terrapin Station Front Royal Hostel, arrived for my shuttle. It was good to get re-acquainted with the Grateful Greenpeace Guy. He told me that only one other hiker, Pilgrim, was staying at the hostel.

After I had the opportunity to do some laundry for the first time since Buena Vista, Mike drove Pilgrim and me into Front Royal for a meal at a Mexican restaurant. It was good to finally meet a hiker whose name I had seen in numerous shelter registers. From California, Pilgrim had been struggling lately. Having gone through two bouts of norovirus, he had lost a good bit of weight. At 66, the white-haired soft spoken adventurer could not afford to drop any more pounds from his frail frame. All thru-hikers lose weight. Pilgrim had just lost too much. Obviously concerned, he was trying, although at times unsuccessfully, to consume massive calories. I felt for my fellow sojourner, hoping that our paths would cross again somewhere up the trail. They would, many times over the next three months.

## June 1, US 522, Front Royal, VA

For the fifth consecutive day I hiked alone. Again I saw no thru-hikers on the trail. At times it seems like I'm the only one headed north even though I know there are still many others. I'm just not finding myself around them. I did pass two northbound section-hikers, Bloodhound from Raleigh and Poncho who lives in Puerto Rico. Poncho was finishing the complete trail in sections in Front Royal. I asked him if he had champagne in his pack. He said he didn't but that he was sure he could find some way to mark the occasion.

With another mundane trail and a very hot temperature, I found myself reflecting for much of the day. I actually felt glad to finally be out of the Shenandoah National Park. Early in the week its uniqueness with the waysides and Skyline Drive captured my attention. By today I had just about seen all that I wanted to see. Plus, the trail continued to consist of stretches of the same old gravelly rocks, leaves, and roots. Being able to hike at a quicker pace was welcomed; however, I missed the variation. In fact, as soon as I exited the park portion, a steep descent with large rocks awaited. Usually I would cringe at such a section. Today I actually enjoyed the change of terrain.

I thought a lot about what I'm doing as I walked today. When I began this quest, I said that I loved to hike but that I only enjoyed camping a little. After about the first three weeks I altered my terminology to: I love to hike and can tolerate camping. Shortly thereafter I mentally moved to I really like hiking, but I hate camping. Now I seem to be in the: I kind of like hiking, but I detest camping. I fear that I may eventually get to: I'm tolerating the hiking. Please don't misconstrue. I have no intention of quitting. I'm just trying to resurrect some more enthusiasm. I am beginning to understand, however, why more hikers quit in Virginia than any other state except Georgia.

Those who really know me understand my competitive nature. So this hike has become more about "getting to the finish line." I find myself more and more comparing the rigors of the trail to the challenge of finishing a marathon. As I approach the literal half way mark, which I should reach around next Sunday or Monday, I'm reminded of the half-way point in a 26.2 mile race. For those who have run one, they know it's not where one would think mathematically. It's the 20 mile mark. It takes as much mental and physical effort to complete the final 6.2 miles as it does to run the first 20. So when I reach the half-way point on the A.T. at mile 1093, I won't really be half way. That will occur somewhere in Vermont or New Hampshire.

When I reached US 522 at Front Royal, Possible, a 2012 thru-hiker, and his wife Lisa had erected a tent and were handing out some trail magic. Even though Mike was already there, I went ahead and had a hotdog and lemonade while chatting with Pacemaker and Runner-up.

Then on the ride back to Terrapin Station, Mike explained that thru-hiker Newton had recently gotten news that his brother had been killed.

Even though I had not met the hiker from Maine previously, I immediately connected with him due to the tragedy in his family. Offering my condolences, I shared some about my brother after listening to him talk about his. At some point in the conversation I asked Newton his brother's name. He replied, "Don."

In the early evening I sat on steps leading up to a deck at the back of the hostel, thinking about my brother Don and Newton and his brother Don. Quiet replaced the sound of a lawnmower. A gentle breeze escorted in a tad of melancholia. Even with thunderstorms in the forecast for the night and the following morning, I looked forward to a night at the Bears Den Hostel, one of the best on the entire trail. I also anticipated the 20-miler on my agenda. Listening to a solitary cricket chirping in the distance, I gave thanks for the opportunity to spend each day among the trees and wildlife, reminding myself often of just how much Don loved the woods.

## June 2, Front Royal to Ashby Gap

Under overcast skies, I set foot on the trail today at 7:40, still holding a half cup of McDonald's coffee. Since the terrain was completely flat for the first mile, clutching both poles in one hand and the coffee in the other worked fine. When I did reach the first climb of the day, I heard talking from up the trail. Getting closer, I realized Bison and Barking Spider were just up ahead. When I reached and passed the brother and sister, they fell in behind me for the next three miles. It definitely felt good to be able to share the hike and a conversation with the Texans. Their dad, Blister, had to leave the trail with a foot problem. He had rented a car and was picking them up for lunch at VA 638.

When the three of us reached the road, to my surprise Shrek was sitting under a tree. Not having seen the strong, young hiker in almost a month, I thought he would be half way through Pennsylvania by now. I offered him a share of my shuttle to Bears Den, but he declined. Trail magic also appeared in the form of cold Sprite and various types of chips. I took a soda and some Cheetos. Thanking Bison and Barking Spider for the opportunity to hike with them, I then headed up the next ascent alone. Almost shoulder high weeds (or maybe they were some kind of flower I couldn't identify) bordered the trail for almost a mile. My shoes and shorts were wet from the morning dew before I escaped the protruding plants.

For the third day in a row I happened upon a couple of trail maintainers. Speedy (A.T. '96) and his wife Katherine stopped their weed-eating to chat for a minute. Just past the couple I began to hear the cicadas. Their deafening song even drowned out the traffic on I-66 that the trail passes under at Manassas Gap. Just past the gap I was asked about my hike by 70-year-young Underdog, a retired gentleman who was getting ready to start a three-day hike. Then I crossed a footbridge and began almost a 900 foot climb to the Manassas Gap Shelter where I took a lunch break.

With a little over half my day complete, I hiked steadily throughout the afternoon. With about five miles to go I was passed by Tugboat and Liferaft. For the remainder of the day I hiked just in front or just behind them as we each stopped for breaks. As I arrived at Ashby Gap to complete a 20.0 mile day the rain began. Fortunately, Mike Evans was already there to shuttle me to Bears Den Hostel. By the time we arrived it was flooding. I didn't get wet hiking, but I sure did walking from Mike's car to the door of Bears Den.

Already at the hostel was a troop of Boy Scouts from Ohio. After the hostel officially opened for business at 5:00, I signed in and took the $30 hiker special: a bunk, shower, laundry, a full pizza, soft drink, and a pint of Ben & Jerry's ice cream. Also arriving were thru-hikers Gator and Pilgrim. I can't say enough good things about Bears Den. The rustic stone building is filled with A.T. memorabilia and history. This year's caretakers, Dana, Johnny, and John, along with Dana's dog Doug, were all most hospitable. Visiting with the other hikers ended another satisfying day of adventure on my journey along the Appalachian Trail.

## June 3, Ashby Gap to Bears Den Hostel

Today was ugly. It took me almost as long to hike 13.5 miles as it did to do 20 yesterday. I staggered, wobbled, and shuffled the last five, feeling totally depleted. If I had been in a road race, an official surely would have pulled me off the course. For 5-milers, be they running, walking, or hiking, today had to have been a PW (personal worst). So am I discouraged? Absolutely not. I'm back at Bears Den, have showered, and now I'm munching on some Pringles and sipping a Dr. Pepper. Life is good.

The day began with a ride with John back to Ashby Gap. Since he couldn't drop me off exactly where I ended yesterday's hike, I had to walk south for about a quarter of a mile and then retrace my steps north. I may not sleep in the woods that often, but I am determined not to miss any white blazes. When I did get headed up the trail north, I saw no other hikers for about the first three hours. Finally, two other fellow north-bounders came into view. Not having hiked with anyone all day, I actually slowed my pace to chat with section-hikers Hickory and Jackrabbit a little while.

It was after I moved on ahead of the duo that my day took a turn for the worse. I paused to photograph a sign on a tree "warning" hikers of the infamous roller coaster, a 13.5 mile section of trail with numerous "tightly packed ascents and descents." Mumbling that the description could be for just about any section of trail, I think I jinxed myself regarding its difficulty. I hiked up and down, up and down, over large rocks, across streams, through the mud, until I felt like I really was on a roller coaster, as much emotionally as physically. It concerned me a little when I found myself singing "They're Coming to Take Me Away." Fortunately, I didn't see any men in white coats on the trail today. Believe me; it wasn't funny.

To try and take my mind off the drudgery, I attempted to recognize some of the vegetation along the trail. Sorry, Mr. Stewart. Despite enjoying leaf identification in high school biology, I failed miserably today. Between swatting bugs and slipping on muddy stretches of trail, I just persevered. And at about my lowest moment I heard a rustling behind me. When I turned I came face to face with a beautiful white-tail deer. When I looked into his eyes, I thought of my brother. It was as if Don had made an appearance to tell me to "suck it up" and get today's hike finished.

So I did my best to listen to my brother's advice internally and work as hard as I could to get to Bears Den. When the sign came into view indicating the blue-blazed 0.2 mile trail to the stone structure, I was again a happy hiker. Even though there was still no zip in the legs, I managed to get to the hostel and into a mood-changing shower. The old hot shower after a hike does wonders. Then I just had to wait until 5:00, when the hostel officially opened, for my pizza and ice cream. For now I'm content to sit on this comfortable wooden bench and enjoy the refreshing breeze.

Shortly after I arrived, Pacemaker and Runner-up hiked in as well. I've now seen the young German couple for several consecutive days. Four southbound former high school buddies from Ohio were also taking a break outside the hostel. Without guides, they weren't sure where they wanted to end their hike. I let them borrow my *A.T. Guide* and suggested Mike at Terrapin Station when they asked about a shuttle. Before the end of the day I suspect other hikers will also arrive for the night. Bears Den is one of those places that is hard to pass up.

As I reflected on my difficult day, I could probably attribute my lack of energy to a number of factors. Most noteworthy was a need to increase my calories at breakfast. I also planned to drink more water and electrolytes early in the day. The following day would take me to Harper's Ferry, the psychological half-way point of the hike. Although looking forward to visiting the Appalachian Trail Conservancy and getting back to a motel, a sudden sense of despair began to creep into my otherwise positive psyche. At this time last year my brother was nearing the end of having the ability to speak. It saddened me to think of how Don had struggled to make us understand. But today I heard him loud and clear as he encouraged me to keep on hiking and reach my goal of getting to Maine on the Appalachian Trail.

## June 4, Bears Den to Harper's Ferry

When the day began I didn't expect to be sitting in a bus on the side of HWY 340, waiting for a deputy sheriff to fill out an accident report. But I'm getting ahead of myself, so first I suppose I need to start with the morning. Actually, I wanted to add some material from last night before I even began the today. I had mentioned that other hikers would probably arrive at Bears Den, and one did. Not only did Ambassador show up, but he also played some on the guitar that he's carrying on his pack. He doesn't seem to mind the extra weight. In fact, he's also packing about a three pound camera.

At 6:00 this morning my alarm and Runner-up's sounded at almost the same time. Wanting to get an early start in order to make Harper's Ferry before the ATC office closed at 5:00, I immediately headed to the kitchen to cook my breakfast. The four large pancakes, a couple of scrambled eggs, and a cup of instant coffee comprised the meal. I also downed 20 ounces of water before leaving the hostel. Pacemaker and Runner-up were having breakfast when I departed. Ambassador was still asleep.

Less than a mile past Bears Den, the trail crosses VA 7 at Snickers Gap. Apparently the speed limit is 80 on the busy thoroughfare leading into DC. It took several minutes before I could find a large enough gap in traffic to dash across. On the opposite side Rock Steady had stopped for a photo-opt with a Snickers bar. Knowing that he would pass me quickly, which he did, I began the first climb of the day. Fortunately, the final four miles of the roller coaster came at the beginning of today's hike rather than at the end.

Just past the 1000 mile mark a spectacular view awaited at Raven Rocks. When I got there Rock Steady was taking a break. We took each other's picture, and I told the Californian about my brother and journal. Rock Steady said he had a good friend who was recently diagnosed with ALS. The personable engineer is only the second hiker that I have met in his 40's. Having only a limited number of days to complete the trail, he hopes to finish in less than three months. Since he didn't start until April 14, he seems to be well on his way to achieving his goal. We would see each other on breaks throughout the day.

The day passed smoothly. I took a lunch break at the David Lesser Memorial Shelter, one of the nicest in Virginia. Rock Steady had also stopped for water. Flare, a southbound section-hiker and veteran, was drying out some gear. The only other hikers I chatted with were father and son, C4 and Hotdog. From Connecticut, they were also sectioning south.

After the end of the roller coaster the trail leveled out for much of the afternoon. Other than some flat rocky sections, with some of the rocks being of the pointed variety, the trail continued gentle until the final two miles when it abruptly dropped almost 1000 feet down to the Shenandoah River. After walking across the lengthy bridge, I crossed a street to where the trail continues to ascend until a blue-blazed trail leading to the ATC headquarters appeared. I walked up the side trail and strolled into the office about half an hour before closing. Peter Pan welcomed me as the 318th thru-hiker to sign in this year. I had my picture taken and filled out the required paperwork to be official.

To my total surprise, Mr. Gigglefits and Paisley were in the hiker lounge along with Carpenter. They had hitched from Luray to get a bus to DC and then a train to NY for some music concert. When I asked how they got 70 miles behind me, with a chuckle, Gigglefits said they had spent six days at Trail Days in Damascus. Ah, the youth on the trail! As we waited together for a commuter bus to Charles Town, Daypack walked up. He had been at the first campsite with me in GA. I hadn't seen him since early in NC.

So after I left the ATC on the bus with Mr. Gigglefits and Paisley, the almost perfect day began its decline. Shortly after getting on well-travelled 340, a compact car with four teenagers inside sideswiped the bus. For over an hour we waited for law enforcement to arrive and for all the necessary forms to be completed. Passengers on the bus (there were only five of us) had to show ID and verify that we weren't injured. The delay kept me from getting to a motel until after 6:00. The bus driver, however, was extremely nice to drive me right up to the registration office rather than let me off at the designated area.

Even with the mishap, it had been a very good day. I recovered nicely after yesterday's fiasco. In nine hours I hiked 19.8 miles with one stretch late in the day where I did three miles in an hour. I met Rock Steady and got re-united with Mr. Gigglefits and Paisley. Unfortunately, it would be the last time I would see the likable couple. Tomorrow I've decided to take a day off after hiking 17 consecutive days and 266 miles. After a day of rest I'll cross into Maryland, the sixth state and second shortest next to West Virginia.

Thinking about my brother, I got a little emotional today crossing the Shenandoah River. Approaching Harper's Ferry, the realization that I was at what many consider the (first) half-way point kind of overwhelmed me. I could just see Don standing by the river, fishing rod in hand. There will be other rivers and ponds and lakes along the way. I know he'll like them all as we start the second half of the adventure on the Appalachian Trail.

# 8

# West Virginia and Maryland

## June 5, Day Off in Harper's Ferry

Sleeping much later than usual on the scheduled rest day, I found myself eating breakfast at 9:30. Then I spent the remainder of the morning planning my next week's hikes. Logistically, it's more challenging to plan using roads as a basis than it is using shelters. Still I eventually choreographed something that appears feasible. With shuttles lined up for tomorrow and Friday, I feel a little more at ease, especially since rain is in the forecast. Hopefully tomorrow's hike will be completed before the bad weather begins.

In the early afternoon I took the bus back over to Harper's Ferry and the ATC headquarters. Fidget was signing in, and Runner-up also stopped by while I chatted with Peter Pan. Deciding that I wanted to begin my hike tomorrow at the end of High St., I walked the blue-blazed trail back to the A.T. and went ahead and hiked the 0.6 mile stretch up to the bridge today. Along the way I walked down to Jefferson Rock. Most have seen the famous picture in a history book. Then I paused at the site of the ruins of the old Episcopal Church and also took a picture of the adjacent newer structure.

When I reached the end of this section at High Street, I walked up the hill to look for a spot for a late lunch. Rock Steady suddenly appeared, so we found a tavern to share a meal and fellowship. After lunch we walked to the outfitter where I purchased some more Aqua Mira, the water purification treatment that I'm using. Realizing that it was almost time for the commuter bus, I quickly walked back to the pick-up location across from the ATC office, making it just in time for the 4:45 shuttle.

After getting dropped off in front of Walmart, I did a little shopping and then walked to a nearby "salon" to get my first professional haircut since the hike began. The hair stylist asked about my hike, so I shared a few details. Then I walked back to the motel. Nearing the building, a smile came to my face. In the parking lot sat the white Volvo with the Ohio plates. Molar Man and Sweet Tooth (formerly Diane) had arrived. When I called the two they invited me to join them for dinner at an Italian place. It seems Molar Man has been hiking some big mileage days, and is only about a half day behind me now.

Overall, today had been relaxing, although for a while there I wondered why I wasn't out hiking. Sometimes it's harder to take a day of rest than it is to hike. My days of the week are also confused. It seemed like Saturday all day. Tomorrow, however, all will be back to the routine of the thru-hiker. I'll arise early, try to consume as many calories as I can tolerate at breakfast, and hit the trail early. The trail in Maryland only runs 41 miles. Virginia seemed to last forever, but now each state should come and go with rapidity as the walk continues north on the Appalachian Trail.

## June 6, Harper's Ferry to Turners Gap

June 6 forty-seven years ago was the last day of school my freshman year of high school. My German teacher, Mr. Russell, wrote the date on the green chalkboard, 6/6/66. He commented that it would be over eleven years before the date could again be written using only one numeral. At the time 1977 seemed so remote that it could have been a hundred years in the future. Little did I know as a lad of 15 that before 7/7/77 rolled around, I would be married, have two college degrees, and be a high school teacher myself. Every year on June 6, I still remember Herr Russell.

Over the years I section-hiked the AT, I would usually begin as soon as the school year ended, so I've often been on the trail on June 6. Today I walked out of the state with the fewest number of trail miles and into the state with the second fewest. The bridge over the Potomac took me from

West Virginia into Maryland, the 6th state heading north. I felt inspired and motivated on the overcast early morning. I had arrived in my sixth state on the sixth day of the sixth month.

Wanting to get started before 7:00, I arranged for a taxi to the trailhead at the east end of High St. in Harper's Ferry. The driver dropped me there at 6:40. After crossing into Maryland, the trail follows the old C&O Canal Towpath for three miles. Along that stretch I saw two runners, a cyclist, and a lady walking six dogs, all hers she said. A deer came into view at a distance but had disappeared by the time I reached the spot. The flat spacious terrain made for fast hiking. Even though I had to wait for a train to cross at the north end of the towpath where the trail begins to ascend toward Weaverton Cliffs, I averaged right at three miles an hour for the first six miles.

Early in the day I took the short trail to the Ed Garvey Shelter. A little later when I reached Gathland State Park, I took another break to briefly visit a museum. Sweet Tooth had parked nearby to wait for Molar Man to hike past. Rock Steady arrived as we talked. Before exiting the park I met trail angel Peggy from Pensacola. She was waiting for a group of hikers that she was supporting on a series of A.T. day-hikes. Hancock and Gypsy were also hanging out at the picnic tables under a pavilion. Just as I left the park the rain began.

Continuing to hike quickly, I hoped to reach my end point for the day before the heavy rain that was forecast began. I did stop at White Rock Cliff for the view. Then I zigzagged my way through a series of small rocks for a couple of miles to the Dahlgren Campground. By then the rain had increased. Rock Steady, Hancock, Gypsy, and two section-hikers from Norfolk were also under the overhang, trying to keep dry. It was then that I changed my plan for the day. Since serious storms were in the forecast for tomorrow, I decided to stop at Turner's Gap for a 17.5 mile day. This way I could get a lift from Molar Man and Sweet Tooth rather than risk being at a hostel or shelter all day tomorrow.

When I finally got back to the trail to hike the final 0.3 mile, the rain had gotten heavier and colder. Rock Steady and I hiked together. He headed on up the trail as I took refuge under the front eave of a church to wait for the Volvo. Feeling a little chilled, I removed my wet T-shirt and replaced it with a dry long-sleeved one. I also put on my raincoat and gloves, knowing that the wait would be over an hour. As soon as Sweet Tooth parked I made a dash for the car. Molar Man soon arrived and we were off to Hagerstown.

So after another comfortable day of hiking, I ended the day in a very nice motel room. I hated to take another day off so soon; however, it was unlikely that many would hike tomorrow if the weather that was predicted arrived. So after a lackluster finish to Virginia, I re-energized in WV and started Maryland in a positive manner. And on another positive note, Molar Man was about to become my hiking partner again.

## June 7, A.T. Museum

Whether one sleeps in the woods or in beds, it takes a lot of planning to thru-hike the Appalachian Trail. Today was one of those "getting ready for the next four days" days. Since it was also my second respite in the last seventy-two hours, I wrestled over the necessity of such a day when I awoke to gray skies, but no rain. Thinking I would rather be hiking, I had to convince myself over breakfast that all was for the best. When the steady, bordering on cold, rain began, I realized that my decision was a good one.

So for much of the day I rode in the back seat of the white Volvo, mentally taking notes on just how a supported hike can be fine-tuned. Molar Man and Sweet Tooth have a method that works for them. We first drove back to where we left the trail yesterday so that Molar Man could navigate, via very precise A.T. maps, where Sweet Tooth could meet him with lunch and also where she could pick us up at the end of tomorrow's hike. Given all the "back roads" and state highways that sometimes don't even appear on a traditional roadmap, the "preparation and rehearsal" phase is indeed necessary.

After arriving at Pen Mar Rd., where we will finish hiking tomorrow, we drove into Waynesboro, PA and then to Caledonia State Park where Sunday's hike will conclude. Checking places to meet along the route, we finally made our way up to Pine Grove Furnace State Park, the half-way point and home of the Appalachian Trail Museum. Visiting the historic building, which truly captures the essence of the trail, was the highlight of the day. It was especially meaningful since I had read about many of the exhibits on display. Taking a break at the Pine Grove General Store was thru-hiker Colin whom I had last seen at the Audie Murphy Memorial. Colin is the only hiker who I have met who actually reverted back to his real name, preferring it over a trail name. The last time we had met, Colin had been Scarecrow.

From the park we scouted out other places where Sweet Tooth could meet Molar Man; however, I only plan to hike with them the next three days. In fact, one of my reasons for rejoining them for a bit revolves around next week. Linda will arrive on Tuesday, so I hope we can duplicate the Ohio couple's scheme for a few days. My mental notes better be good. I wouldn't want my lovely wife lost some place like Rattlesnake Run Rd. Yes, there's one in Pennsylvania. But hopefully after learning Molar Man and Sweet Tooth's strategies, Linda and I will be just fine.

It has been a good day. Despite taking a day off, much got accomplished. Late in the afternoon clouds still lingered overhead. The forecast for the following day called for sunny skies, at least in the afternoon. A few Junes ago, Don would have been getting his gear ready for some bass fishing tournament on a Saturday morning. He competed in many and won a few. For me Saturday would provide another opportunity to move on up the trail. I couldn't be more excited to get to the state famous for its rocks. Great days lie ahead as the adventure continues on the one of a kind Appalachian Trail.

## June 8, Turners Gap to Pen Mar Rd.

Goodbye Maryland. Hello Pennsylvania! Today I walked into the 7th state on the Appalachian Trail, passing the Mason-Dixon Line just prior to Pen-Mar Rd. I guess I'm officially in the north. The blue skies and white puffy clouds enhanced the enjoyment of the final few miles on a comfortable 23.5 mile day. Despite a few tough stretches of rocks, some slanted in various directions, today's hike progressed about as smoothly as any I've done over the entire trip. I continue to be at my best using my motto of "light pack, big miles, and beds." Hey, it's working.

So when Molar Man said he wanted to get an early start, I had no idea he meant that we would be standing in the lobby of McDonald's at 5:00. With breakfast to go, we drove along with Sweet Tooth to the trailhead at Turners Gap, arriving in time to begin the hike at 5:45. Chirping birds and a couple of scurrying squirrels greeted us as we ascended the first gradual incline shortly after dawn. Just prior to the two-mile mark we walked into Washington Monument State Park. A side trail of about fifty yards led to the "original" Washington Monument, a stone edifice erected in 1827. After a brief stop and photo-opt, Molar Man and I picked up the pace.

With a slightly humid, overcast mild morning, we banged out the miles at near record pace. By 8:00 we were crossing the footbridge over I-70. Sparse traffic travelled the interstate on this early Saturday morning. We zipped by the blue-blazed trail to Annapolis Rocks, choosing to make miles rather than check out yet another view. By 11:30 we had already hiked 14.9 miles to Foxville Rd. where Sweet Tooth waited with the cooler and snacks. I had packed two burgers and a root beer, but I did take a bag of chips. While we ate, section-hiker Fis walked up and graciously accepted some of Sweet Tooth's trail magic. Molar Man and I would pass her shortly after resuming our hike. We would see no thru-hikers, however, all day.

As the afternoon began, we encountered a challenging segment of rocks which required some diligent maneuvering. Molar Man continued to lead, and I followed throughout most of the day. When we got to the north end of the High Rock Loop Trail, I convinced my buddy that it was worth the short walk to the scenic view. With a tad of reluctance he agreed. Several folks were hanging out at the site that had formerly been used for hang gliding. A young man from Rockville, MD, Carlo, told us that rock climbing permits can be obtained for the dangerously steep outcrop. A section-hiker at times himself, Carlo offered to take our picture.

Returning to the trail, we were again faced with an extremely rocky descent. I painstakingly navigated the rocks, falling behind Molar Man. After the rock section we arrived at Pen-Mar Park, perhaps the prettiest recreation area on the entire A.T. I commented that this would be an ideal place for some "yogiing" on the busy Saturday afternoon, were we not so close to the end of today's hike. Since Pen-Mar Rd. was less than a mile away, however, we just kept moving, arriving at the road a little after 3:00. Indeed, we had knocked out big miles in good time.

Today was a great day to hike. For Don, it would have been a great day to fish. He often had already launched his bass boat, readying for a day on the lake, at about the same time I started hiking today. On many picture-perfect Saturdays like today, he would in all likelihood have still been casting away. There were no lakes on today's hike, but there were many reminders of my brother's life. Ferns bordered the trail in several areas today. As I passed through them on either side, I was reminded of how Don regularly brought ferns to our mother and how much she appreciated his kindness. Today beauty abounded everywhere as it does so often on the Appalachian Trail.

# 9

# Pennsylvania

## June 9, Pen Mar Rd. to US 30

The story almost read, "A.T. THRU-HIKER 'KNOCKED' FROM TRAIL." Don's Brother, an Appalachian Trail thru-hiker from Georgia, came close to having his hike suspended today when he ran into a large, overhanging tree limb. Briefly staggering backward, DB commented that he felt his teeth rattle before he regained his composure. Hiking companion, retired dentist Molar Man of Ohio, made no effort to check Don's Brother's dental work; however, he did pause long enough to ascertain that there was little chance that a concussion had occurred. For the remainder of the 17.8 mile day, Don's Brother paid closer attention to his surroundings.

Hitting my head on the tree really wasn't that big of a deal. There just wasn't that much to write about today. With another early 6:10 start, Molar Man and I managed to complete the hike in less than seven hours. The first full day in Pennsylvania could be described as boring. We climbed a little, descended a little, walked level occasionally, and confronted a couple of sections of "from washing machine to refrigerator size" rocks. Pennsylvania is often referred to as Rocksylvania, so I suppose what we encountered today is a precursor to what lies ahead.

We also crossed a few streams with footbridges. "Footbridge" has become one of my favorite A.T. words. Every time I hear the sound of distant water, I start wondering whether or not there is a bridge for crossing. Today there were four. There were also some patches of black mud on the trail today. They could be circumvented most of the time, however. And as always, there were several short sections with smaller oddly-shaped rocks. The trail offered up some variety. It just wasn't very interesting.

We passed two locations where two shelters stood side by side. At the Tumbling Run Shelters, pea gravel had been spread to enhance the site's ambiance. "Two" appeared to be the operative number because there were two picnic tables as well. Molar Man and I took a break there. Fis, the section-hiker we met yesterday from Massachusetts, had also stopped for a snack. Other than some day-hikers, we didn't see many folks on the trail today. For the second consecutive day, we saw no other thru-hikers.

When we reached US 30 and the end of today's hike, Sweet Tooth was waiting. We drove back to Pine Grove Furnace State Park where I consumed a pint of Butter Pecan ice cream. Then Molar Man drove to scout locations for day after tomorrow. He was also nice enough to drive into Carlisle, where I plan to pick up a rental car after tomorrow's hike to use while Linda visits. After that we headed to a motel and called it a day.

Indeed it has been a beautiful Sunday. Don might have been sitting on his deck, waiting for a deer to walk up in his backyard on other Sunday afternoons like today. I think he would be happy to know that tomorrow I will reach the true mileage half-way point as I return to continue the journey on the Appalachian Trail.

## June 10, Pine Grove Furnace State Park

Most years some re-routes of the Appalachian Trail occur, which usually means a slight variation in distance. This year's trail measures 2185.9 miles, a 1.7 mile increase over the trail of 2012. The half-way marker, however, dates back a few years, indicating that the half-way mark is 1090 miles. Nevertheless, as of today I have hiked 1095.6 miles by last year's standards. I have now officially completed over half of the A.T. So from now until completion, I will have fewer miles to walk than I have already walked. To be quite honest, that makes me feel pretty good. As a matter of fact, it makes me feel real good.

When Molar Man and I hit the trail this morning at 6:10, there was rain in the forecast. Within about an hour it started. Throughout the day we hiked in a steady drizzle although it never rained very hard. It was late morning before my clothes and shoes were thoroughly soaked. Then I just slogged along, not worried about stepping in numerous puddles on the trail. There were also several water crossings, but for the most part, footbridges were provided. At one place I was trying to select the best rock skipping strategy when I noticed out of the corner of my eye that Molar Man was traversing the stream via footbridge. I hadn't even seen it.

Aside from the rain, today's trail offered very little to get excited about. We passed through Caledonia State Park early in the day and then by another "double shelter" at the Quarry Gap Shelters. Like many of the shelters so far in Pennsylvania, the amenities looked inviting. Hanging baskets even adorned an arbor of sorts. I suppose I should eventually take advantage of one of these impressive structures. Perhaps there is a Pennsylvania shelter in my future. A few hikers were still in their sleeping bags as Molar Man and I passed by Quarry Gap.

If I were rating today's hike on the 1-10 scale for difficulty, with 10 being extremely difficult, I would call today's trail a 1 or 2 all day. With the easier terrain, we hiked the 19.5 miles in less than seven hours, despite the rain and mud. One noteworthy aspect was the numerous road crossings. We crossed 12 to be exact. In two cases, five gravel roads intersected where the A.T. moved from one side of the woods to the other. Most of the roads were hard-packed dirt or gravel, but a few were paved.

When we reached mile 1090, a sign indicated that the half-way point had been reached. Molar Man and I took a brief break for pictures. Then we passed the Toms Run Shelter before finally arriving at the road leading into Pine Grove Furnace State Park. We walked by a hostel before reaching our final destination, the General Store. Sitting out front were several thru-hikers including Finder, Triple Six and Calamity Jane. Finder reminded me that we had met at Woods Hole over 400 miles ago.

Triple Six, another of the Germans on the trail, was trying to finish off his half gallon (it's now really a quart and a pint) of chocolate mint ice cream for the half gallon challenge. It is an A.T. tradition for thru-hikers to attempt to eat a half gallon of ice cream at the half-way point of the trail. I opted for the half pint challenge instead. I'm not sure I could have consumed the larger portion, but the chocolate marshmallow smaller size sure tasted good after my hike in the rain. Molar Man selected a drumstick for his challenge.

After leaving the park, we headed to Boiling Springs and a stop at the ATC Mid-Atlantic Regional Office. Just as we arrived Ambassador and Sugar Bomb also walked up. It had also been some time since I had seen the affable Sugar Bomb. We chatted on the porch, and then I went inside to purchase A.T. maps for the next five days when Linda will be shuttling me. From there Molar Man and Sweet Tooth were very thoughtful to drive me to Carlisle, about five miles away, where I could pick up a rental car that I had reserved.

After saying our goodbyes, until somewhere up the trail, we parted. Inside the Enterprise office I received excellent customer service from Courtney. Next I checked into a motel, showered, and went for a late lunch. It felt luxurious to be able to drive to a meal. The plan for the following day was to take another day off. After that the landscape would change with my wife becoming my helper for a few days. Smiling, I wondered about Linda's indoctrination to the life of the thru-hiker on the Appalachian Trail.

## June 11, Boiling Springs

Some say the most important word for thru-hiking the Appalachian Trail is flexibility. Due to a cancelled flight by Delta Airlines, today's plans indeed required me to be flexible. After we found out that Linda's flight had been re-scheduled to arrive late in the day, I decided to go ahead and hike the 19.6 miles into Boiling Springs with Molar Man. Since my plans didn't change until late last night, I wound up only getting about five hours of sleep. Still, I hiked strong throughout the day, partly due to following behind the "machine." Molar man's ability to set and hold a pace of about 2.75 miles per hour is uncanny. I don't even check the itinerary as we hike. He keeps me well-informed.

When the alarm sounded at 4:15 I had already been up a quarter of an hour. Thinking I might find an all-night restaurant, I headed for our meeting in my rental car at 4:30. A convenience store with hot breakfast sandwiches and coffee met my needs. As daylight approached, I sat in the car having my meal. Then I drove to the rendezvous with Molar Man and Sweet Tooth for the ride back to Pine Grove Furnace State Park and the beginning of today's hike. No one else was around as we made our way through the manicured park and finally back into the woods.

All went well early until we reached a spot where what appeared to be a white blaze led us down to an impassable stream with no bridge. Not seeing a blaze on the other side, I suspected that we had made a wrong turn somewhere. With his pioneer instinct, Molar Man bushwhacked to a spot to cross. Before deciding to go ahead and just walk through the ankle deep water, I retraced my steps up the trail to discover that the trail we were on should have been blazed blue. It looked as if a previous blue blaze had been painted over with white. When we finally got back to the real white blazes, Molar Man picked up the pace to make up for the ten minutes lost in futility.

After approximately a twelve minute lunch break (long, by Molar Man's standards), we continued to make good time until we hit the first of two rock mazes. The boulders of various sizes, from large appliances to small homes, required a degree of patience. With blazes aplenty and an arrow here and there, I thought the navigation of the mazes would be fairly easy. There's that word that has no place on the A.T. again. Then I looked ahead to see Molar Man standing atop a two-story rock looking for an outlet. His choice of directions worked for him. I went another way which required a little rock scrambling. All in all, the variety was almost refreshing.

Like the other days in Pennsylvania, a number of footbridges were provided for most water crossings. Late in the hike we passed Center Point Knob where a statue had been erected to indicate the original A.T. midpoint. A short while past this landmark we found ourselves hiking a path that passed through a cornfield. My dentist/engineer/farmer friend educated me on some aspects of corn growing. He also answered, "alfalfa," when I asked, "What's that?" After we walked through the farmland for over a mile and a half, we finally reached the small one-way bridge leading into the quaint little town of Boiling Springs, home of the ATC Mid-Atlantic Regional Office.

As the trail enters the town, it passes by a lake. A few fishermen sat in chairs at the bank on the warm, lazy afternoon. One young lad cast his rod as his dad watched.

When he said he wasn't catching anything, I noted, "But you're having fun."

The dad replied," That's what it's all about."

On another afternoon, twenty or so years ago, that could have been Don and Brent. My brother loved to fish with his son. And Don would have definitely loved Boiling Springs, a town that seems Mayberry-like in a peaceful way. I could see him relaxing by the lake, just enjoying.

It had been another good day to hike. I shared a special section of trail with someone who has become a good friend. Our hiking styles, as well as our demeanors, seem to complement each other well. Tomorrow we'll hike together again. For now, however, I'm off to the Harrisburg International Airport to hopefully meet Linda's plane. If all goes according to plan, when morning arrives, she too will begin to learn just how special life can be on the Appalachian Trail.

## June 12, Boiling Springs to PA 850

Apparently the section of the Appalachian Trail I hiked this morning is maintained by Old McDonald. From a moo moo here to a cornfield there, farmland existed as far as the eye could see. Over fence stiles and through several cow pastures, Molar Man and I hiked the first 10.2 miles to the Scott Farm Trail Work Center where Sweet Tooth and Linda met us for a short break. Then we covered the remainder of the 16.5 miles at a steady pace, finishing today's hike in six and a half hours. With a few dark clouds overhead on a warm day, it was good to get it done early.

In addition to all the farmland, we also walked across three overpasses. The trail crosses I-76, very busy US 11, and I-81. We also encountered more footbridges in the woods. Some appeared to be new, especially in marshy areas. A portion of the trail ran adjacent to a muddy Conodoguinet Creek. Other than a short climb of about 500 feet just before the Darlington Shelter, the trail remained reasonably flat, muddy, and nondescript for the final six miles up to PA 850 where Sweet Tooth and Linda waited.

When we reached the small parking area, the ladies were talking with Mossy Brown, a 2009 thru-hiker. She had heard about my hike from Walker when he, Whiskers, and Rocket had passed through the area about ten days ago. Walker had referred to me after Mossy Brown mentioned having a friend recently diagnosed with ALS. Not having seen any of these hikers since Damascus, it was good to know about where they are now. We chatted with Mossy Brown for a while before heading back toward Carlisle.

My brother Don stayed on my mind much of the day. From an early deer sighting just off the trail to sections of smashed mulberries, memories abounded. I thought of the mulberry trees he and I had climbed as kids on our grandfather's farm. Then there was another small pond and of course the creek. But the strongest memory was connected to a dog. In his early teens, my brother got an Irish Setter at Christmas one year. Don loved Red and hated to have to have him put down when the old dog got too sick to barely stand. As I walked through the filtering sunlight early in today's hike, two dogs came charging down the trail. The second, an Irish Setter, looked old and tired. His owner said he was nearly deaf. When I asked his name, she said, "Red."

Even hiking with a buddy like Molar Man, there are stretches when neither of us has anything to say. I suspect that he, like me, is often lost in memories. Today is Wednesday. On Wednesdays last year Linda and I regularly shared a meal with Don and Lisa. It became our routine to meet at our condo. Don enjoyed wheeling his power chair on a breezeway out over the river before we would go inside. When he could still speak coherently, he quietly stated one night, "I like this place." He was at peace by the river. I miss those Wednesdays.

So another day has passed on the Appalachian Trail. For me it was day 82. Tomorrow severe weather is predicted, so Molar Man and I are going to wait for morning to plan our day. I'm not sure either of us is interested in any tornado-blazing. Still, if it's just rain, we'll probably be back on the trail. Today proved to be another day that my brother would have liked. So as I walk on I will keep remembering how much.....Don loved the woods.

## June 13, PA 850 to PA 225

Molar Man suggested that I begin today's entry with, "We hiked through a thunderstorm and nobody got killed."

I preferred, "My phone rang at 5:45; Molar Man asked, "You ready to hike?"

With severe weather in the forecast, I had set my alarm for 6:00, expecting to sleep late for a change. My friend, however, had a different idea.

"The bad weather isn't coming until 4:00," he informed me.

"Famous last words," is all I have to say. Because when we reached the trailhead a little before 7:00, the skies were rumbling. We looked at each other, told our wives goodbye, and proceeded to hike into a thunderstorm.

Actually, the thunder, lightning, and rain didn't begin until we had hiked almost a mile. When it did start, it poured, but only for about an hour. Thunder boomed occasionally, but the lightning really never seemed close. As the rain subsided, we both agreed that we were glad to be hiking the trail today even if it was a shallow stream for a few miles. After all, after the feet are drenched, it really doesn't matter whether or not you walk through the puddles. Molar Man would later change socks at the break. I just hiked in wet ones all day.

When the rain did cease, the humidity kept us sweating. Still we made good time, reaching Duncannon before 11:00. A warning that the trail was very rocky the last six miles into town didn't seem exactly accurate. Sure there were rocks aplenty but not nearly as severe as what we would face on the last leg of today's hike. When the trail reached Duncannon, famous among A.T. hikers for the Doyle Hotel, we were greeted with a road walk

155

(or I should say town walk) for over two miles. A short block before the Doyle the trail goes west to High Street, following the street that runs parallel to Market Street until the edge of town. Passing near the Doyle reminded me of the night terror incident that had occurred there on my Pennsylvania section-hike in 2008.

Although they happen rarely, when I do have these night terrors they more often occur when I'm sleeping on my back. The bed in the cell-like room at the Doyle came with a sagging mattress which made it a challenge to sleep on my side. At some point during the night I slipped onto my back and the moaning began. I remember hearing myself moan for what seemed to be a minute or more before I awoke. When I did awake, I heard someone exclaim from an adjoining room, "What in the **hell** was that?" To this day, I'm not sure if the occupant was asking the question of someone else in the room with him, or if he was in the room alone. With the paper-thin walls of the Doyle, I'm surprised Alton didn't hear me as well from his room down the hall.

So before walking up to High St. we took a couple of pictures of the majestic old hotel. We then meandered through a peaceful neighborhood until the trail turned east to head over the Clark's Ferry Bridge and the Susquehanna River. After crossing over the river we met Sweet Tooth and Linda at a parking lot under the bridge. Also parked there was Spirit, Steady's wife. She had been acquainting herself with our ladies in her RV. I also went inside to relax and eat a sandwich that Linda had brought me. With a longer lunch break allotted by Molar Man, it felt good to rest my feet.

When we did start hiking again, we were faced with a climb of about 1000 feet which culminated with a spectacular view of the town of Duncannon and the Susquehanna. It was after the ascent, however, that the hike got dicey. A very rocky stretch of trail, often requiring us to use our hands, slowed our progress over the last few miles. At one point I had to sit on a rock and carefully lower myself down about an eight foot drop. The change of terrain was fun initially, but then it got tedious. When an actual trail finally appeared past the last of the big slabs, we quickly picked up the pace to PA 225 where the ladies were waiting.

*Don's Brother on Springer Mountain, March 23, 2013*

*Rocket and Whiskers on Wayah Bald*

*Crossing a Stream North of Pearisburg, VA*

*Speck in Virginia*

*Don's Brother on McAfee Knob*

*Fields in Pennsylvania*

*Don's Brother and Funnybone on the A.T. in New York*

*With John Teeples and Jimmy Brooks in Connecticut*

*Pilgrim and Banzai in Massachusetts*

*Susquehanna Slim, DB, Banzai, and Pilgrim*

*Mt. Moosilauke in the New Hampshire White Mountains*

*Susquehanna Slim, Pilgrim, Molar Man, and Don's Brother*

*Molar Man, Pilgrim, and Don's Brother in the Mahoosuc Notch, Maine*

*Saddleback Mountain, Maine*

*Don's Brother, Susquehanna Slim, and Molar Man on Avery Peak, Maine*

*With Susquehanna Slim Getting Ready to Cross the Kennebec River*

*Fording a Stream in Maine with Molar Man*

*Molar Man, Sweet Tooth, Double Nickel and Rich*

*View of Mt. Katahdin*

*Molar Man and Don's Brother on Katahdin Summit, September 2, 2013*

*Brent, Lori, Lisa, and Don, 2008*

*Elizabeth, Lisa, Don, and Brent in the Spring, 2012*

*Don and Mike Headed to Church, Circa 1961*

*Mike and Don at Turner Field for a Braves Game, September, 2011*

*Don and Lisa*

*Mike and Linda, Back in the "Regular World"*

*Shortly after Don's ALS Diagnosis*

*Don and Lisa Enjoying a Special Sunset*

Just before arriving at our destination, Molar Man and I were passed by Blazer, a thru-hiker that neither of us had previously met. I'm 1149 miles into my hike and meet another hiker who started six days before me for the first time. Seems odd, but it continues to happen. Blazer hiked with us to the road where he was offered some trail magic by Sweet Tooth. Also visiting at the Volvo was Steady. I had hiked almost a full day with him out of Waynesboro, VA over two weeks ago and had not seen him since then. Before we left the area, Tugboat, Liferaft, and Finder also showed up to partake of some snacks.

When we did finally head for town, I followed Molar Man in our rental car. Within a couple of minutes it felt more like I was following George Costanza on his way to the Bubble Boy's house. I barely had a glimpse of the blur of a Volvo as Molar Man exited onto US 233. Telling Linda to hang on, I somehow maintained contact until we thankfully reached a traffic light. From there we made our way to a motel. In the parking lot stood OB, another thru-hiker from GA that I had not met, but who had heard of me. His wife, Mona, had driven up to visit and slackpack her hubby for a few days. I wouldn't see OB on the trail until Maine.

## June 14, PA 225 to PA 443

With a 25.6 mile day on the agenda, Molar Man and I headed up the trail from PA 225 at 5:50. I'm actually beginning to like these early starts. In less than three miles we passed Peters Mountain Shelter. Several tents still stood. It was also apparent that few had roused themselves from their shelter slumber at the early hour. So we hiked on throughout a partly cloudy, pleasant morning until we reached PA 325 where Sweet Tooth and Linda had parked. Even though it was still early, this would be our only rendezvous of the day.

Pilgrim, whom I hadn't seen since Bears Den, stood by the Volvo. He needed a ride to pick up a package in town, so Sweet Tooth agreed to help the Californian out. Also in the parking lot was Bernie the Whittler. He presented me with a hand-carved whistle. Bernie said that he was supporting his wife and her sister on about a 400 mile section-hike. Under

His Wing and In His Feathers were relaxing in the back of Bernie's van. Before Molar Man and I continued our hike, thru-hikers Finder and Fatty joined the group. The trim, attractive blonde with a captivating smile had acquired her trail name because of the massive calories she was able to consume. I took an immediate liking to Fatty and her smile.

With 16 miles still to go, Molar Man and I hiked at a steady pace for the duration of the day, finishing just after 4:00. Throughout the afternoon we passed and were passed by a few. Blazer and Lentil hiked by on an uphill grade and quickly disappeared. Pfeiffer, whom I had not seen since Daleville, and Calamity Jane also passed us. With gentle terrain except for a few stretches of rocks, it proved to be a good day for big miles. It was a personal best for Molar Man and came within 0.1 of equaling my longest mileage day.

At one point near the end of today's hike, we stopped to briefly chat with the four ladies who said they were having some girl time. Pfeiffer, Fatty, Finder, and Calamity Jane appeared to be enjoying their break. We also took a brief respite by a stream where Blazer and Lentil were resting. Molar Man and I then hiked steadily the final four miles to reach PA 72 earlier than we had expected. Right before reaching the road we caught Steady, who planned to hike the additional 1.4 miles to Swatara Gap.

All in all, today's hike lacked anything really interesting. The trail intersected with a few other trails, and signs indicated where significant structures had stood in the past. It was good to get in the miles. I was even happier knowing that I was going to take my lovely wife Linda out to dinner to celebrate her birthday. What better way to end another day of the adventure that continues on the Appalachian Trail!

## June 15, PA 443 to PA 501

Molar Man asked, "Are we almost to the road?"

"I don't know; we just came up over that rock pile," replied the young man with his family.

"Rock pile" is not exactly what one wants to hear with less than a mile of a 12.8 mile morning hike remaining. As we neared our scheduled meeting with Sweet Tooth and Linda, Molar Man and I met a small army of day-hikers, many of them children, on their way to I'm not sure what. We hadn't really had any views to write home about all day. Still, the single file line of packless people continued. Molar Man and I smiled and said hello to the legion before finally reaching the Kimmel Lookout, the first truly awesome view in quite some time.

For much of the morning the trail had been a continuous stream of various sized rocks. More small ones than large slowed our pace at times. Occasionally, however, we still encountered level, gentle terrain. Early in the hike we missed a turn, which resulted in about a quarter mile walk off course. Fortunately Spirit and Steady were parked down the road. Steady appeared from the RV to greet us as "lost hikers." Retracing our paths for the distance, we found the blaze that had been partially covered with graffiti. We then proceeded to climb over 700 feet. Other than Finder, we saw no thru-hikers.

After reaching the parking area on PA 501, unfortunately Molar Man and I had to bid each other farewell again. While he wanted to continue for a 22.1 mile day, I was content with 12.8 and a final afternoon with my wife before she flies back to GA tomorrow. Somehow, I knew that our paths would cross again. They would, but not until New Hampshire. Before we drove away, I walked the approximately 100 yards back down the trail with Linda, Sweet Tooth, and Spirit so that they could enjoy the Kimmel Lookout view. Linda then said her goodbyes to the other two ladies at the car before we headed into Pine Grove.

When Linda and I reached the outskirts of town near I-81, we stopped for lunch. As we ate I noticed Fatty across the road trying to hitch a ride. Walking outside, I shouted that I would take her back to the trail. She came in and joined Linda and me. A tri-athlete from Nova Scotia, the vivacious young lady started at Springer four days after I began, yet we saw each other for the first time two days ago. A current resident of Alberta, Fatty has plans to visit her Nova Scotia home after finishing her hike in Maine.

So Linda and I drove our new friend back to the trail before finding a room for the night. We then scouted out the best route to the airport and just did some driving, enjoying the countryside. Tomorrow will be a little sad. For the first time in almost two weeks I'll again be hiking alone. I'm losing a wife, a friend, and a car, but the woods await. One never knows what the next day may bring. For me it will most assuredly be more rocks, but it may also be an introduction to a new hiker who might also become a friend. Whatever the new day may offer, the journey will continue up the Appalachian Trail.

## June 16, Pine Grove, PA

With my buddy Molar Man now a day up the trail and Linda en route to the Harrisburg Airport, I must admit a tad of despondency has crept into my psyche. Looking for a panacea, I decided to take Father's Day off and treat myself to the final round of the US Open. Remembering the special times when I enjoyed the tournament with my dad, and later with my son, has brought me comfort on an overcast afternoon. Despite being alone in a Pine Grove, PA motel, the memories are comforting even if they bring with them a little melancholia. There will hopefully be other Father's Days in future years when, in the company of Sam and Rachel, I will nostalgically remember this day. That's what the A.T. and life are all about– a compilation of memories.

Earlier in the day Linda and I shared a leisurely breakfast and then a time of relaxation near the pool. When I sighed that I still had 996 miles to walk, my lovely wife replied, "That's soooo much better than 1000." She qualified her response with, "That's why the price tag says $3.99 instead of $4.00. It's all psychological."

Perhaps she has a point. By this time next week I should be in another state and have fewer than 900 miles remaining. A positive attitude continues to be paramount to success. I never entered a road race without thinking I would finish. So I've tried to maintain the same mindset as I hike. The summit of a mountain in Maine marks the finish line.

I also thought about my nephew Brent throughout the day. This is his first Father's Day without his dad. They shared so much. From fishing and hunting, to Little League, to trips to watch the Braves, they were an inseparable father and son. Don was proud of the man Brent has become. Above all, he felt blessed that his son was and is a man of faith, just like his dad.

As our mom grieved the loss of a son, Brent's wife Lori tried to comfort her with, "Brent is just like his dad and we still have him."

Those of us who have lost our dads cling to those special times of the past. Times of childhood when Dad could make everything OK. Good times they were indeed.

So many have been supportive of my hike. From family to friends, to former students I taught and athletes I coached, to people I have never met, yet who have taken the time to send a guest book entry or write an email, I have truly been blessed every day of my walk. So many people have touched my life over my 62 years. One, Bobby Gardner, who ran cross-country and track on my teams for four years and later excelled in college and the US Army, sent a Happy Father's Day text this morning. He never misses contacting me on this special day. It's rewarding to know how one's life may impact another's.

Those same kinds of special relationships are formed on the A.T. Each day that I hike I meet someone new. Often we just say hello and move on. Occasionally, however, a bonding relationship develops that may have long lasting significance. On the trail as well as in life, we never initially know how we may affect another just as we don't know how another may affect us. We merely accept and appreciate the opportunity to have our lives interwoven with another earthly creature that just happens to be sharing a moment in time with us. I exist for the moment to walk a trail, a trail that leads to a destination that fulfills a goal. And as I walk I become. I become a man of determination and resiliency, a man with a passion for overcoming and defeating. The trail is not necessarily the enemy. Still, it presents all hikers with confrontation and the need to persevere.

So as I sit and dwell on the past and anticipate the future, I am oblivious to the present. It is a Sunday, Father's Day. My mind journeys to a special day when I became a dad. Then it moves to another special day when Don became a dad. Finally, it travels to another special day when

I became a dad to a daughter. Each day is forever transfixed within the memory. I can replay every wonderful moment of each of those memorable days of my life. They provide comfort at a solitary time. They give me strength to confront a new day with its potential tribulations.

Tomorrow I will continue the hike. I will attempt to meet the challenges as I enjoy the beauty of my surroundings. I will focus on each step in the present, realizing that without notice, peril may await. I am grateful for this opportunity to hike. I hope to make the most of what tomorrow has to offer as I continue the northward journey on the unbelievably beautiful Appalachian Trail.

## June 17, PA 501 to Port Clinton, PA

It felt odd starting a hike solo today. It also felt strange hiking with a full pack again after a week of slackpacking. Nevertheless, that's what I did. After breakfast at the motel, I used my first shuttle in several days to return to the trailhead at PA 501. During my meal I overheard a member of a tour group use a phrase I haven't heard in some time.

"Well, I'll be dog!" prompted me to ask where they were from.

When a member of the group said, "Tuscaloosa, Alabama," I shared that I was from Georgia.

After being dropped off at the trail, I began walking at 6:40. Early in the hike I passed Fis and later was passed by Wrangler. I would see no other people all day until the last mile going into Port Clinton. The trail was lonely today, my friend. As the morning progressed I took a break at Round Head to just enjoy the view. Then I hiked steadily until a little past noon when I reached a campsite where Wrangler had built a fire and was cooking some lunch. He explained that the fire was to keep the bugs away. That sounded like a good idea, so I joined him.

After lunch I continued at a quick pace until I reached the Eagles Nest Shelter. I had actually intended to stay the night there; however, since it was only 1:20, I just couldn't force myself to stop with only 15.1 hiked and seven hours of daylight remaining. So I pushed on. In fact, I covered the two miles from the shelter to Shartlesville-Cross Mountain Road in 38 minutes. While the terrain allowed, I kept up the pace. Then when the rocks appeared, I slowed. Even with some lengthy stretches of rocks, usually small in size, I arrived at the small town of Port Clinton, PA before 5:00, having hiked 24.1 miles with a full pack.

One noteworthy occurrence on today's hike was running out of water, which is something that should never happen. As the day got hotter I found myself drinking more and not finding any sources from which to refill my bottles. I tried to conserve when I realized that I had little left and about three miles remaining until town. Then the magic occurred. Within a couple of minutes after I had taken my last sip, I turned a corner to find eight 32 ounce Gatorades under a tree. It could have been 32 ounces of gold and I don't think I would have been any happier. I took one and immediately downed half of it. That drink gave me the lift I needed to carefully negotiate a very steep descent to the road. I thought to myself, "I'm glad it's not raining."

Reaching the road by the train tracks, I took a break at a picnic table before crossing the short bridge into Port Clinton. Arriving at PA 61 going into Hamburg, I thought I'd give a motel a call to check on rates. As I was talking, a truck stopped. The lady in the passenger seat asked if I needed a ride. Fred and his trail angel wife drove me right to the front door of the motel. Also in the truck was Fables, a young lady who started at Springer the week before I did. Like so many others, I had not seen her until today.

Even though I hiked a ten hour day alone, the miles went quickly. At one point I thought about creating an imaginary hiker friend that I could share the trail with when no one else is around. I gave him a name, a place of origin, and a rather bizarre personality. The mind can travel to some strange places. Perhaps it was the "missing" that plagued my mind throughout the warm afternoon. Whatever the case, over two months of hiking remained if there was to be completion of a thru-hike of the Appalachian Trail.

## June 18, Day off in Hamburg, PA

There's something special about waking up at 7:30 in a comfortable bed. When the bed happens to be in a four-star motel within two miles of the trail, it just doesn't get any better, at least not for this "town guy" hiker. Apparently I'm not the only one with an affinity for luxury because other hikers were milling around the lobby as I enjoyed the impressive complimentary breakfast. Section-hikers Jim Dog, from Utah, and Beaker, from Kentucky, joined me at my table for some trail conversation. Jim Dog plans to shuttle up to New York with his daughter today to meet his wife for a section. Beaker is headed back to Virginia to pick up some miles. I told both about Don.

Also in the dining area were Medicine Man and his 23-year-old son, Kudo. The father and son team from St. Louis had also hiked the 24.1 yesterday to reach Port Clinton. They started at Springer ten days before I did, but they had gone home for a few days before continuing their hike recently. So I meet two more thru-hikers for the first time. When Medicine Man said that they hoped to finish in early August, it put into perspective how much ahead of schedule I am. Still, I never know what may occur from day to day. I'd rather be ahead of schedule than behind, trying to catch up.

So as I relaxed in my comfortable surroundings, I waited. I waited for tomorrow when I would again hit the trail. As I waited I was reminded of the days of happiness that the trail had given me. But I was also cognizant of times of loneliness and despair. It seems that every time an ounce of sadness or perhaps a tinge of melancholia surfaces to potentially disrupt the hike, something wonderful happens. I just didn't feel like hiking at the moment, but I also knew that the following day the trail awaited. Perhaps good fortune would also await when I returned to the woods to hike north up the Appalachian Trail.

## June 19, Allentown Hiking Club Shelter

The last time I saw Speck she was walking up the trail out of my hike forever, or so I thought. That day I struggled to limp the final three miles to Jennings Creek where I shuttled back to Daleville to treat my Achilles tendinitis. Today Speck walked back into my hike on a beautiful day in northern Pennsylvania. On the trail for another section-hike, she appeared when I thought I'd be hiking alone for a while. Her company was definitely welcomed and appreciated.

My day began with a hitch from Hamburg back to Port Clinton. Two trail angels with a work truck offered the lift. Dale hoisted my pack into the back of the truck as I climbed up to the front seat. His co-worker, Ben, rode in the back. After the short ride I found myself hiking by 6:55. To begin the day I walked under a bridge and up a steep ascent of 900 feet. Noticing a familiar-looking female in the distance, I quickened my pace. Looking over her shoulder, Speck greeted me with a smile. It was going to be a great day for a hike.

Throughout the day the trail afforded us much variety. At one time Speck and I were strolling down what seemed like a pleasant country road. At another we were faced with various sizes of rocks to climb over or navigate around. We took a break at Reservoir Rd. and then another at Pulpit Rock, which offered another spectacular view. It was hard to leave the beauty, but after a few pictures, we moved on. Then there were the short sections of smaller pointed rocks which made finding a place to step challenging. But that's what the A.T. in Pennsylvania has been all about.....variety. From the farmland to the rocks, it has all been good.

Not having seen Speck in over a month, we spent much of today's hike talking. It was good to catch up with my friend. She told me about the rest of her section-hike in VA after we went our separate ways, and I filled her in on my days with Molar Man. Our conversation made the day pass quickly despite the often difficult terrain. We took another break at The Pinnacle, which afforded us another, OK; I'll use it, breathtaking view. It was there that we saw Scarecrow, or Colin, drying some gear.

One of the highlights of the day came when Speck and I met Under His Wing and In His Feathers. The 80 and 75-year-old sisters have been section-hiking the A.T. since one of them started receiving social security. A true inspiration, they chatted for a good while with Speck who was fascinated with their endeavor. When we reached the road leading to the Eckville Shelter, Bernie the Whittler was waiting by the van. He allowed

Speck to select one of his carved figures. Before we headed on, the two ladies walked up, ending their hike for the day.

The last few miles proved a little more difficult, mainly I think because we were tired. Still even though the trail caused some difficulty at times, we were able to hike 22.2 miles to the Allentown Hiking Club Shelter, arriving a little after 6:00. Speck was nice enough to boil me some water for a hot meal. The lasagna was delicious. I suppose I could get used to this sleeping in shelters and eating trail food if I so desired.

We shared a picnic table, adjacent to the shelter, and good conversation with Shadow and Shade, an older couple from North Carolina. They had begun their hike in Harper's Ferry four weeks earlier, hiking comfortable miles each day. Shade said they hope to get all the way to Maine. They're just not sure when. It appeared that Shadow was happy to follow Shade's direction. Speck called them a "cute couple." They exhibited a sort of cheerful innocence for a pair of sixty-somethings.

So tonight I'm back in the woods. This shelter is nice. There are even a couple of canvas chairs and two bunks. The shelter sleeps eight, so the four of us have plenty of room. Darkness has arrived. The others may already be asleep. What sounds like a family with five or six boys of about ten or eleven just walked up. They appear to be looking for a place to camp. One said he thought he heard a wild animal. I hope not. I'm tired. It's been a good day to hike with a friend. Tomorrow we'll head toward Palmerton, the next town on the map up the Appalachian Trail.

## June 20, Palmerton, PA

When the A.T. experts decided to label Pennsylvania rocky, they must have based their evaluation on the section between PA 309 and Palmerton. "Rocky" seems like an understatement for what I encountered today. The portion of the trail from the Knife Edge to Bake Oven Knob was downright nasty. At times I thought that there must be a better way to get from point A to point B without putting my life in danger. I tried to keep my mind on each step, slowly making my way over the slanted rocks with exposure on both sides. This was probably the most technical section of trail that I have encountered thus far.

The day began at the Allentown Hiking Club Shelter. Awaking at 6:00 after a rather restless night, I couldn't believe that I was the last one stirring. Shadow and Shade were already packing up their gear and Speck was having breakfast. After hastily downing a fruit pie and some water, I hiked out of camp with Speck at 6:55. Early in the hike all went well. We hiked steadily, enjoying a conversation as we walked. At Blue Mountain Summit Rd., we took a break to fill our water bottles at the restaurant right off the trail. Ken, the owner, came out for a chat, offering some information about the area.

After returning to the trail the real hike began. About three miles later Speck and I reached the infamous Knife Edge, only about 0.2 mile in duration, but very strenuous. I hiked ahead for a while; then Speck took the lead. Even though the hiking was tough, we took the time to take a few action shots of each other. Speck called the section exhilarating. I called it scary. Trying to harness the adrenaline rush as best as I could, I just kept reminding myself that a blind man had once hiked this. It didn't really help, but Speck's encouragement did.

When we finally reached the end of the perilous section, Bear Rocks awaited. These rocks, however, were not exactly on the trail, so even though we had to hike over another rocky section, the difficulty was lessened. But at about the time that I had regained my composure, we were confronted with Bake Oven Knob, another technical, rocky segment. As with the Knife Edge, our pace slowed, but Bake Oven Knob proved to be less challenging although still very difficult. After all the rocky sections, I think we both welcomed the more gentle terrain for the remainder of today's hike.

Like so many other days, we saw few other thru-hikers. We did meet several section-hikers, most southbound. When we reached PA 873 and the Lehigh River we were left with a mile and a half to Palmerton. Fortunately, a gentleman in a van, Bob, agreed to drive Speck and me into town where we checked in at the Jailhouse Hostel on Delaware

St. The hostel is located in the basement of borough hall near the police station. Medicine Man and Kudo were going through their gear as we sought bunks.

Even though there were challenges in today's hike, I somehow managed to stay vertical all day. By taking my time, focusing on each step, and remembering that many were offering up prayers for me daily, I succeeded. But that's what the Appalachian Trail is all about, a series of challenges that have to be met daily. Like today, tomorrow would present more difficult sections of trail that would have to be dealt with. For now, it's getting late. I'm writing this from a bench in a park across the street from the hostel. Bugs are circling the street lights overhead. Another good day draws to conclusion, yet tomorrow more adventure awaits as I will climb out of Lehigh Gap on the Appalachian Trail.

## June 21, Wind Gap, PA

The climb out of Lehigh Gap is regarded as one of the most technical segments of the Appalachian Trail south of New Hampshire. At 8:00 this morning Speck and I crossed the bridge over the Lehigh River headed for that ascent. Speck had a smile on her face anticipating some real rock climbing. I had the feeling I sometimes get before a dental appointment. I just wanted to get it over with. Before the scrambling was finished, however, I was smiling as well. After all, a good hike in Pennsylvania wouldn't be complete without a section that requires the use of one's hands.

So after encountering a steep, wooded uphill for the first half-hour, we came face to face with the boulder field. With the bridge over the Lehigh River in the background, Speck and I took aim on the final ascent. We telescoped down our poles, and Speck placed them in the back of my pack. Considering the rockface we were approaching, poles were more of a hindrance than a help. The higher we got, the more I needed to concentrate. Each upward movement required finding the appropriate shelf to place my hands and feet. It took time, but the slower pace was necessary to ensure my safety. Speck again called the climb exhilarating. Today I called it exhilarating as well.

When we finally crested the apex of the mountain after a 1000 foot elevation gain, we found ourselves at the south end of the Superfund Detour. For the next three miles the trail stretched along a ridgeline that afforded a beautiful view of Walnutport and Slatington, PA. The views were so gorgeous that Speck and I stopped often to enjoy. Once the trail headed away from the edge of the ridge we had to walk over a rock bed for a short while. The detour trail not only presented better views but also steered the A.T. away from the old zinc mining fields.

For much of the rest of the day the trail was comprised of a variety of rocks. We hiked over some short sections of rocks about the size of our packs. At times the trail became a path of pointy rocks often protruding through the grass. To put it simply, it contained rocks and more rocks. A stiff neck can be the result of having to continuously hike with your head down. Otherwise, an ankle injury, trip, or fall might be the result. Speck and I conversed some, but mainly we just concentrated on getting through these rocky sections without getting hurt.

Like yesterday we saw no thru-hikers. We did see a few section-hikers like Andy, a young lad from Newcastle, England. When Speck asked him if he had a trail name, he didn't know what she meant. Dressed in a purple fleece and long, heavy-looking camo pants, Andy said he started in New York and was ending his hike in Charlotte. When I told him that Charlotte wasn't exactly on the A.T., he replied that he realized he would have to leave the trail eventually and walk east. We wished him well before hiking on.

As the afternoon waned we saw one extremely long black snake. He had to be seven feet in length. It was the second snake we've seen this week. I forgot to mention on Wednesday the timber rattler that was curled up about a foot off the trail. At first I thought he was a black snake as well until Speck pointed out his markings underneath. In addition to the snakes, we've also seen some wild turkeys, hawks, and a few other familiar critters. And we continuously hear the incessant singing of the cicadas. Speck seems to like their song. I wondered if Odysseus' Sirens may have created a similar sound.

Hiking at about 2.5 miles per hour throughout the afternoon, we finally reached Hahns Overlook, the first view since early this morning. With only a mile left in the day's hike, we only paused briefly to chat with ridgerunner James. From the overlook we quickly hiked the final mile into Wind Gap, finishing the 20.8 mile day at 5:30. For the three days I've hiked with Speck, we have averaged 20.1 miles per day, a very good pace, especially considering the rocky terrain. It's good to have some tough sections behind me as I get ready to say goodbye to Pennsylvania.

## June 22, Delaware Water Gap

When you've just bounded over a series of kitchen table-size boulders called Wolf Rocks, you don't expect to suffer your first fall in over a week while having lunch. That's just what happened on another beautiful afternoon in Pennsylvania. With a 15.7 mile day on the agenda, Speck and I began today's hike at 9:15. After a short climb out of Wind Gap, we meandered our way through the woods on a trail carpeted with more pointed rocks of various sizes. A warm sun made its appearance early in the day to remind us that we needed to stay hydrated.

Nothing of any great significance caught my attention until we reached Wolf Rocks about seven miles into today's hike. Speck smiled, anticipating another opportunity to do some rock hopping. Considering the mundane landscape we had been traversing, I smiled as well. I'm beginning to enjoy the challenge of some more difficult sections of trail. Even though these rocks did not pose as big an obstacle as the Knife Edge or the hike out of Lehigh Gap, they still demanded concentration. I commented to Speck that they reminded me a little of New Hampshire where you have to plan your next step.

Right after Wolf Rocks the excitement for the day occurred. I had packed a ham and cheese sandwich, fries, and a Mountain Dew for lunch. Not being able to open the Dew, I asked for Speck's help. When she proceeded to remove the cap in about two seconds, we both began laughing. In my exuberance I tripped over a baseball-size rock and fell backwards hard into a larger rock. The fall changed Speck's countenance from laughter to concern as I sat motionless for a few seconds, unsure of just how badly I might be hurt. After I ascertained that I was OK, except for a minor scrape and a sore lower back, I got myself to my feet to eat my lunch. When I figured out that I wasn't hurt badly, I turned my attention to the Mountain Dew. Also a fan of the citrus beverage, Don would have still been laughing at my blunder. Over lunch I continued smiling, thinking about how much my brother loved to laugh.

From an early age Don always seemed to find something funny about various aspects of life. And not only did he love to laugh, but he also loved watching or making others laugh. His nine-year-old niece, Anna Kate, said to him in a special card, "You're the funniest man I know." Many others thought the same. When Don was in the room, laughter abounded. He could cheer up the disheartened with a humorous story or a talented impression of one of the many "characters" he sometimes became.

At his job with Atmos Energy, Don regularly brought smiles to the faces of his co-workers. One declared that the workplace would never be the same after Don's death. They felt blessed to share an office with such a genuinely caring man who could in a moment's notice generate resounding laughter throughout the building. Shortly after his death, an abundance of his comical stories were re-told by many who knew him. Those stories, in a minor way, will continue to contribute to his legacy.

One of Don's favorite pastimes was talking to telemarketers. If he were in the room when one called, Don immediately stated, "Give me the phone." Before or in the middle of the unsuspecting salesperson's pre-rehearsed pitch, Don would start to ask a wide array of questions. The first often dealt with the location of the caller as well as the weather in the caller's city. Don had somewhat of a "down home" knack for engaging the party on the other end of the line in what was no more than trivial banter. Still Don would continue the conversation for as long as the telemarketer would comply.

One question that Don loved to pose was "Are the fish biting up your way?"

If the caller took the bait, Don would talk fishing for as long as his newfound friend would accommodate him. As the conversation sometimes lingered, the rest of our family sat laughing in the background at his ability to converse with the caller as if they had known each other for years. And occasionally Don would even get someone who wanted to talk about fishing.

Eventually, the caller would get around to the reason for the call. When the product or service was finally mentioned, Don would assault the caller with a battery of questions, many which had no relevance whatsoever to the aforementioned product. Probably Don's favorite revolved around companies offering roadside assistance. Don would tell the person on the line that he currently didn't own a car, but that he was saving to buy one. He would then add that he did have a cart and a couple of mules. He would next ask if their company could offer assistance if he had a problem with one of the mules while traveling around. One poor girl actually put him on hold for a minute while she checked with her superior. Even though after a while it had to be a certainty that the caller realized that my brother was only having a little fun with her, I imagine that some probably related the story of the call to fellow telemarketers in their office and hopefully laughed when doing so.

When the caller became frustrated or tired of Don's unrelated questions, Don usually just kindly stated that he was not interested in what the person was selling, that is if the caller had not already hung up on my brother. I don't ever remember Don's being outright rude to the person on the other end of the line. Whether the call lasted for five seconds or five minutes, Don maintained what could be considered a pleasant demeanor throughout the conversation.

Don also enjoyed laughing at the antics of characters on various TV sitcoms. One of his all-time favorites was Barney Fife of *The Andy Griffith Show*. Don could recall specific lines of Barney's and bring laughter to anyone in the room when he shared them. Just as Don Knotts had entertained with laughter his audiences over the years, Don Stephens entertained his audiences as well. The only difference was that our Don's audiences were his family, friends, and co-workers.

In more recent years Don became a huge *Seinfeld* fan. I still remember his calling me one night to ask if I had seen the episode where Kramer reconstructs the Merv Griffin set in his apartment. I had missed the show that evening, so Don carefully re-told the plot to me. When I finally did see the episode, I remembered our phone call. The conversation with my brother made the viewing of the show even more enjoyable. Even though we had seen every *Seinfeld* episode numerous times, we still laughed any time we enjoyed a show together, even after Don's diagnosis.

Don could also laugh at himself. In early April of 2011, about a month before he found out that he had ALS, we visited my daughter, Rachel, in New York. Along with Linda and Lisa, we spent an entire Saturday walking throughout the city. Despite having legs that had begun to fatigue easily, Don often pointed out sights that to all of us were amusing. We took many photos over those four days which showed my brother laughing. In the Museum of Natural History, he wanted his picture taken posing next to a primate exhibit. It is one that I will always cherish.

Laughter can be addictive and it can also be therapeutic. For those who spent time with Don throughout his life, and especially during that last year, I think it was both. We laughed along with him then, just as we still laugh when thinking about some of his antics that are fresh in our memories today. Those who have the ability to make others laugh are a blessing to all who know them. My brother was that type of man. Even though Don is no longer with us, his laugher still is. His family and friends will always think of him as we remember the smile on his face and the resounding laughter in his voice. Because Don loved to laugh, all those who had the opportunity to share that laughter have been given a special memory to cling to from now on. And as we certainly all know, Don would want us to still be laughing.

⌇

As the afternoon progressed, Speck and I continued to hike at somewhat of a leisurely pace. At a power line we met John and Brandon, who had set up a ham radio tower. When I asked John how far away he had transmitted, he said Russia. A little later we reached Totts Gap where a cooler of bottled water and some mints had been left. Dolores, the mother of A.T. hiker Olive Oyl, had also left her phone number for hikers needing assistance. Even though Speck planned to camp again tonight, I made a note of the number before signing the card she had placed by the cooler. I figured that Dolores would be a good person to call for a lift from the Delaware Water Gap. When I did reach her by phone, Dolores said that she would be happy to provide me a ride into Stroudsburg.

When I reached the Water Gap, I stopped for ice cream at Zoe's. Leaving just as I arrived was Colin (formerly Scarecrow). He was headed back to the trail. Before I left, however, Medicine Man and Kudo stopped in at the shop. After walking outside, I also spied Pilgrim walking up the street. He filled me in on who was at the Church of the Mountain Hostel. It was good to know who was in the vicinity. It was equally good to have completed half of the fourteen states that comprise the Appalachian Trail. With fewer than 900 miles remaining, I was anxious to walk across the Delaware River into New Jersey.

# 10

# New Jersey and New York

## June 23, DWG to Blue Mountain Lakes Rd.

On a cold, rainy morning three months ago today, I set out from Springer Mountain in GA to attempt a thru-hike of the Appalachian Trail. On that March day I must admit there existed an inkling of doubt that I could accomplish the task. Now 93 days later the doubt is gone. As long as I can stay healthy, I feel the goal will be reached. Even though I sometimes wonder how I continue to follow much the same routine day after day, I do. So as I moved into my eighth state at the beginning of my fourth month on the trail, I hiked happily on a beautiful Sunday.

Trail Angel Dolores again aided my hike by driving me back to the trail at the Water Gap this morning. Speck and I had arranged to meet by the bridge for the walk across the Delaware River into New Jersey. The trail passes the Kittatinny Visitor Center before moving under I-80 toward the trailhead. In the parking lot adjacent to the trail sat the RV of Spirit and Steady. Both came out and met Speck. Shortly thereafter Speck, Steady, and I headed into the woods. A goodly number of day-hikers and runners dotted the trail.

After about four miles we reached the south end of Sunfish Pond. The still water amidst the picturesque landscape created a peaceful setting. Just past the pond, we missed a blaze and got off trail briefly. Retracing our path, however, we found the blaze and continued to hike near the water. Even though this was not Pennsylvania, the small pointy rocks continued.

Steady kept saying the rocks would cease around the next curve, but they didn't seem to be honoring Steady's wishes.

The best view of the day happened at the rocky summit of the Kittatinny Mountains. Ridgerunner Grasshopper patrolled the area. At Camp Rd., Speck, Steady, and I stopped for some lunch. Pilgrim passed by on his way up the road to the Mohican Outdoor Center to purchase food. For some reason it seems that lunch is becoming my downfall, since for two consecutive days I've fallen during or right after lunch. Speck laughed, and I went ahead and laughed along with her, when I just tripped over an innocuous rock step at the very beginning of the next incline. Stumbles is several days ahead of me, but I'm challenging her for her trail name.

At the Catfish Lookout Tower two couples were taking a break. From there we hiked by a swamp where beavers had spent a lot of hours damming up a stream. Past the stream the rocks all of a sudden seemed much less prominent. We continued to hike at a rapid pace, arriving at Blue Mountain Lakes Rd. before 4:00 to complete a 17.7 mile day. Steady said farewell before heading on up the trail looking for a campsite. Speck and I waited for Bob (Shamrock) and a shuttle back to Stroudsburg. Also a hiker, Shamrock said his shuttle business had been booming the last couple of days.

As my hiking day came to an end, I reflected on my three months on the trail. In some ways it felt like three years. At times it still feels like I am stuck somewhere between the regular world and a dreamlike state. I wonder if there isn't another me still living my other world life as I continue to participate in this grand adventure. The mind can be an enemy or our friend. For an A.T. thru-hiker the mental struggle always exists as does the beauty along an ever-changing landscape.

## June 24, Gren Anderson Shelter

I'm sitting on a blowdown at a campsite in the woods. It's 7:17 in the evening, sticky warm, and rain is in the forecast. Several hikers are gathered at a picnic table, some cooking supper, others just visiting. Mosquitoes are in the vicinity. I've used bug spray. It hasn't helped. My red shirt, covered in perspiration, hangs from a makeshift clothesline in the Gren

Anderson Shelter. I've put on a dry shirt but will probably sleep in my damp hiking shorts. Because of the expected warm night, I'll sleep on top of my bag rather than in it. There are eight slots in the shelter. All are full. It may be a tough night for sleep.

The day began with a shuttle back to the trail from Shamrock. Light Bird, an injured section-hiker, was also in the truck. A doctor and soldier who had been deployed four times, Light Bird has been sectioning for a few years. He and Shamrock both expressed concern and compassion when I told them about Don. I thanked them both before heading up the trail with Speck. Shortly after the day began we saw Medicine Man and Kudo resting by a brook. For the remainder of the day Speck and I would hike off and on with the two.

The trail today consisted of a couple of sections of medium-sized rocks, more small rocks, some pine straw areas, and a few ridge views. Rattlesnake Mountain offered the best view of the day. Speck and I took a break there to just relax and enjoy. Despite the intense heat of a 93 degree day, all was good. I drank water and Gatorade regularly. Still, it was tough to stay hydrated.

When Speck and I reached Culver's Gap, we walked about 200 yards up the road to Gyp's Tavern. I'm not sure who Gyp was; however, an auto-graphed picture of him with Babe Ruth resides in a glass case. I had one of those, "I need to call my brother" moments. Don would have loved hearing about the pictures of the Babe. I miss those baseball conversations that Don and I had so regularly.

Gyp's is a nice place. The tavern owners have made it really easy for hikers to find their way around. Signs were posted that told us where we should leave our packs, where we could enter the tavern, and where we should and should not sit. Before Speck and I ordered, Medicine Man and Kudo arrived and joined us at our table. I ordered a burger, fries, and a turkey sandwich for the woods. Along with a root beer over ice, it made for an outstanding meal prior to the walk to the shelter. Before leaving the establishment, a local patron suggested that I take a bottle of whiskey rather than my re-filled water bottles.

On the final three miles Speck and I picked up the pace as thunder re-sounded in the distance. A light shower began just before we hit the short blue-blazed trail to the shelter. When we walked up, Bob, a section-hiker from "just north of Manhattan," Lentil, and Pfeiffer were already inside. Shortly after we got here, Medicine Man, Kudo, and Pilgrim also arrived. So the eight-person shelter is at capacity on a steamy night.

Darkness is approaching. A large group of young folks, who appar-ently drove to the campsite and are tented nearby, are noisily enjoying themselves. My shelter mates are trying to get comfortable in a cramped environment. I am sleeping in the woods and all is well. Kudo, to my left, is gazing toward the bear box. Speck, to my right, is busy with her phone. Pilgrim and Pfeiffer are still seated at the picnic table with Lentil. No one is asleep. I'm not really tired and doubt that I'll sleep much tonight. Still, all is good. I'll wake at dawn, pack up with the others, have a little break-fast, and head north for another day on the Appalachian Trail.

## June 25, New Jersey 23

The tell-tale sign that another hiker was stirring, air being let out of a mattress, awakened me after a surprisingly good night's sleep. I checked my watch to discover that it was 5:00. It was Pfeiffer's mattress I heard. Pilgrim was already at the picnic table cooking breakfast. Speck sat up on her pad. Bob also stirred. Medicine Man, Kudo, and Lentil appeared to still be sleeping. Oppressive heat already filled the air along with the pesky bugs. I immediately knew that it was not going to be a comfortable day for a hike. My instincts would prove correct a few hours later.

Having chosen to sleep in my one pair of long hiking pants and only long sleeve shirt, to try to deter the pests from striking, I needed to change clothes. I quickly removed my pants to put on my still wet from perspira-tion hiking shorts. There is little modesty in shelters. I then pulled my even wetter shirt from the makeshift clothes line and donned it as well. After packing up my sleeping bag, pad, and clothing, I laced up my trail runners over my disgustingly filthy socks. They had been clean yesterday. So with a pack ready to hoist onto my shoulders, I sat down for breakfast.

Even though I realized that I needed something nutritious, I could only manage to eat one cereal bar. So after the meager breakfast Speck and I left camp a few minutes before 6:00. Only Pilgrim and Bob preceded us.

Fortunately today's hike was short. The trail offered absolutely nothing of significance. I took only one picture all day. More rocks, sometimes pointy, covered a portion. At other times the trail was barely visible due to various foliage that had practically overtaken the path. Speck and I climbed a few larger rocks, but those minor sections fell way short of offering anything in the range of exhilaration. I fell twice. Speck showed concern. I laughed; she laughed. I'm beginning to wonder if I have a balance issue. I seem to be tripping when there's nothing there. Even though I keep hearing my buddies back home saying, "Stay vertical," it's hard.

The only noteworthy view occurred at Sunrise Mountain where a pavilion had been erected. The sun had already risen and the bugs had begun their relentless attack, so we didn't pause for long. The bugs must have had no interest in the view either. They pursued Speck and me ruthlessly as we ambled on up the trail. By the time we got to the Mashipacong Shelter, we both had multiple bites on our arms and legs. The Deet wasn't working. Neither was the swatting. We did stop briefly for a snack. Pilgrim, whom we had passed earlier, and later Lentil, arrived before we moved on. Pilgrim removed his head net so that he could apply some bug spray that Speck had given him. The critters were a menace to all. Pilgrim struggled to lift his pack, one that appeared much too heavy for his frail frame.

So on we went, hiking and itching all the way to High Point State Park Headquarters at NJ 23. The Spirit/Steady RV sat in the parking lot. After talking with Spirit, Speck and I walked into the air-conditioned building to sign in as hikers and receive a complimentary Pepsi. I remembered this park from my section-hike with Alton. This is the spot where our Michigan friend Ponder thought he missed a blaze and did a circuitous route to get to the building. I made sure I didn't make that mistake. It was too hot to have to repeat even ten yards of the A.T. today.

Since it was early and we had been promised a ride by "just north of Manhattan" Bob, Speck and I relaxed in some shady grass, awaiting his arrival.

Having covered the rather short 11.3 miles before noon, we were really in no hurry. I felt sad knowing that this would be the last day that Speck and I would hike together. As she shared a special story about her twin four-year-old granddaughters, my mind wandered to the past when Sam and Rachel too were young. Sitting in the grass, I found myself transported in a sort of melancholic reverie. We never know when we are doing something for the last time.

⁓

Last winter I took my mom to buy a new stove. The stove she had cooked on since, in her words, "before your daddy died," had served her well. It had offered up many a Thanksgiving dinner over the years, so it almost seemed appropriate that the oven would cease working on turkey day. In all likelihood, it will be the last stove that she will ever need. Still, like buying an appliance or a baseball glove, we never know when we are doing something for the last time, that is unless we're old or facing death.

When Sam, my son, was only three, we began playing catch in the backyard. Many an afternoon, through his days of T-ball and later Little League, we would toss a baseball back and forth until dusk. He went through a phase where he wanted me to throw high flies and then another where he preferred grounders that he could scoop up and fire to a first baseman dad. I don't know when we last played catch, but we did. It probably was toward the end of his last season of organized ball, but I don't know exactly on what day.

Rachel, my daughter, loved to swing on an old metal playset, also in our backyard. We have photographs and videos, as well, of me standing behind, pushing her into the air. The pigtails of a six-year-old fluttered in the breeze on a chilly winter day. Even in the cold, she still enjoyed this time to spend with her dad. These carefree, innocent days of childhood were fleeting even as they transpired. I don't know when I last swung her, but I did. On one of those days of winter, or perhaps in springtime, we walked back into our home after an hour of happiness that would never be shared the same again.

Throughout the spring and summer, as my mother has cooked on her last stove, her son has been travelling north, working hard to complete a thru-hike of the Appalachian Trail, both for the first and last time. As I have walked from Georgia I have met many other travelers. Some of them have become friends with whom I'll later exchange a Christmas card or perhaps call to wish a happy birthday. Others I'll see for a last time somewhere along the way. We won't know it at the moment. We may not even remember where it occurred. All we will realize, and come to appreciate even more keenly over the years, is that we walked together, fellow pilgrims toward a destination and a dream. As Ulysses says in Tennyson's poem, "I am a part of all that I have met." Each of us will become a part of the other, when we initially exchange greetings, and also when we say our goodbyes, for what very well may be a last time. Life has so much to offer, and so does this journey along the Appalachian Trail.

To make certain that Bob hadn't already gotten to the parking area via a different route, I eventually walked up the road to check. A few minutes later Speck and Bob arrived. Once again a trail angel helped this "poor old, can't keep his balance, hiker." Speck and I were grateful for Bob's kind act since he still had an hour and a half drive to get home.

Later in the afternoon I took a taxi into Port Jervis for a meal and laundry. Unlike last night, tonight I would sleep in a bed, alone rather than in the company of seven other hikers. My room is larger than last night's shelter. It's exponentially more comfortable. Hiking has been and will continue to be my life for hopefully about two more months. Tomorrow, however, I'm taking a bit of a detour on a walk of another kind a little east of the Appalachian Trail.

## June 26, New York City

I'm on a train, the Metro North/New Jersey Transit. The Hoboken Line. Destination, Penn Station. Speck sits beside me. Her second section-hike of the summer has come to an end. Across the aisle sit Medicine Man and Kudo. All three of my hiking buddies are headed to LaGuardia. Medicine Man and Kudo will fly to St. Louis; Speck heads to Atlanta. I'm going into the city for a special visit. I'll ride this same train back to Port Jervis later today…alone. For my friends, home and families await. For me, it will be back to the trail community. I will find a way back to High Point State Park and walk solitarily toward Vernon, NJ. But for now, life on the A.T. is temporarily suspended. Time stands still.

I look through the window at distant ridgelines. Their heights decrease the closer we get to Manhattan. The conductor announces the next stop. Commuters board every time it does. Each takes out a cell phone, or iPad, Kindle, or paperback. All look downwards, just like I've daily focused on my feet, and the ground, as I hiked. The train whistle blows. I reflect on the past, think about future days on the trail, but try to live in the present. I have only hours, minutes, to offer well-wishes, say good-byes, embrace a moment in time that will never be repeated. The train slowly moves into another station. Again the whistle blows. In many ways I envy my friends who are headed home. In others, I long to be back on the trail. We arrive at our destination, Penn Station.

I say goodbye to Speck, Medicine Man, and Kudo at the intersection of 31st St. and 8th Ave. The Joe Louis Plaza. I shake the men's hands. I hug Speck. I've stood here before. I love New York. There are no white blazes, but for some odd reason, I feel more comfortable navigating the NYC subway system than the rocks of the A.T. There's less chance I will fall on the streets of New York. Perhaps I am an enigma. I have over an hour to kill before the meeting. While my friends head north toward Central Park and eventually a cab to the airport to make mid-afternoon flights, I walk south toward the West Village. It's a beautiful day in Manhattan.

I walk down 7th Ave. Sidewalk vendors sell their wares. There's a fruit stand every block. Food is plentiful. Ah, for an available piece of fruit around every bend on the Appalachian Trail. That would be good. It's hot. I get to 23rd St. and decide to take a cab the rest of the way. I don't want to be late. The driver is courteous and jolly. I'm grateful. I arrive 15 minutes early and text Rachel. She comes outside to meet me. I haven't seen her since the first weekend in March. We hug hello. It's a bittersweet moment, knowing how brief the visit will be.

I'm quickly propelled into the working world of my daughter. I momentarily become the center of attention for a group of strikingly vivacious young ladies. They all have beautiful smiles. All are interested in my hike. I meet Lauren, Meg, and Amy. Then I'm introduced to Madison and Teresa. In the next room I'm greeted by another Amy, Rachel's boss, who interrupts her meeting to emerge from a glass conference room to talk. I meet Mary and Dustin and others whose names I unfortunately can't remember. These aren't trail names. These are real people in the regular world. They could be Rocket or Finder or Paisley or Fatty or a number of other young ladies, if they were hiking the Appalachian Trail.

I see my daughter's office and am a bit overwhelmed by the magnitude of the company for which she works. We leave to walk to lunch. I'm reading a distinctly New York menu at Westville. I think of another time, when a nine-year-old sat across from me at a restaurant in Park City. We order and chat. Rachel tells me about her incredibly busy world at Soul-Cycle. I talk about the hike. We speak of the uncle she loved so much. We smile a lot and enjoy the moment. Lunch goes much too quickly. We walk back to her office. I chat with a few others. We take a picture. Rachel walks with me to the corner of Leroy and Hudson. We hug tightly and exchange I love yous. She walks back up Leroy toward Greenwich. I turn to watch for a few seconds more before heading up Hudson. I'm simultaneously happy and sad. The two hours with my daughter have become a memory.

I begin walking north on Hudson. There are no blazes. I need none. I'll turn east to 8th Ave. at W14th St. and keep walking to 31th St. and Penn Station. I pass the Bus Stop Cafe at Bethune St. and remember the brunch there with Rachel and Sam. I notice the Apple store at the corner of W14th, where Rachel and I stopped on the cold January afternoon I left her in her new city before I drove back to Georgia. I think of all that has happened in the past two and one-half years. I see two women walking dogs. They smile when I ask to take a picture. Lindsey, a beautiful young lady, shows interest in my hike and says she will read my journal. I move on. The sun beams down. I think of a day last week when I saw only two other people over a ten hour period. Today there are tens of thousands marching through time on cement sidewalks. They have no blazes to follow; still, they find their way.

I'm back on another NJ Transit train, traveling in the opposite direction the same route Speck, Medicine Man, Kudo, and I travelled this morning. Their flights are near completion. Their families wait. The coach is crowded. The train rolls between one small hamlet and another. Passengers depart at each stop. Outside, clouds and haze have replaced the sun. An older gentleman across the aisle watches a video on his iPhone. The voice sounds like a five-year-old granddaughter. He has no expression. I wonder why. I nap. The gentleman to my left wakes me at Harriman. Commuters depart at each stop. A once full train is now nearly empty. I sit alone, gazing at the ridgelines in the distance. They are increasing. I am nearing the trail.

The conductor announces, "Port Jervis; last stop." I walk from the train. It is raining. I pass by the Burger King where only eleven hours earlier I had shared a meal with three fellow hikers, now friends. I call a cab. I stand near a puddle waiting. I ride back to the motel to remember. It has been a good day, a special day, but a day that now has become a memory. I will rest well tonight because tomorrow a hike needs to be resumed as the northward journey continues up the Appalachian Trail.

## June 27, Vernon, NJ

Today would be in serious competition for my most miserable day on the trail. Not due to the terrain. Just as Steady had promised last Sunday, up around the bend the Pennsylvania rocks finally ended, 45 miles into New Jersey. The reason for my miserable state had little to do with the trail and everything to do with the heat, humidity, and the mosquitoes. If anyone would like to try and simulate what I experienced today, let me suggest the following: Find a place with a 90 degree temperature and 100% humidity where mosquitoes are swarming by the hundreds. Now walk around in that environment for around nine hours. One fifteen minute break in an air-conditioned room is permitted.

My day commenced with a final Port Jervis taxi ride back to High Point State Park. It was the first that was more than $5. One mile into the hike I stopped to climb a wooden tower with a platform and view of another tower which sits at the highest point in New Jersey at 1701 feet. From there I hiked steadily, crossing several roads and swatting bugs as the heat increased. After the rocks diminished, the trail became a fairly flat, soft path for most of the morning. It would have been a pleasant hike on a cooler day. Unfortunately the army of mosquitoes had only recently invaded the area, or so I was told by a local.

When I reached Lott Rd., I walked the half-mile into Unionville, New York. The trail continues in New Jersey; however, it is so close to the line that some trail towns are in New York. At Horler's Store I ordered a turkey sandwich on wheat with a Dr. Pepper. I sat in an old, metal, red porch chair on the front veranda. Also at the store were Johnny Walker, Sinner, and Banzai. I had not seen my old friend Banzai since before the Shenandoahs. My break from the heat and bugs was short-lived. When I walked back to the A.T. I was immediately attacked by a small battalion. I made numerous kills, but many in the army struck me as well.

Sweating profusely and covered in Deet, I tried to outrun the pests unsuccessfully. At one point I put on my head net, which at least kept the critters out of my face. What made matters worse was that the trail passed near water most of the afternoon, especially around the Wallkill Reserve. After the swampy walk around the Reserve, Pochuck Mountain awaited. Ascending about 700 feet, this was the only challenge of the day. It was here, however, that I again suffered what could have been a serious fall. Due to fatigue, I think, I failed in an attempt to pull myself up on a knee-level large slab. As a result I lost my balance and fell backwards on another large rock. This fall evoked no humor. It hurt a lot. My right hand jammed underneath my body as my shoulder hit the rock. And what made matters worse was that I snapped one of my trekking poles. The mosquitoes showed no remorse, sending in reinforcements for multiple strikes as I lay motionless on the ground. Did I say it was miserable?

So hiking with one pole, thoroughly soaked with sweat-laden clothes and triple figure mosquito bites, I painfully proceeded to County Rd. 517 where I took a short break to reassess the potential injury. From there I first had a boardwalk hike followed by a cow pasture crossing before arriving at NJ 94 and Vernon, NJ. I then walked the hundred yards or so west to Heaven Hill Farm, a combination nursery, farmer's market, and deli. I ordered a barbecue sandwich and root beer which I enjoyed on their patio. Land Line, a thru-hiker who is trying to beat his own thru-hike personal record of 74 days, joined me. After the meal, Mike, the deli owner offered a ride to the Episcopal Church Hostel in Vernon.

Several others are at the hostel with me including Banzai, Lentil, Pfeiffer, and Fis. All are young folks. After a shower I walked to a grocery store and now am writing this in the only fast food restaurant in town, a Burger King. Darkness has arrived. I'm about to order a burger and then walk the two blocks back to my home for the night. Today was a tough one, but I've bought more bug spray so that I'll be ready for those varmints as I hike out of New Jersey and into New York tomorrow on the Appalachian Trail.

## June 28, Greenwood Lake, NY

I suppose every adventure needs a little adversity. So today I hiked out of Vernon, NJ with one pole, a sprained hand, and a sore right shoulder and lower back, prayerfully. The day began two hours earlier at The Mixing Bowl. The only thing that would have made my hearty country breakfast better was grits. I got a smile before the "no" when I asked. Several local diners were talking about the trail. When one said he couldn't believe anyone would walk over 1350 miles to Vernon, his buddy said it was no different from walking around a golf course every day. Did I really hear that? I just drank my coffee and kept quiet.

After breakfast I walked back to the hostel to pack up. Everyone had still been asleep when I crept out a little after 6:00. When I returned a few continued to sleep. The youth show no urgency in getting their day underway. Lentil and Pfeiffer, the only ones out the door with me, sought a ride back to the trail at a corner convenience store. I chose to put my thumb out up the road a piece.

After about ten minutes a truck stopped. The driver, who later introduced himself as Walter, told me to quickly get in.

"There are state troopers all over today," he stated. "The governor is expected in town."

Apparently hitching is illegal in New Jersey, so he was trying to get me off the street. I thought it was only against the law in New York. Since Lentil and Pfeiffer had not gotten a ride yet, I asked Walter if he would mind giving them a lift also. He gladly turned his truck around.

When we got to the A.T., the two quickly hiked into the distance. The climb out of Vernon requires about a 1000 foot ascent up Wawayanda Mountain. Many refer to it as "The Stairway to Heaven" since so many stone steps aid in the climb. With only one trekking pole, I found myself grasping for large rocks to help with balance. Taking my time, it took a while to reach the Pinwheels vista at the top. Seated on a rock were Leigh and Ed. When Leigh asked if I were a thru-hiker, I told them about my hike and Don.

The next couple of hours went well. I saw ridgerunner Grasshopper for the second time. Then I took a break at Warwick Turnpike. I'm not sure why a two-lane road in the country is called a turnpike. Just as I was heading up the trail, I heard someone yell my name. Rapidly moving toward me was none other than Chin Music. We had been near each other for a good while but had never met. So for the duration of the day the congenial dentist from Illinois became my hiking partner.

Within minutes I felt like I had known Chin for years. In addition to the camaraderie, I was just relieved to know there would be another hiker around when the New York rocks greeted us. As we hiked toward the state line, we shared some data about our lives. When I told my new friend that I was a retired English teacher, I didn't know at the time that Chin Music and I would be bouncing over the rocks discussing semicolons. I was glad to oblige and explain various rules since the discussion briefly took my mind off the severity of the rocks. Chin equated some portions to walking across a slanted roof.

So across the rocks we bounded for a lot longer than I had anticipated. Each time I thought they were over, another series of the slanted monsters appeared. In many ways I think only having one pole today benefited me. I often used my free hand for leverage when pulling myself up to the next ledge. At one point I didn't think I was going to make it around a sloped rockface with no room for error. Chin braced himself in a position that gave me someone to keep me from falling if I lost my balance. Thankfully, no falls occurred today. At one point an aluminum ladder was stationed next to a precariously dangerous rock slab. The assistance was appreciated.

Like yesterday, the heat and humidity prevailed. There were fewer mosquitoes; however, I still received some fresh bites. One thing that I'm finding recently is how tired I get by early afternoon. I definitely could have used some more water. When Chin and I finally reached NY 17, we walked the two hundred yards or so to the Creamery. Chin's demeanor altered abruptly when he stepped off the side of a road, twisting his ankle. After a water and root beer, I struck up a conversation with a former soldier, Gene, who wound up giving me a ride to Greenwood Lake and the Breezy Point Inn. I dined on the patio with a view of the lake before again enjoying the night in a bed.

## June 29, NY 17 at Arden Valley Rd.

"Old age hath both its honor and its toil," stated Tennyson in his poem "Ulysses." Today I felt old. I don't really know if there is any honor associated with this hike, but there sure is a lot of toil. It took me over seven hours of hard work to cover a mere 12 miles on another hot, humid, buggy day in New York. With multiple rock scrambles and several areas of poorly blazed trail, my frustration level was exceeded by early afternoon. If not for the knowledge that I would again be sleeping in a bed and eating a restaurant meal later in the evening, the hike would have been unbearable.

When my alarm sounded at 7:00 I had to coax myself out of bed. I bid Breezy Point adieu and headed back toward the trail via HWY 210. After a quick stop at the Country Grocery, I started looking for a breakfast establishment. Murphy's, a bar and grill with a prominently displayed sign advertising country breakfasts on weekends, caught my eye. Two couples dined on the front veranda; however, I was the only patron in the dining room. Strangely enough, several folks were already in the tavern. Some were at the bar; others were shooting pool.

My breakfast was quite appetizing even though I still couldn't get grits. The portion of eggs looked outrageously large. It seemed more like four than two. While eating, I inquired of my waitress if there were a taxi service in town. The bartender called for me and even paid the $10 fare. Before leaving the restaurant one of the ladies who had been dining outside stopped by my table to ask about my hike.

Mary, the local librarian, asked, "Are you having fun?"

"No," I replied.

For a second I couldn't believe how quickly and easily I had uttered the word. Finally, I had said out loud, "This hike really isn't very much fun." We chatted briefly about its perils until my cab arrived.

From the beginning of today's hike I kept asking myself why I had remembered this section as enjoyable. My memory is fading fast. It was downright treacherous and frustrating (from this old man's perspective) all day. Beginning with the Eastern Pinnacles, I found myself using my hands often. What concerns me more and more is how tentative I have become on dangerous sections. At one point I sat down to negotiate a rock about ten feet long and three feet across. A short while back I would have just strode over it. Noticing that there were potentially fatal drop-offs on both sides, I just couldn't do it. I fear I have lost confidence in my balance. With the most difficult part of the hike still remaining, I need to regain it.

When I got to Cat Rocks, I took the short trail around rather than use my hands to climb up the boulders. Even the less difficult trail proved challenging. I just don't feel steady these days. Other than because of the falls, I don't know why. The other issue with today was the blazes. At least a half-dozen times, I had to wander around looking for a blaze to be sure I was hiking on the trail. So much of today's trail was undefined. It was leaves, rocks, and roots, but often without a clearly defined pathway. And like the past two days, the heat and humidity slowed me drastically. I was already so depleted after 6 miles that I decided to change my plans for the night. I called the Bear Mountain Bridge Motel and made a reservation. Then I arranged a ride. Four hours later I was thankful I had.

There were, however, some positives today. Fitzgerald Falls, within a couple of arms' lengths of the A.T., captures all that is beautiful on the trail. I also disrupted a doe from her nap. In fact I almost stepped on the deer that was resting no more than a yard off the trail. She stood up, looked at me walk by, and then continued grazing. I also saw a snake sunning itself. After ascending Arden Mountain I gingerly descended a steep, rocky section to NY 17. Unfortunately I had to wait for over an hour for the ride into Fort Montgomery.

The trail today again offered a variety of challenges. Since I stayed vertical, I met most. Still, it was hard. I found myself thinking of Medicine Man and Kudo, who just weren't having fun anymore and are now home with their loved ones. I thought of the 1377 miles I've walked and of the 806 remaining. I thought of the good days and the bad. So even though I kind of envy my fellow thru-hikers who have returned home, I will continue. Despite the pain, frustration, and mental fatigue, there's a finish line that needs to be crossed on a mountain in Maine.

## June 30, Bear Mountain Bridge, Hudson River

WANTED: Full or part time support person for the duration of Don's Brother's thru-hike of the Appalachian Trail. Interested applicants should have valid driver's license and be at least 25 years of age. Applicant should be able to navigate roads of all surfaces including highways where the A.T. crosses. GPS skills are beneficial. Vehicle must be provided by the applicant. A car is fine; however, van, SUV, or RV is preferred. The length of support may range from one day to eight weeks beginning Monday, July 1 from Fort Montgomery, NY to late August at Mt. Katahdin. Don's Brother would prefer a trail angel or angels; however, compensation may be offered to highly qualified individual. I was serious. If this hike were going to be completed, help was needed.

Today was the best I've felt in the last five. The reason can be stated in one simple word: slackpack. With only a light pack containing food and water, I not only stayed vertical, but regained some much needed confidence concerning the balance issue. I even managed some rock-skipping over water and didn't seem to mind as much the boulders at higher elevations. Plus it was much easier to pull myself up the rock scrambles wearing a light pack. So despite the continued heat and humidity, I knocked out 19.8 miles while hiking alone all day. Even though the hike took almost eleven hours, I wasn't totally exhausted at its conclusion. I could have probably gone at least a half-mile more...maybe.

So if I could just find a support person(s) that would make it possible to slackpack every day, I would be good to go. After all, Molar Man has Sweet Tooth, Steady has Spirit (and an RV) and as far as I know, Chin Music's wife is on the trail to help him awhile. Boo Boo's wife was also with him earlier, and I'm sure there are others. Since my wife has obligations back in Georgia, I was soliciting; no, make that begging, for help.

I started today's walk up Arden Valley Rd. in Harriman State Park at 7:20. With the sun already beaming down, I was sweating profusely after the nearly 800 foot climb up Island Pond Mountain. Along the way I had to pass through the infamous Lemon Squeezer, a narrow stone passage that requires a sideways navigation. Since I was slackpacking, I kept my pack on; however, it did scrape the sides of the rock occasionally. After the Squeezer, a rock climb and scramble followed. With the lighter pack I was able to handle the challenging section without too much difficulty.

The trail today actually offered up a good deal of variety. Boulder climbs and rock scrambles were prominent. Occasionally, a gentle trail allowed for some faster walking. There were also sections with foliage bordering on both sides. Like yesterday, I almost stepped on another deer. This one just looked at me as I snapped her picture. The trail also offered up several spectacular views. Even though clouds rolled in in the afternoon, visibility remained fairly good. I paused for a few minutes atop

Black Mountain to chat with thru-hiker Cocoon, a young man who is taking his time to really observe nature and to write some poetry. He was the only thru-hiker I would see all day. There were also beautiful views from West Mountain. On Black and West the trail stays on the ridge for quite some time, with the views in the distance.

Eventually I made my way to Bear Mountain. The ascent is different from when I section-hiked here in 2005. A rock staircase provides an easy route for much of the climb. Easy for most, that is. I fell off near the bottom, but stayed on my feet. At the apex of Bear stands Perkins Tower, from where a view of NYC is visible on a clear day. By the time I reached the top, the sky was overcast. The descent also consisted of hundreds of rock steps. I wondered how long this project took. At the crest scores of people strolled or lounged around the area. Even more were busy at a variety of activities in the park or by the lake at the bottom of the mountain.

The A.T. follows a path around the lake for a while and then goes through the Bear Mountain Zoo. The bear cage in the zoo is the lowest point on the entire trail at 166 feet. Unfortunately the zoo closes at 4:30, so I had to walk back up to the park and out via a road since the blue-blazed trail was closed for work as well. John, a park employee and retired NYC fireman from Brooklyn, left his post to walk me to where I needed to go to get out of the park. When I told him I had gotten a ride with another retired NYC fireman in Greenwood Lake, he said he knew Gene, who was a good friend of John's brother. Small world, we agreed. Since the white blazes weren't available today, I'm glad I had gotten to walk through the zoo on my section-hike.

So tonight I'm back at the Bear Mountain Bridge Motel. The hike was fun today. The trail offered variety and I was fairly comfortable, considering the weather. No day is going to be easy; however, if I can maintain that positive attitude, and maybe get a little support, Maine is within sight. Not really, but it will be soon if I just keep putting in the miles.

## July 1, US 9 to Peekskill

When I attended junior high school, I ordered a copy of a book entitled *101 Elephant Jokes* from my English teacher's book club. One of the riddles asked, "Why did the elephant wear blue tennis shoes?" Because his red ones were in the wash. So why is Don's Brother wearing his blue shirt today? I'll let my followers answer that one. So other than the possibility that I'm really losing it and may need serious intervention soon, why am I talking about elephant jokes? Because today is my 101st day of hiking on the Appalachian Trail. By now I'm beginning to see as many correlations with the hike to jokes as I am with Odysseus. I'm trying to identify the humor involved in order to keep my sanity.

So after a bagel sandwich breakfast at a deli across the road from the Bear Mountain Bridge Motel, I rode the 1.8 miles back to the trail with Doug, who, along with his wife Ingrid, has owned the inn for over forty years. A former soldier, Doug was at one time stationed at Ft. Benning, the military base near my home. The light sprinkle that had fallen an hour earlier had subsided as I headed over the Hudson River via the Bear Mountain Bridge. Cars zoomed by in both directions as I crossed. On the overcast, early Monday morning visibility was minimal. I did notice a large barge headed down the river.

On the eastern side of the Hudson I had to walk up the road a ways before heading back into the woods. Soon after I began the 500 foot climb, the rain commenced. At first it was a mere sprinkle; then it became a drizzle; finally, it poured. With only my slackpack, I didn't even bother to apply my rain cover. I also walked without a rain jacket. At the top of the first incline I came across Pfeiffer and Lentil who were breaking camp. Pfeiffer was preparing for a short day on the trail before heading into New York City. Lentil was going as well.

Hiking carefully over the wet rocks, I still made good time. Eventually Pfeiffer and Lentil passed me. I decided to pick up my pace and try to keep with them for as long as I could. As the rain continued, at first I was glad because it was cooler and kept the bugs at bay. Slogging along in wet shoes proved to be the downside. By the time we reached the Appalachian Market at US 9 I was soaked. I went inside with the others for cover. Funnybone also came into the store. Pfeiffer quickly talked a lady into a hitch into Peekskill, so she and Lentil were off to the train station.

While having a bite to eat I heard that a flash flood warning was in effect for the area. It was at this point that I decided that I really didn't think it wise to continue. So with a 5.8 mile day completed by 10:00, I opted to go back to my room for the remainder of the day. Fortunately, after striking up a conversation with a store patron, the South Bronx fireman took me all the way to the motel. Once again, a trail angel was there when I needed one. For the remainder of the afternoon I just relaxed.

## July 2, RPH Shelter

Alton, my good friend and hiking buddy, recently diagnosed my ailment as, "Not having anyone with whom to share the misery." Today I not only had others around me most of the day, but I met and hiked awhile with Misery, a young man from Buffalo. Misery and I hiked over a trail that offered up a good bit of variety. Most of the rather flat terrain was forgiving even though muddy portions slowed my movement. There were no rock scrambles, and the climbs were minimal.

When I reached Dennytown Rd., I stopped for lunch. Several other thru-hikers had chosen the same spot for a break. Johnny Walker, a short, red-bearded lad with an American flag attached to his pack, commented how rare it was for this many thru-hikers to be gathered in the middle of the day. Not long after, the rain began. For a brief time it kept the mosquitoes away. When it ceased, however, the critters began swarming again. For the past few days the pests have been the greatest obstacle. I must have sprayed myself at least five times. The only relief came when the trail gained in elevation.

When I got to the rocks with a view of Canopus Lake, I took another break with Misery and Funnybone. Then I hiked with Funnybone for about an hour prior to Shenandoah Mountain and the 9/11 Memorial. A triathlete from Boulder, Funnybone is only the third hiker I have met in his 40's. At the memorial I took a brief break but quickly hiked on, leaving Funnybone, Chickadee, and Misery relaxing.

From there I made good time, arriving at the enclosed RPH shelter a little after 5:00. Upon my arrival, it looked like I was getting the last bunk. When I turned in for the evening, however, only Johnny Walker had decided to tough it out in the shelter. After the mosquitoes made their presence known, everyone else set up their tents or hammocks in the grassy area adjacent to the cinder block building. With both ends of the structure open, Johnny Walker and I were fair game throughout the night. With the night too hot and muggy to fully get inside my bag, I opted for a long sleeve shirt and another coating of bug spray. Still, it actually felt rather nice to be sleeping again in the woods.

## July 3, NY 55

I'm not sure how many bites I had this morning, but I actually slept quite well. After awaking at dawn, I dozed until my watch alarm sounded at 6:00. As I began packing up, those who had tented followed suit. The humidity had to be 100% as I hit the trail at 7:12.

Even though I was the first to leave camp, within the initial hour I was passed by Misery, Johnny Walker, Tugboat, and Chickadee. The young folks always smile and speak respectfully as they leave me in their dust. They hop over the rocks as if the obstacles don't exist. I pause and calculate my next step to try to ensure I won't fall. After five consecutive "no fall" days, the streak ended.

Since I had only dined on leftover pizza for breakfast this morning, I walked the 0.4 miles up the road to the Mountaintop Market Deli when I reached NY 52. Even though it was mid-morning, I ordered a breakfast sandwich and drank two chocolate milks. The proprietors had placed a plastic lawn chair next to an outside outlet, so I was able to charge my phone as I ate. I also refilled my water bottles and bought a root beer and Gatorade before leaving. I even napped for about fifteen minutes. It made for a nice interlude to battling mosquitoes.

Before leaving I ran into Torch, a young hiker that I had last seen on McAfee Knob. Torch was farther north on the trail; however, he had returned to the area for a big 4th of July thru-hiker bash sponsored each year by a local fellow named Bill. Unfortunately, however, he said his two buddies, Rango and Half & Half, had gone home. When I got ready to return to the trail, Bill gave me a ride. Bill was shuttling hikers around all day to allow some slackpacking, especially for those who skipped this section, knowing that they could hike it when they returned to the area for the 4th. When I resumed my hike I met two of them, Bulldog and Trucker. The last time I saw Bulldog, he was returning to the Super 8 in Erwin with a dozen cheeseburgers. It was at Cowboys in Damascus that I had last seen Trucker. Both hikers immediately recognized and remembered me.

In the early afternoon I took another break at the Morgan Stewart Shelter. Funnybone, Tugboat, and Chickadee also were hanging out there. Funnybone wasn't sure what his plans were for the day; however, Tugboat and Chickadee were utilizing Bill's trail angel generosity to get in a slackpack as well. I remembered staying at this shelter on my section-hike of NY. After about a ten minute break I headed back onto the bug-infested trail. For some reason they didn't seem as much of a nuisance at the shelter. Perhaps the varmints prefer moving hikers over stationary ones, because once I began walking they attacked again. At least with my continued one pole hiking, I had a free hand to swat.

Maybe it was due to the calories because I hiked with renewed enthusiasm throughout the afternoon. The final 3.3 miles passed quickly. I stopped once for a minimal view, the only one of the day. When I arrived at NY 55 I hitched a ride to a motel near Wingdale. Looking forward to having a hiking partner the next three days, I felt a kind of peacefulness on this, my final night in New York.

# 11

# Connecticut and Massachusetts

## July 4, Bull Bridge, CT

July 4th has always had special meaning for my family. As a child I remember my dad grilling on Independence Day. After I started running, I regularly competed in the Peachtree Roadrace 10K in Atlanta. When my kids were teenagers, our family, along with Don, Lisa, and Brent, would spend a few days at the beach. My brother always enjoyed setting off fireworks late into the evening. Three years ago Don and Lisa joined Linda and me at our downtown condo to watch fireworks over the river. Two years ago we did the same; however, the occasion warranted little excitement since Don had received his ALS diagnosis only a few weeks earlier. I think we all knew it could be our last Fourth of July celebration. At this time last year, Don had lost use of his arms and legs, and he could barely speak. It was a somber Fourth.

So as I hiked today, moving from New York into Connecticut, I thought often of my brother. Having my good friend John Teeples along to share the hike was truly special. John's travel day yesterday reads like an odyssey of its own. After a cancelled flight in Atlanta, a change of itinerary to land in Newark rather than LaGuardia, a cab ride through Times Square, a mad dash to catch a Metro North train, and a taxi from Pawling, he arrived at the Wingdale motel after 11:00. So when we walked up the highway for an early morning breakfast, it was on very little sleep. Still we knocked out 18.8 miles in just over ten hours with an additional 1.2 mile round trip road walk for lunch.

For the most part, John's first day on the A.T. proved rather uneventful. Other than a few minimal climbs, the boggy areas with an abundance of black mud dominated the hike. We saw a few day-hikers but no thru-hikers all day. I suppose most are at the nearby July 4th hiker bash. An accomplished ultra-marathoner, John easily adapted to the rigors of the trail. I suspect there were times he would have liked to run rather than walk. Today, however, was as much about good conversation as it was miles. Among the topics we talked about were John's businesses, Big Dog Running Company, Iron Bank Coffee, and the Run Across Georgia. And of course we talked about the running buddies. I told John I had heard from Jimmy, Kevin, Reynold, and Cecil, all good running companions over the last several years.

With good conversation and a friend with whom to share the hike, for at least today, I didn't even seem to mind the humidity and mosquitoes. John discovered his greatest appreciation for the trail near the end of the day, when we reached the Ten Mile River. After crossing the Ned Anderson Memorial Bridge, John decided that a swim was in order. Not being a very good swimmer, I chose not to join him. After the swim we hiked on to Bull Bridge Rd., where I had arranged for a taxi to take us to Cornwall Bridge, CT. I had given John the option of a shelter after his first day on the trail, but he said he'd prefer my "find a nearby bed" method.

We changed our plans during the ride, however, since there was no place to eat near the motel in Cornwall Bridge. Instead we retraced our route to Kent, where we found a hiker-friendly B & B. After getting to Kent we had a meal at an Italian place before calling the inn for a shuttle. Exhausted from the late night and hiking day, I fell asleep shortly after getting to my room. When I awakened about an hour later the real surprise occurred. Standing next to my bed was Jimmy Brooks, another running buddy from home. John had managed to keep Jimmy's arrival a secret throughout the day.

So as I ended this Fourth of July I felt truly blessed. So many people care about this hike. From strangers I've never met who have taken the time to write, to two good buddies whose friendship I've cherished as we have put in the miles over the years, folks are concerned about me. At one point today, John said I needed to replace the word "misery" with "magnificent." He's right. This is in all respects a magnificent trail and I'm being given the magnificent opportunity to hike it. And more importantly I get to share it with two special friends when tomorrow John and Jimmy join me for a jaunt on the Appalachian Trail.

## July 5, CT 4

Over the years I have always considered myself to be extremely fortunate to have a number of really good friends. Many of those really good friends are my running buddies. Between 1998 and 2006 a group of these buddies would meet me at the high school where I taught for a 5:30 AM run every Wednesday. A certain camaraderie develops when runners meet before dawn to pound out 8-12 miles before a busy work day. As I've gotten older and slowed down considerably, the long Wednesday runs have ended for me. The friendships, fortunately, have not. So at a time when despondency was creeping into my everyday psyche, two of these really good friends arrived to again pound out miles of a different kind. Today I hiked with enthusiasm, and without a pack, as John Teeples and Jimmy Brooks took an 18.3 mile hike with me on the Appalachian Trail.

I was still a little stunned this morning over the late night arrival of Jimmy. I knew of course that John was coming up to hike with me for three days; however, Jimmy's arrival was truly a surprise. Actually, it was a shock. The second surprise came at the breakfast table of the Cooper Creek B & B (note the name, my Columbus friends) when Mary placed a bowl by my plate. Staring in disbelief, I asked, "Are those grits?" Jimmy had not only arrived to hike but had brought grits with him. I quickly dubbed Jimmy "Grits" for his time on the trail. Along with the scrambled eggs and cheese, sausage, toast, and coffee, the breakfast had to rank among the top five I'd enjoyed since the hike began.

After breakfast Cooper drove the three of us back to Bulls Bridge Rd. What made today's hike a little different was the opportunity to hike without a pack all day. We carried only one, stocking it with food and water. I should say my friends carried one pack. My two buddies insisted on alternating carrying it, so I got to hike packless. With some fairly challenging climbs and high humidity again, it certainly felt good to have the weight off my back.

Throughout much of the day we shared some of the best conversations I've engaged in on the hike. At one point I found myself talking about Don. Both of my friends listened compassionately as I related aspects of his life, illness, and death. For me, I guess one could say, it was kind of therapeutic. Regardless, I appreciated their understanding. We also talked about John's businesses, Jimmy's practice, our families, running, and of course my hike. It was all good.

The trail today posed a few more challenges than yesterday. There were several water crossings that required some rock hopping, an occasional series of rocks to negotiate, and some mud. My buddies wanted me to hike in front; however, I'm sure both could have easily increased the pace at any time. Not having seen any other thru-hikers yesterday, I hoped that John and Jimmy would at least get to meet one of my fellow Maine-bound pilgrims. That finally occurred at a stream in the early afternoon. Colin, a hiker I've been around many times since early in Virginia, was taking a break by the water. We would see him again throughout the day.

The most challenging part of today's hike was hiking down St. John's Ledges. I should say it was a bit of a challenge for me. John and Jimmy had expected something more technical. Near the end of that section we came across two rock climbers. Dave and Lacey had affixed a rope to a tree at the top of a rockface. Dave began the climb up as we watched. I sensed that John would have liked a turn, having done a little rock climbing himself. From there we hiked on toward the Housatonic River.

For much of the final six miles the trail parallels the river. At one point my two companions decided a swim was in order. I watched from the bank as John and Jimmy cooled off in the rippling water. After their swim we picked up the pace until a final climb commenced. I needed a short rest before we completed the last mile. Just before we reached CT 4 near Cornwall Bridge, we spotted Cooper walking up the trail to meet us. After a stop for a Mountain Dew, we headed toward the inn.

After cleaning up we ventured into Kent for a little grocery shopping and a meal. Good conversation resumed over supper. Like so many times throughout my hike, someone special has helped to make my day less difficult. With good friends to accompany me on today's hike, I barely thought about the miles. My buddies, however, have real jobs in the regular world, so tomorrow will be the last day they will hike along with me. As John would say, I know it's going to be another "magnificent" day on the Appalachian Trail.

## July 6, Falls Village, CT

Sometimes we take friendship for granted. We go through our day to day lives aware of who our friends are; however, at times we fail to grasp the significance of the bonding process that has occurred over a period of years. I first met Jimmy when we trained together for the Marine Corps Marathon in 1995. John and I became acquainted when he started running with a group of my buddies a couple of years later. Over the years, we've shared many a mile and story on the roads of Columbus, but none may have been as significant as those we shared over the past three days on the Appalachian Trail. As I sit at a laundromat in Salisbury, CT, I'm already remembering how important and special those past few days have been.

For the second consecutive day I was able to start my day with grits, thanks to Jimmy. Mary was reluctant to serve them with her blueberry pancakes, at least until we assured her the combination would in no way offend us. Having been told that we were seven minutes late for breakfast yesterday, we hustled to arrive in the dining room six minutes early today. I continue to be astounded by what irks some people. I suppose we all have our shortcomings. Nevertheless, starting the meal thirteen minutes earlier than yesterday meant that John, Jimmy, and I could begin hiking a bit earlier as well. So after the ride back to the trailhead, provided by Cooper, we were walking at 8:00.

From the outset, the hike went smoothly throughout the day, that is if my slipping off a rock in the first five minutes can be overlooked. After I stepped about ankle deep into a stream, Jimmy suggested that I just wade across rather than try to get back up on the wet rocks. I took his advice and paid no attention to my wet shoes and socks. John chose to tightrope a blowdown. This was only the first of several water crossings we would encounter throughout the day. Fortunately I did not step in again. In addition to the streams, a "lemon squeezer" type rock formation added a little variety to another rather mundane trail.

But like yesterday, it wasn't the trail, but the fellowship among friends that made the hike enjoyable. Neither the heat nor the humidity nor the various biting bugs could detract from our time together. I again talked at times of Don. My thoughts today seemed even more poignant since today was his birthday. And again John and Jimmy listened with heartfelt compassion. We continued to reminisce about our running pasts and share stories about our many running friends. It was such a satisfying way to conclude my buddies' brief visit to the trail.

Today's 14 mile hike concluded in Falls Village, CT. John, Jimmy, and I walked the short distance into Main St. and the Toymaker Cafe. We shared a final meal before the two headed toward the train station for a ride into NYC. John even offered some sound advice for the remainder of my hike. Then they were gone. I momentarily turned to wave before walking the 0.2 miles up the road for a lift to Salisbury and a night in the home of Maria McCabe. So I rode in with Maria, did my laundry, and had supper with Pilgrim at a local bistro. As John would want me to say, it's been another magnificent day on the Appalachian Trail.

## In Memorium

On July 6, 1957 Donald Andrews Stephens was born in Columbus, GA. On August 28, 2012 he died at the age of 55. ALS took my brother's life, but his memory lives on in the hearts of those who loved him. He is missed every day by his friends and by his family. The world is a better place because he lived; we are at a loss because he lives in this world no more. I remember all that we shared with happiness. And I celebrate his life every day by remembering how much Don loved the outdoors. Happy Birthday, Donald.

## July 7, Salisbury, CT

Maria McCabe has been welcoming A.T. hikers into her Salisbury, Connecticut home for well over a decade. Alton and I stayed a night with her on our section-hike of this area in 2004. Even though her prices have risen a bit, the house on Grove St. is still a bargain. When she picked me up at the bridge in Falls Village yesterday afternoon, she seemed genuinely happy to see a hiker who had stayed with her before. With all the hikers who have passed through her doorway, I obviously didn't expect to be remembered. Asking me when I had previously boarded with her, Maria said she could barely remember last week, or something to that effect.

Part of Maria's "Hiker Special" is a ride to the laundromat. On the return trip Maria enlightened me with a restaurant review for the area. One of the more swank dining establishments got a thumbs down from the feisty, 80-something young lady of German stock.

"It's too dark inside," she stated without malice. "The next time I go I'm going to borrow one of the hikers' headlamps."

She did add that the food was pretty good, but expensive. All in all, it was an entertaining ride both going and coming back to her home. She also reminded me that she couldn't cook breakfast, but that hikers were permitted to use her kitchen to cook their own.

Maria also noted that she couldn't shuttle me back to the trail the following morning until 9:00. Since I had only planned the short 8.3 mile stretch between Falls Village and Undermountain Rd., the late start was fine. What I didn't realize, however, was that apparently most of Salisbury slept in on Sunday. When I walked the two blocks to the center of town, not a person was stirring at 7:00. Walking around, I quickly determined from posted signs that no businesses opened before 8:00. So I found a comfortable weathered wooden bench under a shade tree and just sat. For a while there I thought I was in one of those *Twilight Zone* episodes where an entire town had disappeared. Finally, a car pulled up and a young man entered a bakery across the street from my bench.

When a local church's bell tower eventually tolled eight, I walked the block to the bistro and ordered a bacon and egg breakfast. I wish I had thought to bring a package of the grits Jimmy left with me. I wonder if my waitress would have supplied a bowl of hot water. Just as I finished my meal, Colin walked in. Having hiked in from a campsite, he chose to dine outside. I asked for a third cup of coffee and joined him. After a short chat, I ambled over to the market around the corner before heading back to Maria's. As soon as I retrieved my pack, we were in her car on our way back to the A.T.

Starting at the bridge, I had barely walked into the woods when I stopped to view the falls cascading into the river. At the next road crossing I met for the first time Miles From Nowhere who was hiking the same section as I was today. After these two short breaks, however, I just took off and hiked at a steady, fairly fast pace all morning. Again today, I walked up on another deer grazing on the trail. She moved over to let me pass but really didn't seem too affected by my presence. There was a fairly good view from 1475 foot Mt. Prospect and an even better one of the field called Rands View. Despite missing my buddies, I felt OK hiking solo today.

When I arrived at Undermountain Rd., I walked the approximately half-mile back to Maria's home, ending my trail day before 1:00. For the remainder of the afternoon I just relaxed. The two brothers from Germany, Restless Cowboy and Fresh Coke, are also staying the night. Fresh Coke is having a lot of trouble with the humidity. He looked a bit whipped. Hopefully, the town night will restore some of his energy. Eventually I strolled back down to the bistro for another opportunity for some fine dining. I really never get tired of the "town life" just off the Appalachian Trail.

## July 8, MA 41, South Egremont, MA

Ten down; four to go—states, that is. On another extremely humid, buggy day, I hiked out of Connecticut and into Massachusetts with a slackpack and a positive attitude. Like many other recent days, things went well early in the day, but by mid-afternoon the energy level had plummeted. Still I managed to hike 17.8 miles in ten hours over some pretty challenging terrain. Were it not for a hard rain late in the day, I could have finished at least an hour earlier. Nevertheless, I'm not complaining since I again had a room to return to on Grove St. So everything considered, I'd call the day slightly closer to John's "magnificent" than to my oft-used adjective, "miserable."

At 5:30 I started the day by cooking myself breakfast in Maria's kitchen. After my three fried eggs, toast, and orange juice, I walked the approximately half-mile back to the trail on Undermountain Rd. I then headed back into the woods at 6:10 and was immediately greeted with a climb of 1000 feet over the first 2.6 miles to Lions Head. This would be the first of several spectacular views throughout the day. After Lions Head I was faced with an additional 580 foot ascent of Bear Mountain. It's interesting how some names are used more than once on the A.T. There have been at least three Deep Gaps, for instance. Today was the second Bear Mountain. The climb wasn't too difficult; however, the descent was trouble.

After scrambling down the steep rock slabs, including twice on the seat of my pants, I reached the CT/MA border. Just after crossing into Massachusetts, Sages Ravine and all its beauty came into view. The trail parallels a fast-running stream with multiple waterfalls for 0.3 of a mile. Having expected a bridge over the rushing waters, I was a bit disillusioned when I realized the manner to cross was over slippery, potentially dangerous, rocks. Knowing that my feet were going to get wet really didn't matter. I just didn't want to fall in and get swept downstream. All went well with the crossing until the last two partially submerged rocks. I had to leap from one to the other and maintain my balance. Prayers must have been being lifted up at the moment because I stuck the landing without any slippage. Breathing a sigh of relief, I looked back thankfully at the beautiful natural crossing that I had fortunately handled.

Shortly after leaving the Ravine I noticed a southbound hiker who looked familiar. Susquehanna Slim recognized me before I did him. We had first met way back in Erwin, TN when we shared a shuttle. Slim said he was doing a modified flip flop hike due to some off-trail obligations. He started a few days ago on Mt. Greylock and is hiking south to the Delaware Water Gap, where he left the trail. When he gets there, he plans to return to Greylock and keep walking north. I had been reading Slim's journal occasionally, so it was an unexpected treat to see him again.

The best views of the day appeared about a mile after I saw Slim. The trail elevated to a 0.6 mile ridge walk on Race Mountain. The continuous vistas to the east were beautiful beyond description. Although somewhat challenging, I never felt that any part of the ridge walk could be construed as dangerous, that is unless you got too close to the edge. I made sure I didn't. It was after Race and during the climb up Mt. Everett that I began to droop. I kept downing fluids and consuming fruit and protein bars, which finally restored some energy. After the ascent I reached the Guilder Pond Picnic Area where someone had left several gallons of water labeled, "for thru-hikers." With almost five miles remaining, I refilled my bottles before continuing through a swampy segment of trail. Like all recent days, the mosquitoes and various species of flies attacked relentlessly throughout the day.

As I headed toward one final difficult section, the descent of Jug End, the rain began. This gave me the chance to try out my new emergency poncho. The rain also afforded me the opportunity to practice descending wet rock slabs, which would have already posed a major challenge had they been dry. Using caution and the seat of my pants when necessary, I managed to navigate the slippery menaces without falling. It just took time. When I reached flat trail again, I picked up the pace to arrive at MA 41 a few minutes ahead of my shuttle. After a rather tiring as well as trying day, it felt good to have this section behind me.

## July 9, MA 23, Great Barrington, MA

When Fresh Coke asked me how I slept last night, I immediately knew that he and Restless Cowboy had heard my "night terror" screaming. I explained the malady to the German brothers as best as I could. Restless Cowboy replied that he wasn't sure if he should have come across the hall to check on me. Assuring the two that I always eventually wake myself, they still seemed a little befuddled by the wailing that had awakened them in the middle of the night. It was only my third such episode since the hike began. None have occurred in the woods, thankfully. This one, I think, was also the first that had been overheard by another hiker. Oh well. Maybe it will give the lads from Europe a story to tell when they return to their homeland.

The brothers are leaving the trail for a few days to do some sightseeing in the New England area before Fresh Coke departs for Germany. His hike is over. He just points to his head and says, "Mental." Restless Cowboy plans to return and finish the hike solo. The first leg of their off-trail excursion involves a hitch to Hartford. Both the brothers seemed very sure that they would have little trouble finding a lift.

After again cooking myself some breakfast, I moseyed down to the U.S. Post Office to send a few items up the trail. Since Franklin, NC I've travelled without a tent. As of today I'll be minus a sleeping bag as well. Since I was still carrying my winter bag and recently hadn't used it except to lie on, I figured why not trim some more weight from the pack. I also shipped my rain pants and gloves ahead. Andy, the postal worker on duty, found me the perfect size box for the items, which I forwarded to Norwich, Vermont, the last trail town before New Hampshire. With all the towns I'm hitting, I don't know why I hadn't sent these items ahead long ago.

After mailing the package, I walked to a cafe on Main St. for a cup of coffee. Inside, "A Whiter Shade of Pale" played in the background. When I made a reference to the Procol Harum lyrics, it quickly became obvious that the young lady behind the counter failed to understand my comment. I, therefore, decided not to get into the Chaucer allusion from the late 60's hit. Not seeming too interested in my small talk, almost smiling, she turned to help another customer. I took my coffee to a table outside where I joined Banzai, who was sipping on some juice and munching a muffin.

Old Banzai looked a little down. We talked for a while about the morale on the trail.

Banzai observed, "Some people may say they're still enjoying the hike, but deep down, everyone is miserable."

Can't say that I disagree with my friend. When I offered him part of my shuttle at no expense, after a brief rumination, he accepted. So we walked back up to Grove St. for the ride to the A.T. Maria was at her sassy best during the eleven mile trip up MA 41. She had both of us laughing and exchanging jibes with the delightful lady for the duration of the ride. I said my final goodbye to the A.T. legend and then began the walk with Banzai.

We hiked together for the first 3.8 miles, a level stretch through a section of untrimmed foliage. The mosquitoes began their barrage early and never let up for the 12.0 mile day. Banzai left the trail at US 7 for Great Barrington. I hiked on to MA 23, which also leads into town. After Banzai's departure I saw no one else all day. Fortunately I covered the last 8.2 miles in well under four hours. The trail today was about as nondescript as any over the past three weeks. Mud, pine straw, a few moderate-size rocks, roots, and vegetation summarize it well. What made the hike utterly miserable (in no way magnificent) were the merciless mosquitoes. I've come to the conclusion that these varmints have a plan. The first unit's task is to lick all the Deet off of hikers so that the second unit can come in for the strike. Quite frankly, I don't think any bug spray is effective. Despite multiple applications, I stayed covered and under attack all day.

With no one else around I was left with a lot of time to think about how miserable I was. At one point I felt downright mad, which is a characteristic I almost never display. I used to tell my students that I only got angry twice a year and that I didn't intend using one of the times on them. Today I used one on the mosquitoes and biting flies. I kept thinking about all the people who have tried to encourage me and other hikers with comments like, "I really envy you," or "you're doing great," or "you're almost there." If anyone had popped out of the woods with one of those comments today, I might be in the Great Barrington jail charged with assault.

I hiked mad all day, and actually felt pretty good doing so. At least I'm being honest with how this hike is going lately.

So now that I've vented for a while, life is good here at the Travel Lodge. I got a text followed by a phone call from Pilgrim this morning. He has decided that he wants to try my plan for a few days. Having lost too much weight and suffering from the heat and humidity, the fellow sojourner needs new direction. Tomorrow he'll ship some gear home and learn my method for "light pack, big miles, and beds." The "big miles," unfortunately, may not be quite as big with the adverse conditions right now. Vermont, however, is only a few days away where the elevation increases substantially. For now, Massachusetts and mosquitoes continue as Pilgrim and I will try a little duo hiking tomorrow up the Appalachian Trail.

## July 10, Tyringham, MA

What a difference a day makes. With two hiking buddies, a slackpack, gentle terrain, and fewer pests, today came close to being a magnificent one on the Appalachian Trail. I sensed that a lot of folks must have been offering up prayers because the mosquito population appeared to be substantially decreased today. Armed with a new supply of Off, I walked behind Banzai and ahead of Pilgrim for most of the comfortable 12.2 mile day. After having covered my arms and legs with the oily substance at the outset, I only re-applied once throughout the five hour, twenty minute hike.

The day started with breakfast at the Great Barrington McDonald's before we headed up to the intersection of US 7 and MA 23. We had barely stuck out our thumbs when Marty, a local resident driving a van, pulled over. Commenting that we were in a very hiker-friendly town, he seemed pleased to assist us with a ride back to the trail. That's two rides, in an average of about one minute's wait, that I've scored in the past two days. Banzai noted how it must be a good sign that he's now hiking along with Don's Brother. Pilgrim and I were just grateful for a quick pick-up, knowing that we had to finish the hike by 2:00 to meet our pre-arranged free shuttle.

With two hiking companions for conversation and a room to return to at the end of the day, my attitude had improved tremendously.

Banzai commented, "You can learn more about a person in two hours on the trail than you might otherwise learn over years in the regular world."

And so I hiked and talked, following a 31-year-old mechanical engineer from Michigan and being trailed by a 66-year-young retired systems analyst from Los Angeles. I think all three of us felt genuinely pleased to have fellow travelers with whom to share the day. Such is life on the Appalachian Trail.

Able to walk without swatting so much and with the aforementioned almost continuous conversation, the miles evaporated quickly. Early-on two northbound hikers caught and passed us, stopping briefly to chat. I literally couldn't believe that I had run into Puffy again. The young man that I had last seen in North Carolina had taken some time off with an infection but was now hiking strong. His buddy, Pigpen, who hails from Georgia, followed him in stride. Seeing Pigpen reminded me just how significant these brief meetings can be. I not only remembered talking with him also back in NC/TN, but even recalled the day. Pigpen had offered me some water from his Sawyer Squeeze as we took a break at a shelter. I remember clearly it was the day of the Boston Marathon. Also a runner, Pigpen talked about the marathon with me that day. Obviously neither of us knew of the events that were unfolding as we spoke. It was awesome seeing the two again.

When my buddies and I reached the trail leading to the Shaker Campsite, I sent Sub Zero a text to ask if he could pick us up an hour earlier than planned. The section-hiker and general contractor quickly responded with an OK. With a little more zip in our steps, Banzai, Pilgrim, and I covered the final 3.1 miles in an hour and fifteen minutes. That included a climb over Cobble Hill, a spot with an abundance of some kind of yellow wildflower and the best view of the day. With impending rain holding off and the mosquitoes at bay, I didn't even mind all the muddy, swampy sections we had to negotiate the final two miles. I was especially grateful at one point that I avoided stepping in some of the oozing black mud that sucked up almost half of my hiking pole.

Getting to the Main Rd. going into Tyringham a little before 1:00, we waited at an A.T. parking area where Pigpen was having some lunch. Just after 1:00 Sub Zero arrived. The trail angel who had given me a hitch yesterday was happy to offer the complimentary shuttle today. Pilgrim and Banzai rode in the back of his truck while I joined my new friend in the cab. Sub Zero enlightened me on some of the "famous" people who live in the area during the ride back to Great Barrington.

As a conclusion to a really good day, Banzai, Pilgrim, and I enjoyed a meal at Ena, a Greek establishment owned by Tom. Originally from Greece, and a former acrobat and nightclub owner in New York, Tom seemed to take great pride in entertaining three hungry hikers. Sharing pictures of his past, a few stories, and jovial conversation, Tom was quite the host while we waited for our meal. Once again, I was treated to a great "town experience."

So after a tough day yesterday, good fortune surrounded me today. In fact, I'm beginning to understand again why some folks envy me. Still, however, I'm not "almost there." There are still 647 miles to be hiked, which include the remainder of the Massachusetts Berkshires, the Green Mountains of Vermont, the notoriously challenging White Mountains of New Hampshire, and rugged Maine. When I get to Baxter State Park, I'll "almost be there." For now, tomorrow offers me another opportunity to hike with companions as the three of us continue northward on the Appalachian Trail.

## July 11, Washington Mountain Rd.

The hiking day is over. I'm sitting in a Friendly's in Pittsfield, MA. It's late. Pilgrim, Banzai, and I are waiting for our meal. Pilgrim and I ordered from the senior menu. Our meals include a complimentary two scoop, one topping sundae. The service is slow. We are hungry but patient. It's been a long day on the Appalachian Trail.

My day began with a ride from Great Barrington back to the trail near Tyringham, MA. Roy Wiley, another A.T. legend and the husband of the "cookie lady," has been shuttling hikers for over twenty years. So with an old plan and two fellow hikers for companions, I covered the 18.0 miles in less than nine hours. Other than two beautiful lakes, there really wasn't much to get excited about throughout the day. Still we all hiked with newfound energy and enthusiasm, mainly due to lower humidity and fewer mosquitoes.

The picturesque, placid lakes we passed today made me think about my brother. As I stood by the banks of Upper Goose Pond I thought about how much Don would have loved to be fishing here. I could see him casting from the bank on the lazy afternoon. This was the type of day he loved to be out on his bass boat, appreciating an opportunity to enjoy nature. Don would have really liked Upper Goose Pond.

Just past Upper Goose Pond the trail crosses over I-90 and then heads back into the woods toward US 20. At the road we walked the 0.1 mile to a small inn with a picnic table by another lake where we could have some lunch. Pilgrim and I had each packed a couple of burgers from McDonald's. When we went inside to use a soft drink machine, we also discovered a microwave. This hike keeps getting better. Not only was I able to purchase a Coke, but I got to heat up my burgers.

After lunch the three of us faced only the second substantial climb of the day. Regardless of the elevation change, all continued to go well. Sure, there were some rocks, a good bit of mud, and a few pests, but overall we were only pleasantly tired at the end of the hike. Banzai said he definitely liked what he referred to as the DBM (Don's Brother's Method).

Late in the afternoon Banzai hiked on ahead for a while. When Pilgrim and I arrived at Washington Mountain Rd., and the home of Roy, Banzai was sitting at a picnic table having a cookie. Roy returned shortly with cookies for Pilgrim and me before he drove us to Pittsfield. A little later we checked into a motel, cleaned up, and headed to dinner. So despite the slow service at the restaurant, we eventually were served a good meal. Tomorrow I'll move closer to Vermont as I hike along with Banzai and Pilgrim northward on the Appalachian Trail.

### July 12, Cheshire, MA

Tom Levardi asked, "Are you having fun?"

I paused briefly, remembering the same question posed by Mary the librarian in Greenwood Lake, NY. "Yes, I'm having fun again, at least for now."

With cooler weather, good companionship, and fewer mosquitoes, life once again is good on the Appalachian Trail. At least it was at Tom's home on Depot St. when Banzai, Pilgrim, and I walked into Dalton, Massachusetts. For the past 35 years Tom has been allowing A.T. hikers to tent in his yard. So as we strolled by just before noon, we were greeted by Colin and Misery.

The day had started five hours earlier with a shuttle back to Washington Mountain Rd. When I arrived back at the Quality Inn from McDonald's, the silver Subaru had already pulled up in the parking lot. In place of Roy, however, Marilyn "the cookie lady" Wiley was behind the wheel. It was a real pleasure meeting the somewhat famous lady known for her delicious treats. So as soon as Pilgrim and Banzai made their way to the car, we headed out of Pittsfield and back to the trail.

Today's hike went quickly. With only a minor climb and few challenging sections, we hiked into Dalton right on schedule. When I spotted Misery sitting at the picnic table in Tom's yard, I was surprised that he wasn't a couple of days farther up the trail. The young man from Buffalo may have acquired a new reason for his trail name. Earlier in the day Misery explained that he had undergone a root canal. That's not something one expects while hiking the trail. So since he needed to return to Dalton for a follow-up appointment in two weeks, Misery was getting ready to bus to Lincoln, NH and southbound back here. Then he would go back to Lincoln and continue north.

Also at Tom's was Nomad. After having to end his thru-hike attempt at 400-plus miles, the former youth pastor from Austin said he felt God had other plans for him. So for the past three months he has been helping out hikers up and down the trail. I chatted with Nomad about Don and his faith. Nomad asked me to sign his van, a tradition that other A.T. thru-hikers were following. He provided Banzai, Pilgrim, and me with cold soft drinks as well.

While my hiking buddies and I were hanging out at the house, Tom offered to meet us at the corner where the A.T. turns up High St. and drive us to the Dalton Restaurant. He also made a stop at the post office so that Banzai and Pilgrim could pick up mail drops. After lunch Tom drove us back to where we left the trail. For the next mile we followed white-blazed poles by quaint New England homes on High St. before heading back into the woods. When we reached the woods, we were again greeted with a climb. That was followed by more mundane terrain until the final mile of the day.

Late in the afternoon Banzai hiked on up the trail ahead of Pilgrim and me. Just before the final descent into Cheshire, Pilgrim and I encountered him resting on a rock chatting with Longskirt, a section-hiker from Indiana. Just past this outcrop a blue-blazed trail led to the Cobbles, another marble outcropping with a view of the town of Cheshire. Longskirt and I ventured up the short side trail for the view while Banzai and Pilgrim kept going. After Longskirt and I retraced our path back to the white blazes, we hiked together at a steady pace to an ice cream shop on the outskirts of town. A short while later the Wiley's arrived to drive us to Williamstown.

So tonight I'm in another "mom and pop" motel in Williamstown, MA.

Pilgrim just declared, "I'm going to keep the bathroom door closed because the sink drips and the toilet runs."

Banzai responded, "Why can't we just have one problem?"

Ah, such is the life of the A.T. hiker on the DBM. As I've been saying about this hike since Georgia, "You can't always get what you want." Hey, who's complaining? We've slackpacked 18.3 miles on a cooler day, had three restaurant meals, and are sleeping in a room tonight. Considering all things, life is pretty good these days on the Appalachian Trail.

## July 13, MA 2, Williamstown, MA

The story goes that when he observed the slope of Mt. Greylock in the winter, Herman Melville was inspired to create the 19th century novel *Moby Dick*. The eventual classic, published in 1851, would be one of only two that I did not finish reading the semester I took The American Novel. I have a theory that only a handful of people in the entire world have ever read every page of the prodigious masterpiece. So today when I made my assault on Mt. Greylock I took about fifteen seconds to pay homage to Melville. Those were the only seconds I could spare on what turned out to be an almost relaxing 14.7 mile day. With varying weather patterns to contend with, my two hiking companions and I not only scaled Greylock, but we did so at a steady pace and without a break.

The day commenced with another hearty breakfast of pancakes, eggs, bacon, and coffee at the Chef's Hat outside Williamstown, MA. Banzai, Pilgrim, and I were then transported back to the trail in Cheshire by Tom Levardi. We greatly appreciated Tom's taking the time to do a rather long shuttle. Longskirt also joined us for the ride.

We all began today's hike together from where we had left off yesterday at the post office. The trail continued through the sleepy town of Cheshire for a short distance before turning into the woods. Then the first of several climbs confronted us. Banzai and I hiked ahead as the elevation increased from 1007 to 3252 feet over five miles. This was the first time the trail had been above 3000 feet since Virginia. With the higher elevation, mosquitoes suddenly became non-existent, at least for the day.

After passing the Jones Nose Trail, we braced for the ascent of Greylock. What we had anticipated as being strenuous actually turned out to be just another moderate climb. When we reached the summit we found ourselves in a cloud and light mist. The highest peak in Massachusetts, Greylock is also the home of Bascom Lodge. Banzai, Pilgrim, and I had the good fortune to eat a hot meal right on the trail for the third consecutive day. Lots of folks were hanging out at the lodge. Most, however, had driven up. There was even some kind of Native American drum presentation underway. We just had our lunch and walked back out into the fog.

As we started our descent the cloud cover came close to concealing the blazes. In fact, we wandered briefly before finding the correct direction. When we did get going Banzai quickly hiked away from Pilgrim and me. With only 6.3 miles to walk in the afternoon, we had high hopes of finishing much earlier than the last two days. Knowing that we still needed a shuttle from the trailhead at MA 2, I called Ellen McCollum from the ATC list. What a terrific surprise it was to discover that Ellen was not only a former thru-hiker (2000), but that she had been reading my trail journal. Bagel was happy to provide my buddies and me with a ride.

After a very steep, time-consuming descent to 660 feet, Pilgrim and I walked the 0.5 miles on Phelps Ave. to MA 2 where Bagel was waiting. Banzai had already arrived and was enjoying an extra-large cookie with a bottle of juice. Trail angel Bagel had cookies and juice for Pilgrim and me as well. After some brief getting acquainted, Bagel drove us back to our motel.

All of a sudden everything seems to be going great again. Another potential trail angel, Steve from Bennington, VT, sent me a message today offering any help we might need while we're in his neck of the woods. When I called him about a ride after tomorrow's hike, he suggested he pick up our gear here in Williamstown so that we can slack into Bennington tomorrow. Things are really coming together. Banzai and I have gone so far as to declare this "The summer of George." Pilgrim has no idea what we're talking about. It's all coming together, folks.

# 12

# Vermont

## July 14, VT 9, Bennington, VT

Time moves slowly on the Appalachian Trail. Time passes quickly on the Appalachian Trail. Time often seems irrelevant on the Appalachian Trail. Four weeks ago today was Father's Day. I said goodbye to Linda after her brief visit and took the rest of the day off. There were 996 miles still to be hiked. Three weeks ago today I dined happily in Stroudsburg, PA after a satisfying first day in New Jersey. Two weeks ago today I arrived at the Hudson River, having walked alone all day. Last Sunday I spent a pleasant day in Salisbury, CT after hiking in from Falls Village. Sundays continue to be the only day of the week that somehow seem to set themselves apart from the other six. I remember Sundays.

So today I crossed the state line in the middle of the woods, entering Vermont with Banzai and Pilgrim on a tiring 18.4 mile day. Now in Bennington, VT in the comfort of another "mom and pop" motel, I find myself with a mere or staggering (depending on how one looks at it) 580 miles remaining. If all continues to go as scheduled (if planning is truly possible) I should have six Sundays left of my thru-hike of the Appalachian Trail. As I ponder the magnitude of what still awaits, I reflect on "the day that the Lord hath made." Despite periods of loneliness, discomfort, and fatigue, I try "to rejoice and be glad in it." Whatever the circumstance, Sundays always seem to offer some semblance of purpose for this endeavor that I have undertaken. I appreciate the Lord's Day on the trail.

So after another wholesome breakfast at the Chef's Hat, I joined Banzai and Pilgrim for the ride back to the trail near North Adams. Once again, Steve Labombard provided the trail magic transportation. After crossing a pedestrian bridge, we walked briefly on a neighborhood street before heading back into the woods. And folks, I mean the woods. Our streak of three hot lunches abruptly ended as we didn't even cross a paved road until we reached the end of today's hike at VT 9 near Bennington. This was the most isolated section of trail I have hiked since.....honestly, I can't remember a section this much in the wilderness in some time.

Even though we climbed over 2000 feet during the course of the day, it wasn't the elevation change that caused the most frustration. It was the MUD. Seeping, oozing, "sucking up a shoe" black mud was everywhere. Although we had been forewarned, my frustration level increased with each new section to navigate. After a while it became obvious that there weren't enough rocks and sticks to step on to avoid the yucky substance. My blue trail runners quickly took a new appearance. The only saving grace was that no rain fell on us today.

Early in the hike Banzai continued to fascinate Pilgrim and me with his wealth of knowledge on such a wide variety of subject matter. For all practical purposes, Banzai is a walking encyclopedia. From Roman history to Greek philosophy to Christian theology to classic literature to the NBA, Banzai can conduct a walking lecture while scaling rocks or attempting to circumvent mud. Whatever subject I broached, Banzai immediately began an oration that left me admiring his intelligence and Pilgrim shaking his head in disbelief that the young man is so knowledgeable. We both suggested *Jeopardy*.

About four miles into today's walk we passed the sign welcoming us to Vermont. For the next few days the A.T. and the Long Trail are the same. Eventually, the Long Trail will bear off to travel northward until it reaches the Canadian border. After stopping for some pictures at the state line, we hiked steadily until noon when we took a lunch break on some rocks under a power line. A cool breeze kept the bugs away while we ate. In the afternoon we met three southbound thru-hikers, Danko, Four Meals, and Righteous. All had started between May 31 and June 6.

As the afternoon waned Banzai hiked ahead, leaving Pilgrim and me to walk quietly for the last three hours. Other than the mud, nothing else stood out except for the dangerously steep descent to the road at the end of the day. Even though there were rock steps for much of it, the final mile required a concentrated effort and extreme caution. Pilgrim followed as I tried to select the least perilous path to the highway. When we finally reached the road Steve was waiting with a cold Mountain Dew for me and chocolate milk for Pilgrim. Banzai was already there, sitting on the tailgate sipping a Coke. We quickly drove the five miles to town and a motel. After sharing a room the past three nights, we decided to each get our own.

It's almost dusk. My buddies have gone for an early meal. I wanted to write first, so I'll be dining alone tonight. A little solitude can be comforting at times. After all, tomorrow I've planned a zero day. After hiking 18 consecutive days, I feel like it's time for a break. I can't think of a better place for a respite than Bennington, a town with some nice shops, cafes, and a good bit of history.

## July 15, Bennington, VT

I first set foot in Bennington, VT in the mid 90's. Linda and I had flown to Boston, rented a car, and were doing a B & B vacation throughout New England. We stopped off in Bennington for lunch at the Madison Brew Co. before driving up to Manchester Center for the night. At the time I doubted that I would ever visit Bennington again. Less than ten years later, however, Alton and I ended an A.T. section-hike of CT/MA here the day Ronald Reagan died. Then in 2007 I hitched in from VT 9, just to get a Friendly's burger, before hiking to the Melville Nauheim Shelter at the beginning of our Vermont section-hike. So today I'm walking around Bennington for the fourth time. I like this town.

The day began with the appearance of another trail angel. Alan, the proprietor of the motel, graciously offered to drive Banzai, Pilgrim, and me to the Blue Benn Diner for breakfast. A favorite of hikers, the Blue Benn looks like it belongs on a 50's movie set. With a juke box at every booth, I wondered what would happen if multiple people chose to select a song simultaneously. Fortunately only one patron needed to be serenaded on the already hot morning. My friends and I listened along for free. It doesn't get much better than classic country music during breakfast in a small town America diner. With homemade raspberry jam from a jar, bacon and eggs never tasted so good.

After our meal Alan even returned to offer another ride to wherever we needed to go. I chose a trip to the laundromat. From there I walked to the post office to pick up my packages. Thankfully, I'll now be able to hike with two poles after finally getting the replacement parts from Leki. They honored their lifetime warranty with a complete new shaft. Since I've hiked with only one pole for over three weeks, it may take an adjustment to acclimate myself to two again. Really it should be no issue. I'm sure I'll once again be grateful for both as I resume the Vermont A.T. tomorrow.

So with a free afternoon I decided to go for a walk. At one point I asked a pedestrian how far it was to the Old First Church. She said it would take me about an hour and a half if I were a fast walker. I arrived at my destination in twenty minutes. After a brief tour of the 208-year-old current structure, I ventured to the cemetery behind the church to pay homage to my favorite American poet, Robert Frost. Frost had owned a home in the nearby town of Shaftesbury and was present at the Old First Church for its re-dedication. While visiting the site, a couple from Manassas, VA engaged me in a conversation regarding my hike. I told Greg and Nora about Don and some of the facets of the trail. Seeming very interested, they asked lots of questions. Before leaving the graveyard, I sat on a shady bench by Frost's grave for a while and wrote.

For the remainder of the afternoon I just rested. Much has certainly transpired over the past week. For instance, last Tuesday when I saw Susquehanna Slim sitting on a bench in Salisbury, CT, looking tired and dejected, I shared with him a little about my method of hiking the AT. A few days later he had temporarily left the trail, suffering from exhaustion.

So I emailed Slim an invitation to embrace the Don's Brother's Method for the remainder of his hike. Last night Slim accepted the offer. With a prior commitment next weekend, Slim plans to continue his southbound hike toward the Delaware Water Gap for now. Then one week from today he intends to join Banzai, Pilgrim, and me for the assault on Katahdin. Yes indeed, it's all coming together. Our trio will soon become a foursome as our motley bunch marches northward up the Appalachian Trail. "One could do worse than be a swinger of birches."

## July 16, USFS Rd. 71

I'm tired. Really tired. Too-tired-to-write tired. It's been a long day on the Appalachian Trail. Banzai, Pilgrim, and I are waiting for a shuttle at Forest Service Rd. 71, essentially "in the middle of nowhere." It's the first road we've crossed all day. It's the only "out" if we want to continue with Don's Brother's Method. Knowing that a shower, meal, and bed are in our immediate future, we are happy to wait. It's 7:40. This is the latest I have been on the trail the entire hike. Hopefully, Steve will arrive at the pre-determined time. I didn't bring my head lamp. Pilgrim has his. Darkness is still an hour away. Biting flies and mosquitoes have infiltrated our space, or are we the interlopers? I'm really tired.

Earlier this morning Banzai asked, "What state are we in?"

"It's the damn sameness of this thing that kills me," Pilgrim grumbled, as we took a short break after about five miles of a planned 20.6 mile day.

We could still be in Georgia based on the redundancy of the terrain. With only twenty-five percent of today's hike complete, we are already a little edgy. It's hot and humid even though it's still morning. Isn't Vermont supposed to be cool? What state are we in?

We walk on, still grumbling about the mud, bugs, and humidity. Even Banzai isn't as eager to lecture today. I eventually mention Tennyson's "Ulysses," and the discussion is on. Miles go by more quickly with conversation. So we hike and talk. Pilgrim lingers fifty yards behind. We pause occasionally and he catches up. He adds a comment now and then. We hike toward the first shelter of three we'll pass today, three

A.T. thru-hikers caught somewhere between happy and miserable. Time passes......time passes.......time passes.

At the Goddard Shelter we stop for lunch. We each have a bag of Mc-Donald's hamburgers that we purchased in Bennington. I have a root beer as well. The shelter is one of the nicest I've seen. If it were later in the day and I had all my gear and my gear included a sleeping bag and I had more food, I might even enjoy staying here. We eat a leisurely meal. Pilgrim leans against the back of the shelter with closed eyes. Banzai suggests we make it a long lunch since we aren't getting picked up until 8:00. We eventually decide to continue the hike before Pilgrim falls asleep. I save one burger and half my root beer for later.

What state are we in? The trail looks the same. We stop at the Glastenbury Mountain lookout tower. Banzai and I climb the metal steps. Banzai reaches the top. I stop two rungs short when a strong wind rocks the structure. Pilgrim waits below. Banzai and I take photos and then descend the steps. This would be our only view of the day. The trail in fact is so remote that there is a six mile section in the *A.T. Guide* that has no listings. No roads, no streams, no shelters, nothing to write about for six miles. We are definitely miles from nowhere.

We hike on to the next shelter, Kid Gore. This shelter has a reputation as being a haven for porcupines. We see none in the mid-afternoon. James, a section-hiker who has only been on the trail three days, plans to stay the night. I warn him about the porcupines. He says no one has mentioned them in the registry. Maybe they've moved elsewhere. I eat my final burger and finish my root beer. Banzai thinks we should take a longer break again. We do. I'm already tired and we still have six miles to hike. A rare breeze momentarily replaces the hot, humid, stagnant air. The biting flies continue to annoy. What state are we in?

We hike over rocks, through black mud, across streams, avoiding roots and swampy areas. As the afternoon diminishes, fatigue increases. My two buddies and I stop at another shelter for a final break. Story Spring Shelter offers a picnic table at which to rest. I'm bordering on exhaustion when I remember a new bag of jelly beans in my pack. I tear open the package and share them with Banzai and Pilgrim. With only 1.6 miles to the road and the end of the day, I pick up my pace. Banzai hikes ahead. Pilgrim maintains my pace. The jelly beans are working. At least temporarily, I've regained some strength.

Steve Labombard arrives with a cooler of soft drinks. We head up the gravel road for the hour drive back to Bennington. Steve comments that he saw a moose feeding on the way up. The moose is still there. We stop. I get out for a picture. The moose ambles away. A calf suddenly emerges from the marsh and follows. Steve offers an informative lecture of his own on the drive. Banzai is captivated by Steve's knowledge of the surrounding area. Agreeing to stop for us to pick up food, Steve goes beyond our expectations. I easily elevate his status to #1 among trail angels I've met.

It's late. I feel less tired now, however, than I did three hours ago. My alarm is set for 6:00. We need an early start tomorrow to make Manchester Center, the next town in Vermont. We're in Vermont on one of the most remote sections of the trail. It's been a tiring day, but I feel good. Banzai and I decided today that we would start focusing on the miles remaining in addition to those we've already hiked. So we now have 557.6 miles left to hike. Tomorrow we'll attempt to erase 19.5 of them as we continue walking through Vermont on the Appalachian Trail.

## July 17, VT 11, Manchester Center

In July three years ago I spoke with my brother several times a week. We talked about baseball, our families and our futures. He took his bass boat out regularly and spent hours walking in the woods. Life was good. Two years ago in July Don and I rode bikes we had bought after his ALS diagnosis. He said riding made him feel like a kid again. We hoped progression of the illness would be slow. He talked of death and dying. I listened. Last year on July 17 I sat with my brother after he had lost his ability to talk. I spoke of life and death. He listened. Six weeks later he was dead. Today when I walked past Stratton Pond, quite possibly the prettiest lake on the A.T., I thought about my brother.

Our day began with another shuttle back to the trail from Steve. Banzai, Pilgrim, and I walked back into the woods at 8:00, beginning a 19.5 mile day. Like the first two in Vermont, isolation dominated the day. Banzai chose to hike ahead for much of the morning, and I also put space between Pilgrim and myself. I suppose we just didn't have much to share with each other. Even when hiking with companions, sometimes it feels good to be alone. Today I hiked in a solitary mood, contemplating on various aspects of what waits ahead, on the trail and in life.

The trail remained the same. It consisted of mud, rocks, mud, roots, mud, rocks over streams, footbridges, mud, leaves, mud, and dirt. There were uphills and downhills. As Pilgrim stated yesterday, it's the sameness that gets to you. Other than Stratton Mountain with its lookout tower and Stratton Pond, there was nothing noteworthy the entire day. The gentle terrain made for a reasonably comfortable day even though the heat, humidity, and biting flies detracted from any potential enjoyment.

The climb up Stratton Mountain in the morning highlighted the day. At the crest we met the caretaker Hugh who enlightened us on some of the history of the Long Trail. It was here that Benton MacKaye conceived the idea for the Appalachian Trail. Pilgrim and I climbed part of the way up the lookout tower for a view of Greylock to the west and Killington to the north. Banzai chose not to do the climb. He has decided to avoid what he calls "extra credit." Past the mountain we stopped at Stratton Pond Shelter, another nice one, for lunch. Then we passed Stratton Pond. I paused and took some pictures before moving on.

Throughout the afternoon we continued to hike alone. Banzai stopped at Prospect Rock to let Pilgrim and me catch up. From there we steadily made our way to VT 11 to Manchester. Needing to hitch a ride into town, we were fortunate to get a lift from Walter, a day-hiker from the area. When we reached town we ate at an Italian place before getting a ride from Jeff to his Green Mountain House hostel. Other hikers are here including Spoon and Blue Eyes.

So after today I have 538 miles remaining on my A.T. thru-hike. If all continues to go well, I should finish my hike in around six weeks. Six short weeks. Six long weeks. Six weeks of beauty and grandeur. Six weeks of potential distress and loneliness. Six weeks to define existence. Six weeks to realize the fulfillment of a promise. Don lived six weeks after that hot afternoon last July 17. Six weeks to reach a goal, a destination, an end. Tomorrow starts the final push. Six more weeks on the Appalachian Trail.

## July 18, Danby-Landgrove Rd.

Blue Eyes, a pretty section-hiking physics teacher from Minnesota, told me last night at the Green Mountain House that I needed to hike happy. She suggested I take more time to essentially "stop and smell the roses." Or according to A.T. lingo, sit and enjoy the view whenever one occurs. Banzai doesn't like to do "extra credit." Blue Eyes thinks we always should. Today I tried to remember what my new friend said. I hiked happy, or at least I tried to. My newfound positive attitude carried me through a moderately challenging 17.8 mile day.

After a quick stop for breakfast, Jeff shuttled Banzai, Pilgrim, and me back to the trailhead off VT 11 at 7:00. One of two major highlights of the day occurred during the first three miles. The trail travels up a ski slope on Bromley Mountain, with supposedly a view of five states from the tower at the top. The morning was reasonably clear; however, I wasn't sure which distant mountains were in which states. Remembering what Blue Eyes had advised me, I did take some time to actually "play around" on top. I walked out on the gondola platform for some pictures and spent some time talking with Jamie and Marcia, section-hikers from Tennessee. Banzai eventually informed me that it was time to continue the hike.

A little over two miles later we reached Mad Tom Notch. No one seemed to know who Mad Tom was, so I decided I would equate him to Pilgrim in song. The tune is to "Big John," a ballad sung by Jimmy Dean.

He stood 5 foot 10, weighed 135;

Had to change his plan, just to stay alive, Mad Tom

Came from California across the great divide

To hike the A.T. before he died, Mad Tom.

Mad Tom....., Mad Tom......, Old Mad Tom

Pilgrim seemed to be a good sport about my unpoetic drivel. It sometimes amazes me to think of the depths to which we have sunk to find ways to entertain ourselves on a hot, humid, sweaty nine-hour day of hiking. Mad Tom!

The next view of the day at Styles Peak required a climb of about five feet. It took me approximately 20 seconds. When I tried to persuade my buddies to join me on the outcrop, both opted to remain on their perches below. I fear that Pilgrim may be adopting the "no extra credit" philosophy as well. As for me, I was hiking happy, and getting some nice pictures to share with friends. While the morning passed into afternoon I continued to embrace the "hike happy" theory.

A final spectacular section of trail greeted us at Baker Peak. Although the elevation was lower, the gorgeously clear views were the best since Race Mountain in Massachusetts, at least according to this happy hiker. Northbound thru-hiker Spoon had been hiking with or around us all day. On the slanted jagged rocks of Baker Peak I followed him and Banzai to the top. Pilgrim trailed. Again I took my time to just enjoy and appreciate. With the White Mountains of New Hampshire in the not-too-distant future, I was actually glad to have a mildly technical section for practice. Exhilaration describes the fifteen minute ascent well. I was grateful it wasn't raining. That would have definitely been a dangerous climb in wet conditions.

During the final five miles of the day, the trail passed three shelters, two of which were directly on the A.T. We took a short break at Lost Pond

Shelter. At Big Branch Shelter I remembered the night Alton, Ponder, and I stayed there on a section-hike. The gushing stream in front of the shelter made for some good sleeping. I had wanted to continue hiking happy by taking off my shoes for a soak; however, since we only had a mile to the road and a ride, I kept going.

When Pilgrim and I reached Danby-Landgrove Rd., Banzai was already at the SUV talking with Jeff. We had picked up some soft drink trail magic just prior to the road, so once again, I enjoyed an ice cold Mountain Dew on the trip back to Manchester Center and the Green Mountain House hostel. On the way Jeff stopped for us to buy some groceries. I purchased the ingredients for spaghetti and cooked up a pot for the group. We invited southbounder Rooster to join us. After supper I just relaxed, anticipating another "hike happy" day tomorrow as I work my way through Vermont on the Appalachian Trail.

## July 19, VT 103, Rutland, VT

During the course of this A.T. hike, my general attitude has fluctuated almost as much as the elevations on the trail. I've hiked with enthusiasm and excitement at times. At others I've walked with sadness or melancholia. Occasionally I've hiked with anger and despair. Yesterday I hiked happy. Today I simply walked with indifference. What little variety the trail offered seemed of little interest on another very hot, humid, uncomfortable day. The weather and bugs make it impossible to truly enjoy the sights along the way. As I write this in the early evening, the temperature outside is still 91. I thought Vermont was supposed to be cool.

There were a few highlights on a tiring 14.8 mile day. Early in the hike we passed another beautiful lake in a picturesque setting. Once again I thought of Don as I gazed into the calm, soothing water. I even took a photo and sent it to Brent in a text. He commented that the fish would certainly be biting. A canoe next to the pond indicated that someone surely had been paddling around. It possibly belonged to the caretaker of the nearby shelter. Spoon, who had stayed at the shelter the night before, noted that the caretaker hadn't been in the area the previous evening.

Most noteworthy among today's highlights were two areas that consisted of some rock artwork. Numerous rock structures of various shapes and sizes have been erected adjacent to the trail. Spoon commented that he wondered if some art students had been assigned the task of constructing the sculptures. I imagine that hikers have been contributing to the gallery, so I took a little time to create my own tiny masterpiece. Spoon was so captivated by the cairns in the middle of the forest that he shot some video. Banzai, Pilgrim, and I also lingered in the area for quite some time, honestly fascinated with all the varying creations.

Eventually we hiked on to VT 140 where we took a lunch break. Spoon joined our band for the meal. I walked down to a stream near the road to wash my face and hands. The cool water felt refreshing on the blistering day. I was always grateful for the occasional breeze that temporarily supplanted the heat. Unfortunately, the wind was often short-lived. Still I appreciated the brief respites. I always offer up a prayer of thanksgiving when they occur.

After lunch we were faced with an 1100 foot climb up and over Bear Mountain. This is the third Bear Mountain we have encountered. New York and Connecticut each have one as well. Were it not for the heat, this climb would have proven rather insignificant. With the heat it was tough. I stopped often to drink and at one point almost was walking in place. When we crested the mountain and started down the other side, we took one final brief break at the Minerva Hinchley Shelter. While there Banzai noticed a posted message on the wall offering rides to hikers needing to go into Rutland. I put the number in my phone before we resumed the hike.

The final highlight of the day occurred on a rock outcrop with a view of the Rutland Airport. From there I called the ride number. Tom said he would meet us at the road in half an hour. On the descent over soft, minced pine straw, with an occasional slick rock blended in, Pilgrim fell twice. There's always a potential fall around every corner on the A.T. After we crossed Clarendon Gorge over a suspension bridge, we easily made our way to the parking lot. Tom arrived a couple of minutes later.

We drove into Rutland, got two rooms, cleaned up, and went out for a good meal. Tomorrow our plans take a new turn as we will have a full-time support person for a few days. Banzai's brother drove up from Virginia today to lend a hand. With a car at our disposal we will have more options for better planning as to where to end each day. Cooler weather is also in the forecast, so with better hiking conditions, light packs, a car for shuttling, and a team, all looks positive for further advancement up the Appalachian Trail.

## July 20, US 4, Rutland, VT

When my home phone rang on the morning of July 20, 1993, twenty years ago today, I didn't even know what states the Appalachian Trail went through. What I did know was that a friend was offering me four dugout level tickets to the Braves game that night. It took me about three seconds to accept. I then immediately called my brother to inform him that we would be sitting four rows behind the visiting dugout with our then seven-year-old sons for the Braves/Cardinals game that evening. I'm not sure why dates stick with some people. In this case it was because of the fire at the old Fulton County Stadium before game time. Fred McGriff made his debut in a Braves uniform as the Bravos overcame a 5-0 deficit to win 8-5. Even though the game didn't begin until after 9:30 and concluded well after midnight, Don, Brent, Sam and I stayed for every pitch. So as I hiked today I relived that wonderful memory of my brother from 20 years ago today.

The day started a little differently in that our trio now has the good fortune of having a full-time driver, at least for the next two weeks. Mike drove up from Virginia to offer support for his twin brother, Banzai, and his buddies. So we cruised down to a local diner for breakfast before hitting the trail at VT 103. With rain in the forecast, followed by a cold front, we didn't even mind the humid start to the morning. After a rock scramble within the first half mile, up the mountain we went, climbing about 1000 feet to start our day. At the time I didn't know it, but a really good day it was going to be. In fact, before the 18.4 mile day had come to an end I would be hiking happy exponentially.

243

Shortly after the initial climb we came across a detour predicated by Hurricane Irene. We had been pre-warned of the road walk that circumvented a potentially difficult stream crossing. Since it had rained the previous night Banzai, Pilgrim, and I chose to follow the advice of the trail maintainers and take the detour. It took us past several very nice rural homes. At one a Vermonter tended his horses. Eventually we arrived at where the trail wound back into the woods. We then walked a short distance to the Governor Clement Shelter. A southbound thru-hiker, who was taking a break, informed us that there were a lot of roots and rocks in Maine. Sorry to disappoint you friend, but that's the entire Appalachian Trail.

From the shelter we started the climb up Killington, the highest mountain on the A.T. in Vermont. The actual peak is 0.2 off the trail. Attempting to follow Blue Eyes' suggestion, I tried to hike happy. For some reason I thought of Fatty, someone with a similar personality to Blue Eyes, that I had not seen since central Pennsylvania.

"I'd like to see Fatty again," I said to Banzai and Pilgrim, "but she's probably over a week ahead of us."

Just the thought of the positive, vivacious young lady motivated me to keep trying to hike with enthusiasm.

Near the top of Killington the Cooper Lodge Shelter stands. Banzai was already inside the fully enclosed structure having lunch when I got there. Also inside were Roboticus, a 2012 thru-hiker, and her friend. Pilgrim arrived shortly after we did. With a cool breeze blowing through the windows, we took a longer break than usual. Roboticus shared some miniature Hersheys as we talked about our hikes. Just as we were about to leave, the door of the shelter pushed open. Banzai was the first to see the hiker as she entered. He indeed looked surprised. When the door fully opened, displaying her usual beautiful smile, Fatty stepped inside. For me it was more shock than surprise. Bizarre might be an even more appropriate explanation. Only about an hour after I had mentioned Fatty's name, she suddenly appeared.

So for the remainder of the afternoon I had the pleasure of hiking with one of my favorite people on the trail. She explained that she had gotten behind me when she went into New York twice. One time she did "touristy" things in the city; the other she went rock climbing for a few days in another NY town. With the cooler temperatures after the front had moved through, I hiked with rejuvenation throughout the afternoon. Fatty seemed content to follow me and chat. It was easy to hike happy with Fatty.

When we reached the road, Banzai and Mike were standing by a car where some serious trail magic was occurring. Jen, a local resident, had an array of goodies. Most impressive was a cooler filled with Klondike bars. I had two. Fatty had four. We also partook of some cherries, raspberries, and cheese. After having spent the past nine nights in the woods, Fatty accepted our invitation to a night in town. When Pilgrim finally arrived at the road, we gave him time to enjoy a couple of ice cream bars before we headed into Rutland.

Tonight Steady and Spirit joined Banzai, Pilgrim, Fatty, and me for dinner at a local establishment. As we waited for our meal I thought about how fortunate I was to have these hiking friends. From California and Michigan, Oregon, Alberta, and Georgia, we had all set out on different dates to thru-hike the A.T. Good food and good conversation made this day one of my best. With a starting temperature in the 50s forecast for the following morning, I hoped to continue hiking happy on my way to a mountain in Maine at the end of the Appalachian Trail.

## July 21, VT 12, Woodstock, VT.

As a young boy I would spend time each summer at the home of my grandparents in rural Alabama. My parents would typically leave me on a Sunday. My mom would return for me at the end of the week. Even though I loved my grandparents and knew that I was in for a fun time with them, it always felt lonely when my parents drove away. Today I felt that same "Sunday lonely" on the Appalachian Trail.

One thing I learned today is that if you want to dawdle while hiking the A.T., don't plan a 22.3 mile day. Still trying to hike happy and enjoy all the sights along the way, I found myself trailing my buddies early in the day. For the first four miles the terrain was about as gentle as any the trail has had to offer. The hiking day began with Fatty and Mike joining Pilgrim, Banzai, and me. At the trail to the Inn at Long Trail where the A.T. and the Long Trail split, Fatty left us to pick up a package. A little later Mike also turned to head back to the car. He plans to do a little out-and-back day-hiking while serving as our support person.

Early in the day we walked through Gifford Woods State Park. Many weekenders were busy at their campsites. From there we soon passed Kent Pond. I couldn't resist walking out on the dock for some reflection. Peering into the water, I hoped to see a fish. None appeared. Canoes and kayaks lay on boggy grass near the bank. One lone canoe could be seen at the far end of the pond. Since I took a long break I had to hustle to catch my friends within the next couple of miles. It was there that the first surprise of the day occurred, and it wasn't a pleasant one.

I had thought that the A.T. in Vermont only had three significant mountains: Stratton, Bromley, and Killington. Somebody forgot to include Quimby. Everyone in our group agreed it was the toughest of them all. We ascended almost 1300 feet over just one mile. That's a climb folks. After the struggle up Quimby we walked at a steady pace to the Stony Brook Shelter where we stopped for lunch. While there Fatty joined us. It was the last time we would see her all day.

For the remainder of the day I just hiked, seldom even looking to see how many miles were left. Feeling often like the day would never end, I hiked alone for at least three hours. That's when the loneliness set in. At one point I hummed "I'm So Lonesome I Could Cry." Still I hiked. Even though there were no significant views, the climbs in the afternoon were minimal. I would go so far to call the final nine miles kind of boring. At the turn for the Lookout, Banzai and Pilgrim had taken a break to let me catch up.

So for the final three hours Pilgrim and I hiked together as darkness approached. I commented that it was the right time of day to see a bear. We didn't. We hiked without talking for a while; we hiked and talked for a while. Despite a hiking companion, that Sunday lonely feeling continued. I thought about having 465 miles remaining after today and felt lonely. I thought about having already hiked over 1700 miles and felt lonely. It was almost 8:00 when I finished what I can only describe as a day in which I couldn't get past a feeling of loneliness on the journey to Maine along the Appalachian Trail.

## July 22, VT 14, White River

The Appalachian Trail has sometimes been referred to as "a footpath through the woods." After having hiked for almost four months and over 1700 miles, this afternoon I finally found that footpath. Unfortunately, the A.T. only took this appearance for less than a mile. Yep, just as suddenly as the beauteous trail had appeared, it was gone. From a wide bed of soft, rockless pine straw, the trail took a sharp right turn into the roots, rocks, and mud that we have been experiencing for most of Vermont. Still it sure was nice while it lasted.

Our day began with a stop at a country store for breakfast and a visit to an outfitter in Woodstock for a couple of items. Then at 9:20 Banzai, Pilgrim, and I headed back into the woods. With a shorter 13.9 mile day scheduled, we decided to take the later start and enjoy the day. As usual I hiked behind Banzai from the outset. Pilgrim followed, mumbling "ah, damn," as we were immediately faced with an almost "straight up" ascent. Even with the climb Banzai talked. I listened until we crested the mountain. Then I contributed to the conversation.

As usual, the conversation, like the trail, travelled in many directions. Before long I found myself in a literary discussion.

Banzai asked, "Which novels do you feel are most significant in AP classes?"

After mentioning a few, I found myself offering an analysis of Kate Chopin's *The Awakening.* I'm not quite sure how we got there. I also suggested he read *A Prayer for Owen Meany* by John Irving. We talked of other writers and books for a few miles before he disappeared into the distance. The discussion did make the time go by more quickly and the climbs a little more tolerable. This helped me because I was hiking rather sluggishly from the start.

After Banzai pulled away I waited for Pilgrim to catch me, which didn't take long. When he did I commented that I felt like I had been walking uphill for the past two days.

Pilgrim replied, "That's because you have."

At the top of one of those hills Mike was waiting to warn us of some serious boggy mud. All of us tried to circumvent the swamp; however, it was downright impossible to avoid getting our shoes wet. With ankle-deep mud and water, as well as head-high foliage, we had no choice but to slosh ahead. Finally we again found the woods.

When we reached Pomfret Rd., Mike called it a day. My buddies and I hiked on to the Thistle Hill Shelter where we stopped for lunch. A few mosquitoes made their annoying presence known while we ate. Still we enjoyed the sandwiches and beverages we had brought with us. From the shelter Banzai hiked on alone, hoping to reach the road before his shuttling brother got there. I suddenly felt re-energized, so I also picked up the pace throughout the afternoon.

The trail at least provided me with some variety. From open fields to pine straw ups and downs, nothing seemed too difficult. Unlike yesterday, I didn't feel lonely despite hiking by myself the last three hours. I thought about Owen Meany and his baseball card collection. Tomorrow I'll walk into Owen's state. Owen Meany certainly knew a thing or two about the granite state. I hope I can handle the Whites with the same fortitude that Owen Meany displayed when faced with adversity. The mind goes to many places while walking solitarily through the woods.

When I reached Quechee West Hartford Rd., I stopped to wait for Pilgrim. We walked together up the highway to VT 14 where we saw a kayaker getting ready to put in at the White River. I borrowed his kayak for a photo, hoping I would see Steady again soon. Across the road from the river Mike and Banzai were waiting. Apparently Mike had thought this was a better ending location for today's hike. So our day officially became a 13.0 which leaves a 9.9 to Hanover for tomorrow.

And tomorrow begins a new chapter of the DBM. Susquehanna Slim has arrived in White River Junction and will join the caravan. Pilgrim, Slim, and I got better acquainted over dinner at a Chinese buffet tonight. In the morning the journey continues as Susquehanna Slim adopts the DBM for the hike toward Katahdin on the Appalachian Trail.

## July 23, Hanover, New Hampshire

Mike's text message at 6:15 this morning read, "Banzai asks, 'do you really want to hike in this rain?'"

My response without even consulting Pilgrim and Slim was "Yes."

With only a 9.9 mile day planned into Hanover, I wasn't about to let a little rain interfere with reaching New Hampshire. It was only moderate rain. OK, the rain was coming down pretty hard. Regardless, I just couldn't see forfeiting a day to weather. Slim agreed. When Pilgrim and Banzai finally bought in, we were off to a morning of slogging up the Appalachian Trail.

The trail today began and concluded with road walks. As soon as the four of us emerged from Mike's car we were greeted with a steady drizzle. I wore my rain jacket with a light poncho that also served as a pack cover. Despite both, I got pretty wet as the rain fell with varying degrees of intensity for the almost four hour duration of our hike. Some of the trail was already saturated; however, the mud didn't seem to be any more severe than other recent days. We did encounter two swollen streams. At the second I just walked through rather than risking falling from a wet rock.

The order in which we hiked varied with Banzai and me alternating in the lead. To take our minds off of the dismal weather I proposed that we sing rain songs. I offered up a verse of The Temptations' "I Wish it Would Rain." Slim crooned CCR's "Who'll Stop the Rain" and then Pilgrim chimed in with "Davy Crockett." Not quite sure where rain fit in with Pilgrim's selection. It did lead me to bellowing out a little of "Rawhide." Such is life on the A.T., especially on a rainy day.

Alter my rendition of the theme song from the popular early 60's western, I decided to put some distance between myself and the others. As I hiked ahead, however, I could hear an ongoing conversation between Banzai and Susquehanna Slim. With a new audience of one, Banzai was on a roll. I only heard bits and pieces of his discourse, but it also seemed that Slim was getting in his two cents worth as well. So on I sloshed through the standing water and mud up a quagmire of a trail toward New Hampshire. With minimal rocks and negligible climbs, I pounded out the miles in near record time. Eventually Banzai and Slim caught me. When we reached Elm St., which began a 2.5 road walk into Hanover, we waited for Pilgrim to catch up. Then we walked together as the rain increased.

As raindrops kept falling on my head, I thought of another cold, rainy 21 mile day and a green poncho. That was over two months and 1000 miles ago. It could have been yesterday or in another lifetime. I hiked on toward the Connecticut River and the 13th state of the A.T. When I reached the western edge of the bridge I noticed several rowing teams. We stopped briefly for the perfunctory picture of the etched VT/NH on the bridge. Even though a steady drizzle continued, I was determined to have this photo memory. After the pictures we made our way on up the road into Hanover and onto the campus of Dartmouth College. The trail then made a right turn onto Main St., moving through the center of the popular New England town.

Within minutes we had connected with Mike and the car. After a trip to the motel for a shower and dry clothes, we headed back to Hanover for lunch. Later in the evening all of us had dinner at the home of Short 'n Sweet, a section-hiker whose son, The Brain, thru-hiked in 2007. It felt good celebrating my four month anniversary on the trail with Short 'n Sweet, her husband Graybeard, and my buddies. Our hosts also provided some valuable information about New Hampshire, the state we'll begin tomorrow on the Appalachian Trail.

# 13

# New Hampshire

**July 24, Hanover to Dorchester Rd.**

Every day presents challenges on the Appalachian Trail. From rugged climbs to an often continuous sea of roots, rocks, and mud, I have to remember to focus virtually every step of the way. Twice today I lost that concentration and fell. Neither caused any harm; however, each just reminded me of how important it is to watch every footfall. The first occurred when I lost my balance on a wet, mossy rock. I was suddenly staggering forward unable to stop my momentum until I hit the ground. Slippery black mud caused the second. Or should I say my inability to stand on the slippery mud resulted in the mishap. Regardless, I'm reminded that potential danger is always lurking. With the Whites in my immediate future, I best beware.

The day started at Lou's Restaurant and Bakery, a mainstay in Hanover, NH since 1947. Located just a block from the Dartmouth campus, decor in the establishment doesn't seem to have changed much over those 66 years. The gang and I ate heartily inside before adding a complimentary thru-hiker pastry from the assortment outside. As we prepared to hike on up Main St. (Lou's is on the trail), several other hikers walked up including Johnny Walker, Puffy, Spoon, and Gator. We would see all of them throughout the day as we began the first day in New Hampshire.

Today's hike began simply enough. With a road walk up Main St. and then past the Dartmouth football stadium, we didn't hit the woods again for nearly a mile. Friendly folks on bikes and in cars appeared to be headed to classes or work on a pleasant New England morning. When we did reach the woods, the trail only slightly changed elevation for the first six miles. At that point we commenced the climb up Moose Mountain for around 1500 feet. With less than treacherous terrain, the gradual ascent didn't pose any real demands. At the south peak Banzai, Slim, Pilgrim, and I stopped for lunch. Several other northbound hikers had also taken a break including the group we had seen at Lou's.

Mike was also slackpacking Johnny Walker and Puffy. Spoon decided to walk without a pack. Banzai carried Spoon's water for him. At another break Spoon entertained us with a stand-up routine about thru-hiking. The retired postman from Minnesota may have found a new career. After the show we continued to make good time to the north peak of Moose Mountain and then down to Goose Pond Rd.

From the road we climbed a steep unnamed mountain to Holts Ledge. I don't know why the 1000 foot climb over two miles had no name. It surely deserved one. From there we descended to Dorchester Rd. where we ended today's hike. It was during this last downhill stretch that I had the falls. After going completely through Vermont vertical, it was disappointing to see my streak come to an end. Trying to stay positive, however, I think perhaps someone was sending a reminder that I need to always remain cautious. If there's one thing I need to do, it's stay on my feet because there are many tough days ahead on the Appalachian Trail.

## July 25, NH 25A, Wentworth, NH

After a rather mundane introduction to New Hampshire on yesterday's hike, my buddies and I got the full welcome on Cube Mountain this afternoon. Finding ourselves close to tree-line, Banzai, Susquehanna Slim, Pilgrim and I realized that the Whites are just around the next corner, or should I say, just over the next ridge. With spectacular views from the south peak of Cube, we took our last lengthy break, before tackling the 2000 foot descent over the final three miles. The less-severe-than-we-had-anticipated terrain helped to alleviate some of the cumulative fatigue from a 16.0 mile, ten hour day. Still, when we arrived at NH 25A, we were all very tired.

Our day began at Dorchester Rd. near Lyme, NH. With light packs and cool weather (48 earlier this morning), we scooted up the first significant climb to Lambert's Ridge in two hours. We were greeted with the first of several awesome views that we would experience throughout the day. Despite having to traverse several large rock slabs, the variation was nice. Large patches of squishy black mud detracted some; however, the somewhat challenging boulders didn't pose any major difficulty. From the ridge we could see our next climb, Smarts Mountain and its fire tower, in the distance.

The distance between the two locations was only two miles with about an 850 foot elevation gain. Surprisingly the climb didn't prove to be very difficult. Arriving on Smarts Mountain just past noon, we took a break for lunch. Spoon had also stopped for a break. Slim climbed the tower to the enclosed top. I sat on a rock below and enjoyed a sandwich. At this point in the hike a jovial crowd we were. In fact, Banzai serenaded the rest of us with a chorus of "Rawhide" as we continued the walk. It appears that this has become our theme song. So on we walked down to Jacobs Brook and then on toward the Eastman Ledges.

The ledges provided the four of us with some more difficult rock climbs, but the views were worth the effort. From the ledges we ascended to Mt. Cube where we took a final break on the south peak. Mike had hiked in to meet us and was waiting at the top with Banzai when Slim, Pilgrim, and I arrived. After hiking tentatively most of the day due to yesterday's falls, I tried to resume my normal pace for the final three miles. Hiking behind the others, I still exhibited caution. When we all reached the road we drove in to Lincoln where we will set up a base camp of sorts for the first few days of the Whites. Then after a stop for pizza we headed to a motel, tired and dirty after another exhausting day on the Appalachian Trail.

## July 26, NH 25, Glencliff, NH

Over breakfast at the Longhorn Palace Pancake House, Mike noted that coffee is the ubiquitous drink. When I commented that "ubiquitous" didn't often come up in hiker conversation, the college professor said that one could become an expert on anything with a little research. From there he lectured briefly on Faroe, some Scandinavian island near Iceland. Having taught *Macbeth* a couple of hundred times, I said I suppose I could talk about the Shakespearean tragedy for a while. Pilgrim said he didn't know the story of "Macdeath." Fortunately we were about finished with breakfast as the conversation took the downward spiral.

As for the trail today, rocks, mud, roots, leaves, and a minuscule amount of pine straw prevailed. Mud overwhelmingly led the way with roots taking a distant second. Views came in last since there were none on the 9.9 mile section from NH 25A to NH 25. I'm not quite sure why different New Hampshire roads have the same numbers with a letter affixed. It can get downright confusing. But before I start rambling too much, there really wasn't anything noteworthy to report on in regards to the trail today. It was simply more of the same. To relieve the tedium, at one point I was requested to summarize *Macbeth*. I did so over about a mile. Banzai followed my lecture with a discourse on *Job*.

Like most of the past few days, we met some southbound thru-hikers. One, Flip, said he got his trail name because he did backflips on the trail, without his pack of course. I failed to mention Puck, another SOBO that I met earlier in the week. Puck carries a hockey stick in lieu of a trekking pole. Almost all of the southbounders have been young men. I've only encountered two women and three folks around my age. The closer we get to the Katahdin, the more hikers we'll see headed to Georgia. Some already look a bit weary. When asked, they also gladly provide information on what lies ahead. The only problem, however, is that each perspective differs from the others. For instance, Puck can't understand why we aren't all carrying hockey sticks.

Throughout the day we only took one break. We did so at Mt. Mist, a spot where section-hiker Laura and her teenage son Sam were resting as well. We had seen the duo yesterday. I shared my website with Laura and listened as she talked about some of her previous hikes, including her first climb of Katahdin. From there, Banzai, Pilgrim, Susquehanna Slim, and

I hiked at a steady, rather fast pace all the way to the road. About a mile before reaching it, Mike met us. He continues to enjoy doing some out-and-back jaunts for exercise. A former collegiate cross-country runner, Mike typically hikes at a pace equivalent to his brother.

Before driving back to Lincoln we stopped at a nearby hostel in Glencliff to gather some information about the Whites from Legion, an A.T. and PCT finisher. When we got back to town we had lunch and visited the post office. Walking around a bit, we ran into several other northbounders. I hadn't seen Salad Days and Risscuit since Daleville, VA. They offered some advice and strategy for our first significant climb up Moosilauke. Sadly, their description of the mountain didn't alleviate my trepidation. Still it was good to hear the perspective of someone who had just ascended it.

So tomorrow we begin the notorious Whites. Like most marathon runners, I have always held the belief that the half-way point of the race is 20 miles. It takes as much physical and mental energy to complete the final 6.2 as it does the first 20. I have now reached the "real" half-way mark of the Appalachian Trail. Everything up to this point has been a warm-up for what now awaits. Tomorrow my hiker friends and I will enter the Whites. This is like being promoted from Double-A baseball to the major leagues. Where I have been averaging two to two and a half miles an hour, I'll now need an hour or more just to cover some miles. It's going to be tough. I'll also need to be even more cautious as I try to meet the challenge of the White Mountains of New Hampshire with only 398.7 miles left to walk on the Appalachian Trail.

## July 27, NH 112, Kinsman Notch

I first hiked in the White Mountains in 2001. Today I returned. Filled with a combination of apprehension, excitement, and fear, I accomplished exactly what I set out to do. For 9.3 miles I enjoyed the beauty of Mt. Moosilauke, shared the experience with good hiking friends, and didn't fall. I hiked with caution and deliberation all day, anticipating potential danger and watching each footfall. Even with the careful approach

I still had multiple opportunities to pause and admire God's wondrous creation. Yes, the views all day were breathtaking and beyond. Banzai, Pilgrim, Susquehanna Slim, and I could not have had a better day for our first day in the Whites. It is a day I won't soon forget.

Today was especially important because I knew I needed to get past that queasy feeling left over in my stomach from that initial trip here. The hiker that entered the White Mountains today at 62 differed greatly from the one who struggled to survive a three-day trip twelve years earlier. The fear had subsided; however, a tremendous amount of respect would be offered to these majestic mountains each day I set foot in them. They command a certain degree of reverence. Their difficulty supersedes anything the A.T. has served up thus far.

Our day began with a short road walk detour. Due to a swollen creek without a footbridge, the trail had been diverted up NH 25 to High St. From there we entered the woods where the A.T. crossed. As we entered, a section-hiker, Step Lightly, was also beginning her hike. We would walk with her most of the morning until the summit. During that time the trail elevated from 1068 to 4802 feet at the crest of Mt. Moosilauke. The gradual ascent did not pose any significant challenge. We took a couple of short breaks prior to reaching a 0.1 mile side trail to the south summit. Banzai even chose to do "extra credit" and join Slim and me for the short walk. We all smiled with exhilaration when we first found ourselves above tree-line. It was quite a sight.

After retracing our steps to the white blazes, we rejoined Pilgrim and Step Lightly for the final approach to the summit of Mt. Moosilauke. And what an awesome site it was when we got there. A sign marked the spot of the 4802 foot crest. What appeared to be at least 50 day-hikers were just lounging around enjoying the panoramic views. My buddies and I ate our lunch even though it was only 11:20. While relaxing we chatted with several folks who were interested in our thru-hikes. One lady had a small black poodle, Duncan, who showed interest in my burger. Step Lightly's boyfriend, Mark, also arrived after hiking up from the north trailhead. Mike did the same hike as well. With hikers mingling in all directions and dogs romping, the summit of Mt. Moosilauke took on a circus-like appearance.

Eventually we realized that there was still much hiking yet to be done. So just after noon we began the treacherous descent. The sign warned of its danger. "This trail can be extremely slippery when icy or wet. Be cautious and consider an alternate route." Later in the afternoon we would see this sign's counterpart at the northern terminus. "This trail is extremely tough. If you lack experience, please use another trail. Take special care at the Cascades to avoid tragic results."

The first 2.3 miles of the 3.8 mile descent were rather tame. But with 1.5 remaining, the work truly began. It took me almost two hours to make my way down the very steep, rocky, slippery trail. For much of the downward trek, a cascading waterfall bordered the trail on the left. At one point the trail was so close that it may have been tempting for some hikers to reach over and touch the water. Keeping my eyes on my feet, I had no such thought. My only consideration was maintaining focus. I just wanted to stay vertical.

During the walk down I was passed by numerous day-hikers. All were young. Two couples from the Manchester, NH area hiked near me for a brief time with their dog. Greg, Dan, Carrie, and Jen expressed interest in my hike when I told them I had started in March. Rudy, the dog, bounded down the rocks with an agility that made me envious. Unable to maintain their pace, I soon watched them walk into the distance as I continued to hike deliberately. I was grateful that Slim would occasionally wait on me, often with a warning of an upcoming extremely troublesome area. With a quickly fatiguing brain, I eventually managed to reach the final challenging section which was followed by the road. In the parking lot we visited with Spirit who was waiting on Steady.

So my first day back in the Whites could be classified as a success in all respects. For the moment, I am a relieved, contented hiker. There are still many miles left to be completed and even more difficult and potentially dangerous mountains to be climbed. But for now I'm pleased that I met the challenge of Mt. Moosilauke. All in all today proved to be about as exhilarating as I could have imagined. Tomorrow my buddies and I will continue the hike through the Whites as we work our way through New Hampshire on the Appalachian Trail.

## July 28, Franconia Notch

For the first time since I began this thru-hike of the Appalachian Trail, four months and five days ago, last night I was just too tired to write. After quite possibly the most demanding physical and mental day of any athletic pursuit, I lay my head upon a soft pillow, completely exhausted. I'm still feeling the after-effects as I sit under a gazebo at a motel with a view of these majestic Whites. With tired bodies and thunderstorms in the forecast, my buddies and I easily concluded that a zero day was a wise choice. So with 373.1 miles remaining, I'm resting. It feels good to prop my feet up and know that I won't have to think about every step as I walk today. I'll try to live normally, at least for a day.

Quite honestly, I don't think Banzai, Pilgrim, Susquehanna Slim, and I realized just how challenging the day was going to be when we entered the woods at Kinsman Notch. We knew it would be hard. I just didn't expect to take 14 hours to walk 16.3 miles. The first surprise came with the ascent of Mt. Wolf. Since Wolf is not one of the 4000 footers, we failed to recognize its difficulty. Like so many of the mountains in the Whites, it was more rock scrambling than hiking. In fact, there was little "hiking" today. When we did rarely come across a seemingly level section, it almost always consisted of large areas of oozing, squishy, black mud. When I put my pole down to check its depth, the mud sucked up one-third of it. Figuring out a path around or finding small rocks or sticks to step on also posed a challenge. Every step of the day necessitated total focus. My brain ached. Not like a headache. It can best be described as mental fatigue.

The terrain down Wolf demanded just as much concentration. I kept telling myself to be deliberate. Twice I had near falls but managed to stay upright throughout the morning. When we reached Eliza Brook Shelter we took a lunch break. Still in good spirits, I didn't realize at the time that it was going to take me over eight hours to cover the remaining 8.8 miles.

The trail from the shelter parallels Eliza Brook for almost a mile. It also, however, begins ascending again. At one point Slim paused to look over his shoulder at me. Three young hikers headed in my direction stopped to allow me passage.

"I'm old, I'm slow, and I'm a little bit frightened right now," I stated, holding my position until the group passed.

"You look like you're doing fine," the prettiest of the trio replied.

I managed a feeble smile with a "Thank you."

And so we climbed and climbed and climbed up South Kinsman Mountain. My trekking poles often proved worthless since I needed both hands to hoist myself up the rocks. It was hard. At one point I jabbed my neck and scratched my hand on a jagged tree limb as I tried to balance myself near the edge of the trail. Every step required precision. A serious fall constantly awaited. Focus and deliberation were essential.

When we finally arrived above tree-line at the summit of South Kinsman Mountain, like yesterday on Moosilauke, the views were unbelievable. It's like being in an airplane with no fuselage. While we were taking a break, our friend Steady walked up. Banzai decided to hike on with him, so after reaching the peak of North Kinsman a mile later, I wouldn't see either Banzai or Steady again for the remainder of the day. From the peak of North Kinsman at 4293 feet, Slim, Pilgrim, and I started the slow, tedious, time-consuming, treacherous descent. It was brutal. At least five times I found myself purposefully on the seat of my shorts trying to inch my way down the perilous, slanted rock slabs. The climb down from Kinsman required as much or more mental effort than physical. At some point Slim also got ahead. By the time Pilgrim and I finally reached the Lonesome Lake Hut, I was spent.

Throughout the White Mountains the Appalachian Mountain Club maintains a series of huts that sleep between 30 and 90 hikers. They allow a few thru-hikers to work for stay. Otherwise, the cost is in the vicinity of $100, which is actually a discounted fee for thru-hikers. Amazingly, most huts are full many nights with short section-hikers and tourists. When Pilgrim and I reached Lonesome Lake I went in to see if Banzai and Slim were there. They were not. So Pilgrim and I ate a snack and then set out for the final three miles to Franconia Notch. It was already after 6:00.

The trail flattened for those final three; however, we encountered two more obstacles. The bridge over Cascade Brook was out, so we had to figure out how to get across the rushing waters. I first tried the rock hop method but changed my mind when I slipped on a wet one and went down hard. For the third time today I bled. The cut on my knee was minor, but still I set a record for blood loss during one day. After the fall I just walked through the knee-deep water to the other side. I did the same when we got to Whitehouse Brook, a half mile from the notch. My feet were freezing from the icy cold water.

When we reached the Notch Slim was waiting. He, Pilgrim, and I still had to walk about a mile up a bike path to the Liberty Springs parking lot. After 14 hours the day on the A.T. had finally come to an end. I had scratches on my neck, right hand, and right knee. Each of my buddies had also fallen at least once. Bruised and battered, we drove through a light drizzle as nightfall arrived. We found a restaurant and then settled in at the motel at 10:30. It was a long day, a tiring day, a day that I will remember. A day of rest should help. We are OK. Soon we will continue our journey through the Whites, a little more cognizant of the perils that may await. Perils of the trail sometimes, however, are no different than the perils of life.

A year ago my brother had one month to live. He struggled daily to just exist. He couldn't move. He had difficulty breathing. He could do nothing for himself except think. Only he knew his thoughts. I believe one of my reasons for this hike was to try to find a way to suffer just a fraction of the way Don suffered during that final month of his life. Today was hard, really hard. But what I encountered today pales in comparison to what Don had to undergo during that painful last month. There are tough days ahead. There are mountains to be climbed and descended. There are rivers to be forded and nights to be slept in the woods. There is also beauty and tranquility to be appreciated and enjoyed. One more month on the Appalachian Trail.

## July 29, Lincoln, NH

Today as I sit in a comfortable motel room watching a hard, steady rainfall, I'm reminded of what a significant role weather plays in the White Mountains of New Hampshire. If I were on a ridgeline in this downpour there would be no escape. I would have to keep walking to the next shelter, which might take hours. So it looks like a day off was a good plan. Still, we will hike tomorrow, hopefully under the forecasted sunshine.

On this zero-day I'm also reminded of all I have to be thankful for. Right now I'm especially grateful for the three hikers who have joined with me for the final push toward the end. Their companionship has sustained me through some difficult times already. Knowing that someone is nearby, just in case an emergency arises, is also reassuring. Hopefully, we can all stay together, healthy and content, throughout the remainder of the journey.

The day off has been good. We've been able to plan for the next few days and rest. We never know what awaits on any given day. Tomorrow we hope sunshine will prevail and we will have the strength and perseverance to continue the pursuit of a mountain in Maine at the northern terminus of the Appalachian Trail.

## July 30, Franconia Ridge

"Ahhh MAN" is a favorite expression of mine when something really spectacular occurs on the trail. Today I uttered the expression multiple times while summiting three 4000 footers and walking along the Franconia Ridge. It may be time to check a thesaurus to find more descriptive adjectives for the views I have had the privilege of observing over the past three days. Breathtaking, spectacular, awesome, and majestic just don't seem to do justice to the White Mountains of New Hampshire. These mountains are beyond description. Today I felt like I was a part of a postcard for much of the morning. It's just hard to fully capture the grandeur of these mountains.

Before Banzai, Pilgrim, Slim, and I could begin the hike, we had to walk a one mile side trail back to the A.T. These extra miles don't count for official mileage, so our total A.T. mileage for the day was 13.0. Like Sunday, the miles were rough. In fact, it took me almost twelve hours to complete the hike. With continued difficult, treacherous terrain, by the end of the day I was drained both mentally and physically. A 13.0 mile day used to be simple. I could hike that mileage and have half the afternoon free. In the Whites, however, I'm exhausted after completing the day.

When my buddies and I did reach the trail we were immediately greeted with almost a 4000 foot climb to the Franconia Ridge. With a fairly navigable trail early in the morning, we made good time to the Liberty Springs Campsite. Cam, a caretaker at the area, emerged from his tent to give us some information about the trail conditions. From there we continued the pursuit of our first of three 4000 footers, Little Haystack. Totally overwhelmed with the surrounding beauty, I shot some video as I exclaimed my first, "Ahhh MAN." With the wind blowing at a predicted 35 miles an hour, I put on my rain jacket and later gloves. At one point the wind actually blew me over.

After Little Haystack we walked along the Franconia Ridge to Mt. Lincoln at 5089 feet and then Mt. Lafayette at 5289. We all paused often and took numerous pictures along the ridgeline. Even though we were sporadically in the clouds, views prevailed in most directions. I literally felt like I was on top of the world. It was beyond exhilaration. The ridge walk was by far the highlight of the day. Unfortunately, we eventually had to come down from the ridge and re-enter the trees.

The trail then became another time-consuming sea of large rocks. Some required precise maneuvering in order to get down the wet slabs. Interspersed were some uphill sections which required rock scrambling. These weren't as difficult as Kinsman, but they still demanded focus and concentration. The most challenging section for me came after the fourth 4000 footer of the day, Mt. Garfield. After the climb we encountered a very steep, precipitous descent. With numerous wet rock slabs to negotiate, I had to sit on the seat of my pants and inch my way down on a couple of occasions. The treacherous descent took its toll. Feeling mentally fatigued, my pace slowed radically.

At some point Banzai hiked on to Galehead Hut, hoping to get a work for stay at the AMC-maintained facility. Eventually, Slim also hiked ahead to make sure he, Pilgrim, and I had a bunk. Meanwhile I kept working hard to find ways down the rocks without falling. It proved to be a definite challenge. Pilgrim and I hiked deliberately, finally reaching the hut just as dinner was beginning.

By far, the past three days have been the toughest. I'm physically tired. I'm mentally tired. I'm seriously ready for this hike to reach its final destination. The beauty on the ridges, however, easily surpasses the difficulty of the dangerously perilous rocky ascents and descents. I'll try to keep remembering that as I journey north on the Appalachian Trail.

## July 31, Galehead Hut to Crawford Notch

As the hike gets tougher, so does finding the time to write about it. Although not as difficult as yesterday, today's hike still took us almost ten hours to cover the 14.7 miles. With a fairly flat path over the final eight miles, it actually felt like I was hiking again rather than rock climbing. For the first time in the last week I didn't have to watch my feet hit the ground with every step. At one point Slim and I even engaged in a conversation for a couple of miles. Lately it's been almost impossible to hike and talk at the same time.

After an evening at the Galehead Hut, Banzai, Pilgrim, Susquehanna Slim, and I headed up the trail at 6:45. The initial climb of over 1000 feet in 0.8 of a mile was one I remembered from a previous trip to the Whites. That time I had been hiking south. The climb north didn't seem quite as challenging. We reached South Twin at 4902 feet in less than an hour. Unfortunately cloud cover eliminated the view. From South Twin we had to walk over a short boulder field before reaching another 4000 footer, Mt. Guyot. By this time the clouds had dissipated enough for a view to the west.

From Mt. Guyot we descended almost 2000 feet to Zealand Falls Hut where we stopped for lunch. Several day-hikers and section-hikers were milling around. One hit us with a barrage of questions after discovering that we were thru-hikers. Banzai answered most. The questioner said, "That's amazing!" approximately 87 times during the ten minutes of interrogation. Like so many others, he and his wife marveled at what we are doing. No one yet has looked at me and said, "That's insane." I kind of wonder why. The hut crew offered us some complimentary soup since we were thru-hikers. I declined but the others accepted their generosity. I've never much cared for black bean soup.

After lunch we embarked on the final 7.9 miles to Crawford Notch. The gentler terrain was welcomed. Along the way we met a southbound thru-hiker from Georgia. A recent graduate of Emory in Atlanta and a Braves fan, Gospel said he planned to go into the ministry in the United Methodist Church. Gospel is the first hiker I've met from my home state in a good while.

So with comfortable temps and hikeable terrain, my buddies and I reached Crawford Notch before five. Mike was waiting to drive us to Gorham for a meal and a room. Our driver and support person leaves tomorrow, so we will then have to go back to hitching rides and using shuttle services. It's been good having Banzai's brother with us for the past two weeks, but now he must return to the regular world. In some ways I'd like to join him. That time, however, will come soon enough. For now the Presidential Range awaits as Banzai, Pilgrim, Slim, and I meet Jackson, Pierce, Eisenhower, and Monroe tomorrow on the Appalachian Trail.

## August 1, Lakes of the Clouds

It is 5:50 PM. I am sitting on a worn wooden bench at the Lakes of the Clouds Hut. Banzai, Pilgrim, Susquehanna Slim, and I all received work for stay. Thru-hikers Finder, Fatty, Roadrunner, Red Rocket, Star Child, Hermes, and Splash are also here. This AMC hut has bunk space for 90. It is full tonight. Most of the occupants are day-hikers who walked up on one of the many White Mountain trails. Lakes of the Clouds is nestled between Mt. Monroe and Mt. Washington. We crossed Monroe in a heavy fog to get here about an hour ago, just before the rain commenced. We will tackle Washington in the morning. We are in the midst of the Presidential Range, arguably the most spectacular section of the Appalachian Trail.

Earlier today Mike dropped my hiking buddies and me at Crawford Notch before heading back to Virginia. We immediately faced a 2000 foot climb up to Webster Cliffs to start our day. Within the first half hour I took a fall when I lost my balance at the beginning of a rock scramble. Other than a couple of minor scratches, I came out OK. During the climb I was passed by Fatty and later saw Finder at a scenic outcrop. I had not seen her since PA. Goose and All the Way also passed me. I had last seen All the Way just south of Bland, VA. Banzai hiked ahead with the faster folks, leaving Pilgrim, Slim, and me to fend for ourselves.

The trail presented us with numerous technical segments as we eventually climbed to over 4000 feet at Mt. Jackson. Unbelievable panoramic views were visible in all directions for much of the day. After summiting Mt. Jackson we made our way to the Mizpah Springs Hut where we stopped for lunch. While there I talked a good while with crew member Eric. The young man gladly provided us with trail and weather information. Expecting afternoon storms, we wanted to be sure we could reach the Lakes of the Clouds before they hit. The 3.9 miles between the huts usually requires four hours to hike. Pilgrim, Slim, and I would do it in just over three. With exposed ridgeline, we continued to enjoy unbelievably beautiful views all afternoon.

From the summit of Mt. Pierce we had views of Eisenhower, Monroe, and Washington in the far distance. After Pierce it was on to Eisenhower. The A.T. does not go over the summit of Mt. Eisenhower; however, there is a spur trail to the summit. Within a few hundred feet of the summit, the trail circumvents Eisenhower toward Mt. Monroe. Crossing Monroe, we noticed the increasing clouds. Literally within ten minutes, all views were gone. The wind velocity increased as visibility diminished. I hiked ahead, hurriedly trying to make the hut before the inevitable rainfall. When it came into view I waited at an intersection, where four trails meet, for the others. Then the three of us hiked the last hundred yards to the hut together.

Waiting for dinner I thought about how fortunate I was to experience the awe-inspiring vistas that surrounded me today. The hike was tough but manageable. I'm hiking with care and deliberation at times, yet when the trail offers the opportunity, with more speed. Today was a good day. Even though it took over nine hours to hike the 11.2 miles, I definitely felt encouraged with my effort. It's all good.

After dinner the thru-hikers were given their work for stay duties. Slim and I were assigned the task of rebinding visitor log books that dated back to 1961. Sarah, the lead crew member, made the assignments. We were grateful since the others had kitchen chores. We both liked chatting with nine-year-old Avery, a lad who gravitated to thru-hikers, asking an assortment of questions. The little fellow, who said he aspired to a thru-hike himself someday, told us his trail name was Puke. It seems a couple of thru-hikers had dubbed Avery after he had gotten sick at Madison Hut the previous night. Young Puke seemed to be thoroughly enjoying his hut-to-hut adventure. Finally when Puke's mom beckoned him to brush his teeth, Slim and I finished our job before joining the others on the floor of the hut. Settling into my sleeping bag, I lay and thought about the future. Another challenging day awaited with the ascent of Mt. Washington, the next major climb on the Appalachian Trail.

## August 2, Mt. Washington

I'm at the summit of Mt. Washington, elevation 6288 feet. The greatest wind velocity anywhere was recorded here sometime in the 1930's. It is cloudy outside, or should I say, the mountain is in the clouds. There are no views. The forecast is not encouraging. The temperature is 52 with wind gusts. It is not a pleasant day for a hike. So after hiking the 1.3 miles from Lakes of the Clouds hut, Banzai, Pilgrim, Susquehanna Slim, and I are taking the remainder of the day off. We are waiting for a shuttle to Gorham. The weather has dictated our plans for the day.

After a restless night on the floor at the Lakes of the Clouds hut, I awoke to the sound of pots and pans clattering in the kitchen at 5:30. The space I chose to repose for the evening happened to be near the path to the restrooms. It seemed like each of the 90 bunkers must have gone twice because the traffic flowed steadily throughout the night. Since the thru-hikers who were working for stay were relegated to a small portion of floor space in the dining hall, we had to arise by 6:00.

This morning after a breakfast of cold leftover oatmeal, I volunteered to sweep bunk rooms. Others in the group of ten also straightened and cleaned the rooms. So after our work was completed, we didn't find ourselves leaving for the trail until almost 10:00. With the late start and a less than desirable weather forecast, an adjustment to plans was necessary. In fact, when we emerged from the hut, visibility was at 75 feet. Due to the cloud cover we had zero views on the hike up Mt. Washington. Needing to watch every step over the various-sized rocks, it really didn't matter. It took us about an hour to cover the 1.3 miles to the summit. Due to the adverse conditions, I wore my rain jacket, gloves, and long hiking pants.

At the top we took some pictures by the summit sign and then ate an early lunch. Still debating what to do, eventually we all agreed that starting a hike in these conditions was not smart. So Pilgrim, Slim, and I bought tickets for the van shuttle via the auto road. Patty, our driver, told us that since we were thru-hikers and had left the summit due to weather, that our tickets would be good for a round trip. We were most appreciative given that the tickets were $30. Pilgrim and I got the $5 senior discount. Banzai decided to forgo the shuttle and try to hitch. Turns out he arrived back in Gorham ahead of the rest of us.

When Pilgrim, Slim, and I reached Pinkham Notch, we still needed to find a way to town. While we were trying to find a shuttle Steady walked up. Spirit had just dropped him off. She gladly drove us to Gorham. So for the rest of the afternoon I relaxed. Later in the evening Spirit joined us for dinner and drove us to drop some gear at a hostel where we will stay tomorrow night. With 332.9 miles remaining I'm getting anxious. I know I need to be patient, but after four months it's hard. Tomorrow will be another grueling day with potential rain in the forecast. There are more mountains waiting to be climbed on the northward journey up the Appalachian Trail.

## August 3, Gorham, NH

Weather always becomes a factor in any thru-hike attempt of the Appalachian Trail. For the first time since I began this odyssey, the elements forced my buddies and me to not only alter our plans but to shift the order in which we were navigating the trail as well. With a 30 degree wind chill and wind gusts of 50 MPH, hiking off of Mt. Washington today just didn't seem practical. Since rain is in the forecast for the next two days, we have decided to wait until Tuesday to continue at the summit. In the meantime I'll take today off before hiking from Pinkham Notch to US 2 over the next two days. This will also necessitate a night in the woods. Meanwhile plans are in motion to get the group to Maine.

Having pre-arranged a ride back to the Mt. Washington auto road with Spirit, we kept the part of the itinerary which included a stop by the Gorham McDonald's for breakfast. Also partaking of a meal were Johnny Walker, Puffy, Gator, and Misery.

"Looks like you made it through the root canal recovery OK," I commented to Misery.

The likable goateed lad responded, "I feel great. We are about to be in Maine!"

The four young folks went on to tell our older group how they had spent the previous night in an abandoned house in Gorham. Banzai appeared to be regaining enthusiasm and excitement as he listened to Misery's account of their last few days.

With only minor hesitation Banzai suddenly declared, "I'm going to hike ahead with Misery and the others."

We had recognized the younger hiker's growing impatience since Mike had departed for Virginia. So Banzai was asking to be released from his DBM contract so that he could immediately join the group of Johnny Walker, Puffy, Gator, and Misery. The younger lads were all hiking today, and Banzai was itching to get out of New Hampshire. Susquehanna Slim, Pilgrim, and I hated to see our young friend go; however, we understood his request. Reluctantly, we all agreed. It had been good having Banzai as part of the team since Connecticut. We will miss him.

After breakfast Spirit graciously agreed to take the three of us to Walmart where we could purchase supplies. While we were shopping she even baked us some cookies in the RV oven. Then she drove us to the Hiker's Paradise Hostel and wished us well on the rest of our hike. I had first met Spirit near Buena Vista, VA. The soft-spoken lady, who always has kindness in her eyes, has helped me on many occasions. This would be the final time that I would say goodbye to Spirit. So my buddies and I checked in at the hostel, got our bed linens, and made ourselves at home in a place about as far removed from paradise as I could imagine. Receiving Ninja Turtle sheets for my bunk brought back a memory or two.

After settling in I decided to give Sweet Tooth a call. She informed me that Molar Man was hiking a section just south of where we are today. As the conversation continued Sweet Tooth said that she was also in Gorham. I invited her to join us for a pizza at an establishment just up the road. Over lunch we discussed our hiking plans for the next few days. Coincidentally, Molar Man plans to hike off of Mt. Washington on Tuesday as well. With a spot on the team after Banzai's release, it looks like we could have a new member if we can work out the contract negotiations.

After lunch Slim, Pilgrim, and I spent a goodly amount of time discussing logistics for Maine. First, however, we have to finish the Whites and get out of New Hampshire. That will take at least four more days. So for now we wait. I'd rather be hiking, but I feel better knowing that we have a sane plan in place. Rain or shine, early tomorrow we'll be back on the trail at Pinkham Notch, leaving the treacherous Madison descent for Tuesday. I think it's still all coming together as my hiking buddies and I prepare for the next step in the journey on the Appalachian Trail.

## August 4, Carter Notch Hut

So again, Burns' quote rings true: "The best laid plans of mice and men." When Bruno dropped Pilgrim, Slim, and me at Pinkham Notch this morning, our intention was to hike a 13.1 mile day to the Imp Campsite. But when cold rain started pelting us a little before 2:00, after only a 6.2 mile day which took over six hours, we realized an early stop was mandatory.

Thankfully, there were four bunk openings at the Carter Notch Hut. We bit the bullet and paid the $93 fee for the night. None of us wanted work for stay. We were happy to pay for the bunk and hot meal. I drank six cups of hot tea during the cold, rainy afternoon and at supper.

The day had started well. With a gentle trail for the first quarter mile, we were able to quickly get back into the hiking regimen. The flat terrain around a pond was short-lived. And when the climbing began, it was intense. The task was to ascend four peaks of Wildcat Mountain. The climb was over 2000 feet to the first, peak E. I have no idea how they are labeled; however, the second peak we reached was D. At the top of D were two picnic tables next to an operating gondola. On this overcast, cold morning, the gondola operator looked kind of lonely.

Early in the day we hiked near Goose and All the Way. After the break on peak D we helped each other find the correct trail. At times few white blazes can be found in New Hampshire. It seemed like a long while before we located one on the short descent.

Finally Goose hollered in the distance, "I've found a blaze."

From there we had to ascend again to peak C and eventually to 4422 foot peak A. The trail then got really tough on the descent. Even though it was only 600 feet, the rocks continued to present great difficulty.

For me, these downhills posed the greatest challenge. I often found myself needing to hug a ledge to keep my balance. I hiked most of the day with only one pole. This allowed me to have a free hand to pull myself up the rockfaces or to grasp small trees at the edge of the trail for support. Still I had to sit on my seat and slide a few times due to the slanted, slick slabs. It was just all real time-consuming and frustrating to be hiking one mile or less an hour. After averaging over 18 miles a day through Vermont, the slower, deliberate pace tries my patience. It also requires a concerted focus at all times. Being someone who likes to think and daydream while I walk, this method of traversing the trail is downright torture.

So when we reached the Carter Notch Hut in the cold rain, we called it a day. Pilgrim and I are sharing a bunk room with Rodney and his 12-year-old son, Josh. Josh is working on summiting all the 4000 footers in New

Hampshire. Slim is in another room. At dinner we sat with members of a large family who were out for three days. Bill from Philly was to my right. When he discovered that we were thru-hikers he asked many questions. Another member of the family said her father had worked at this hut in the 1940's. Carter is the oldest original hut in the Whites.

So now I'm in my bunk writing. Pilgrim is trying to sleep. He strained his back washing dishes at Lakes of the Clouds, and it's still bothering him. The father and son appear to be reading. It's dark outside. We are all using our headlamps. I will sleep soon because my alarm is set for 5:00. With predicted wind chills below freezing on the higher elevation summits and wind gusts up to 60 MPH in the afternoon, we plan to get an early start. Hopefully we will have the strength and willpower to reach US 2, a hike of 14.9 miles which could take 15 hours, as we desperately try to soon get out of New Hampshire, the toughest state by far on the Appalachian Trail.

## August 5, US 2, Gorham, NH

Howling winds awoke me several times throughout the night. When my watch alarm sounded at 5:00, a blustery day awaited. It took a tremendous amount of determination to leave the comfort and safety of Carter Notch Hut for a day in the elements. When Pilgrim, Susquehanna Slim, and I departed from our overnight accommodations, the wind chill was below freezing and wind gusts on the peaks were expected to reach 60 MPH. Fortunately there was no rain in the forecast. I began the day in running tights under my hiking shorts, a fleece, my rain jacket, gloves, and a toboggan hat. It was downright cold!

The hike today began with a climb up to Carter Dome at 4832 feet. At the summit the wind gusts made it impossible to stay very long. From Carter Dome we descended briefly before summiting another 4000 footer, Mt. Hight. It was here that we made a tactical error, or should I say another tactical error. When we reached the summit we took the wrong trail off the top and inadvertently hiked in a circle for about a mile, eventually standing by a trail sign that we had already passed. It was disheartening to have to repeat a portion of trail, especially since we were only hiking about a mile an hour.

When we got going in the right direction, we walked through Zeta Pass before summiting two more 4000 footers, Middle Carter Mountain and North Carter Mountain. The surprise of the day came on the descent of North Carter. We were greeted with a series of extremely slick, dangerous rock slabs. On a scale of 1-10 my stress level registered about a 12. Perilous is an understatement. To try to keep from falling to my demise, I hugged the tree-line at times and at others sat down and inched myself down the wet, slippery rocks. It was nerve-wrenching.

By the time we got to the trail to the Imp Campsite, it was past 1:30. We had only hiked 6.9 miles in almost seven hours. Realizing we still had 8.0 miles to hike and less than seven hours of light, we considered our options. The preferable one was to reach US 2 and a motel room in Gorham. Option two was to stop at the Rattle River Shelter, a little less than two miles from the road. Darkness would dictate our decision. After the trail to Imp we were confronted with one more climb, 3991 foot Mt. Mariah. With only a few stretches that required rock climbing, we reached its peak around 3:15.

From there the trail became much more agreeable. Running parallel to the Rattle River for a while, and crossing the river twice, the trail finally allowed my stress level to fall back to a one for the remainder of the afternoon. The final three miles, in fact, consisted of a gentle path. It was the first I can remember in the Whites. So Slim set his three-mile-an-hour pace as we headed for the road. We reached it a little before 7:00, still having taken 13 hours to hike 14.9 miles.

When we arrived at the road Slim phoned Bruno for a shuttle. In the meantime a car with Tennessee plates stopped to ask if we needed a ride. When Bruno showed up in his small truck Pilgrim and I took the offer from Rainman. Rainman and Professor plan to continue a section-hike tomorrow on Mt. Washington, which will end in a few days at Grafton Notch in Maine. Slim rode with Bruno. When we got to the hostel my buddies and I decided to upgrade to a motel room with three beds.

Today proved to be another challenging one. The steep, rocky descents and ascents can unnerve even the most seasoned hiker. For me, they can be downright petrifying. Every time I find myself in a precarious position, I think that I just want to be on firm ground at sea level again. Then when I get to town I have to immediately begin getting myself prepared mentally for another day of danger. The Georgia poet James Dickey once said, "if you're bored with life, risk it." I'm not bored with life, but sometimes I surely feel like I'm putting it on the line. So tomorrow I'll head back up to Mt. Washington to walk north off its summit up the Appalachian Trail.

## August 6, Madison Spring Hut

Molar Man made his debut as the new fourth member of the "Rawhide" gang in the Mt. Washington to Madison Spring Hut episode today. On a beautiful, sunny 42 degree morning, visibility at the summit was listed at 120 miles. A worker said there are only about six days a year with this nice a forecast. Our decision to forgo this 13.5 mile stretch until today and tomorrow turned out to be an outstanding one. The summit we experienced today compared in no way with the Mt. Washington of last Saturday when visibility was listed at 75 feet. After a day in the clouds then, we enjoyed panoramic views throughout the day today. The awe-inspiring vistas made me appreciate God's creation to its fullest. Again I don't think there are suitable adjectives to describe the enormity of the landscape.

My day began with breakfast at McDonald's in Gorham with Molar Man, Sweet Tooth, Susquehanna Slim, and Pilgrim. After the meal we drove to the auto road at the base of Mt. Washington. At 9:00 our van driver, Dexter, drove us to the summit. We started the descent northward on the A.T. a little before ten. Almost immediately Molar Man and Slim put distance between themselves and Pilgrim and me. I hiked deliberately from the outset, paying close attention to each footfall. The trail consisted of moderate-size boulders slanted at various angles. The downhill always presents a greater challenge for me which is why my pace was slow all day.

As we hiked off the summit of Mt. Washington, the cog railroad, which runs parallel to the trail, came into view. All the remaining mountains in the Presidential Range loomed in the distance. I admired with respect and reverence the prodigious formations. Over the course of the 5.7 mile day I would hike near the summit of Mt. Clay, Mt. Jefferson, and Mt. Adams. The rocky terrain made the miles go slowly, but that mattered little with the scenery. Every few minutes I just stopped to admire.

About a mile before reaching the Madison Spring Hut, I met day-hiker Emerald from Vermont. A retired teacher, he told me that he was working on completing something called "the grid." He hopes to climb each of the forty-eight 4000 foot mountains in each month. I told him I'm motivating myself these days with the motto, "Every step I take is a step I will never have to take again." I can't imagine climbing each of these New Hampshire mountains in every month. The thought fatigues my mind even more than it already is. I really appreciated Emerald's company over about half a mile.

Just past the intersection with the Airline Trail, I reached a peak where I could see the Madison Spring Hut in a valley. When I arrived all my buddies were already there. We had the option of work for stay or to pay $10 for leftover food and a space to sleep on the floor. We opted to pay. Still we have to wait until 7:45 to eat. Hey, it's a roof and much nicer than a shelter. This is my fourth hut. I've been a paying guest twice and eaten after the guests twice. The main difference is the temperature of the food. That's the only downside. Our food is often cold.

So as I write this the guests are being served. It smells good. My buddies and I have been relegated to a table in the corner with no food. It beats standing outside in the cold. More importantly, I'm among good company. Another thru-hiker, Bird, who is from Germany, has joined us at our table. Stretch and Barking Spider also just arrived as did Restless Cowboy who I last saw in CT. As I wait to eat at least I have a view of the mountain ranges in the distance. It's all good. Tomorrow I'll hike back to Pinkham Notch, leaving only 16.5 miles to Maine on the Appalachian Trail.

## August 7, Pinkham Notch

The Whites are done....and I survived. On another postcard-like day, I hiked up and over arguably the most difficult mountain in the Presidential Range, Mt. Madison. It was tough. No, it was beyond tough. It was ridiculously difficult. It is a mountain I may admire at a distance in the future. It is a mountain I never intend to step foot on again. Once was definitely enough. On that stress level of 1-10, this time I hit about a 15. With focused, deliberate steps, I managed to stay upright. Still it took almost two hours (1:50 to be exact) to reach the summit from the Madison Spring Hut. Distance: exactly one mile. And after reaching the summit, there still remained the equally perilous descent. It was tough, even rougher than the climb, but I survived.

The day started with the clamoring of pots and pans at 5:30. We thru-hikers who were sleeping in the dining area had to pack up and be gone by 6:30 when the tables were set for the paying guests. I had pushed two benches together to make myself a bed last night and slept rather well. After packing my gear and consuming two pop tarts and some cheese with a cup of hot tea I purchased for $1.00, I was out the door. Official start time for today's hike was 6:44. Since Molar Man wanted to do some reconnaissance work for the next few days, he and Susquehanna Slim left about an half hour earlier.

Looking up at the massive Mt. Madison made me a bit queasy even before I began the ascent. A sea of various-size boulders, many at a variety of angles, awaited my every step. Few were flat. Many required hand maneuvering to navigate. Each offered a challenge. A false step at any moment could have proven disastrous. I walked carefully, often using my hands to steady myself. I even telescoped down one pole and placed it in my pack. That allowed me to have one free hand at all times. The painstakingly slow climb played on the nerves. Still I paused often to admire the views in all directions. The day was so clear that the buildings atop Mt. Washington were visible.

After over three hours Pilgrim and I finally found ourselves below tree-line. The steep downhill continued, but at least trees lined each side of the trail. A stepping stone pattern offered an easier descent at times. At others rockfaces required more thought. Occasionally, although rarely, a level portion of trail appeared. Usually it was short-lived and often muddy. Even in the Whites, black mud regularly appears. Despite the mud, these brief respites were appreciated. It was over four hours into the hike when Pilgrim and I finally reached the Osgood Trail intersection. We had walked three miles.

About this time we caught Bird and Bella, a hiker from Pensacola. I hiked behind them for much of the afternoon and enjoyed chatting with Bella. She told me that she had recently retired from the US Navy. I also met southbounder Potter, a young man from Tennessee. Potter is a potter who said he had started his thru-hike exactly a month ago today.

So as the afternoon progressed the trail became more agreeable. At each intersection Pilgrim and I conferenced to make sure we were on the A.T. Blazes are often infrequent in New Hampshire, and the A.T. coincides with other named trails. The final trail it uses before reaching Pinkham Notch is the Old Jackson Rd. Trail. This trail crosses the Auto Rd. to Mt. Washington. Pilgrim and I took our final break there before "taking it to the house." The trail gratefully transformed into a "trail" again for those last two miles.

When we reached the visitors' center at Pinkham Notch, I phoned Maryann at the motel/hostel for a shuttle. Bird and Bella shared it into Gorham. Slim already had a room and had bought some special snacks for Pilgrim and me. Later we went out to eat and then to Walmart to re-supply for two nights in the woods. I am about to be in one of the most remote parts of the entire trail. As I get ready to head into Maine, I continue to appreciate all the support and prayers. After tomorrow, one more state on the Appalachian Trail.

### August 8, Gentian Pond Shelter

I'm sitting in the Gentian Pond Shelter. It is raining. I have been here since before 4:00. It's going to be a long night. There are three SOBO's here: Prism, Foxy, and the Doctor. Prism had not heard of her namesake from Oscar Wilde's *The Importance of Being Earnest*. I keep hearing in my mind Lady Bracknell asking, "Prism, where is that baby, Prism?" This Prism shows me a picture of her rainbow Mohawk. Now much of the color and form have disappeared. Prism has much information to offer about Maine. Many of her descriptions are in the form of warnings. I keep telling her that I am not interested. She keeps talking anyway. Northbounder Padawan, a high school student from Florida, just walked up, drenched. The shelter sleeps 14, so there is plenty of room. Others may also arrive. It could get crowded. Time will tell.

With the Whites now history, I awoke in a much more relaxed frame of mind. Pilgrim, Susquehanna Slim, and I rode with Molar Man and Sweet Tooth back to the trail at about 7:30. The first mile of today's hike was on two roads. When we finally reached the woods, a 1700 foot ascent of Mt. Hayes greeted us. Most of the trail consisted of smaller rocks, dirt, roots, and mud. In other words, the A.T. of Vermont had returned. I did not complain. After the treacherous terrain in the Whites, the mundane tree-lined trail of today was a welcome sight.

At the summit of Mt. Hayes we took a break. Slim wondered if the mountain was named for Rutherford B. Hayes. Since he had missed the Presidentials, maybe old Rutherford B. had been assigned a lesser mountain. We went on to suggest other prominent Hayeses for which Mt. Hayes may have been named. Helen Hayes, Isaac Hayes, Gabby Hayes, or "Bullet" Bob Hayes perhaps. We thru-hikers continue to struggle for worthwhile conversation at times. So on we hiked toward Cascade Mountain.

The trail continued to be agreeable for the most part; however, some sections of rock slabs that required the use of hands still existed. Whether up or down, they took more time. Even though the trail for most of the day presented few difficulties, we still needed seven hours to hike the 11.8 miles. We did take several breaks. We also passed three beautiful ponds. Each made me think about my brother. They seemed so peaceful and isolated.

So now there are still three hours to good dark, and there's really nothing to do. If I get in my sleeping bag now, I'll fall asleep and wake up at ten or eleven. Then I'll lie awake until past midnight. There is no good way to relax in a shelter. But I am dry and among interesting people. This is also my last night in New Hampshire. We are 4.7 miles from the Maine border. Even though the next few days will still be tough, at least I'll be in the final state. About three more weeks on the Appalachian Trail.

# 14

# Maine

**August 9, the Cabin**

Hard rain awoke me in the middle of the night. At daylight a steady drizzle continued. Young Padawan walked away from the shelter as the rain's intensity increased. With a 9.6 mile day planned, which included going over potentially dangerous, slippery rock slabs on Success and Goose Eye Mountains, we hesitatingly changed our plans. Pilgrim has been experiencing troubling back pain for almost a week. Molar Man, Slim, and I agreed with him that hiking today bordered on insanity. Our two options were to zero at the shelter or hike the 3.5 mile Austin Brook Trail to a road where we could get a shuttle to Andover, ME. We opted for the second.

So in a light rain we bailed for today to the alternate trail. Earl, from the Cabin, said he could pick us up at North Rd. around 10:00. Over some slick rockfaces, on a trail that had overnight transformed into a stream, we headed to the road and safety. Fortunately the rain subsided for the most part during the two-hour walk. The trail eventually became a very agreeable woods road for about the final two miles. Despite the slippery roots and standing water, we hiked rather quickly.

The only difficulty with the alternate trail was the water crossings. Due to the heavy rains, stepping stone rocks had become submerged. At one stream I slipped from a rock into the water. Since my feet were already wet I didn't worry about the other streams. When I didn't feel like I could plant my foot safely on a rock, I just stepped in the water. This occurred three times. I think we all got our feet wet before we reached North Rd.

Just before another hard downpour Earl arrived to shuttle us to the Cabin in Andover. Earl and Marge have been welcoming hikers for nineteen years. Hikers themselves, they also are more than willing to share a wealth of trail knowledge with anyone who cares to listen. Honey and Bear, their trail identities, are some of the most genuinely kind and sincere folks I have met since I started the hike. They open their main home to hikers and even offer breakfast and supper for extremely modest prices. The bunkhouse, which is attached to the home, sleeps eight. Susquehanna Slim, Pilgrim, and I got the last three bunks. Molar Man and Sweet Tooth were able to land the one private room.

After cleaning up we all drove to The Red Hen for lunch. The continued hard rain didn't deter us from an enjoyable meal. I topped mine off with a piece of homemade blueberry pie. For the rest of the afternoon I just rested. I took a nap and chatted with other hikers. Late in the day I received a text message from Speck.

"You guys are smart to watch the weather. Hopefully you'll have nothing but blue skies for the rest of your hike."

After texting about running for a while, Speck asked, "How are you?"

My reply was straightforward. "I'm very tired physically and mentally. The next 80 miles will be very tough. After that hopefully we can pick up the pace. With good weather I may still make the 28th. No later than Sept. 3, hopefully. This is just so hard. I'm just glad I'm still healthy and hiking."

In her usual encouraging tone, Speck responded, "I am sure it is extremely exhausting in every way. It has to be hard to be forced to take more time when you're so ready to be done. Hang in there. EVERYBODY that has done it says how difficult NH and ME are. You are healthy and will do just fine. Take your time and stay healthy! It'll soon be a memory— a wonderful, wonderful memory!"

Smiling, I thought, "Yes. It will soon be a wonderful, wonderful memory."

## August 10, Full Goose Shelter

On a sunny, mild, windy day I entered my 14th and last state on the Appalachian Trial. Along with Pilgrim, Susquehanna Slim, and Molar Man, I also passed the 1900 mile mark. So as I sit in the Full Goose Shelter this evening, I've found myself thinking back on some early days on the trail. On what should be a cold night, I commented to Molar Man that I'm glad we're not in the Smokies. It was at Spence Field Shelter that we first met. Seems like years ago. Time continues to have little relevance on the Appalachian Trail.

My day began when the alarm on my watch sounded at 3:30. Since we wanted breakfast and an early start, the before-dawn beginning to the day was necessary. Plus we had to hike the 3.5 miles back to the Gentian Pond Shelter on the Austin Brook Trail and the 0.2 from the shelter to the A.T. We only get credit for a 9.6 mile day even though we hiked a total of 13.3 miles. The miles on the Austin Brook trail went quickly. We then stopped briefly at the shelter before heading on to the A.T. Pumpkin Head, a northbounder that I had heard of but never met, and Spacey were still there. When we did finally begin the A.T. portion of the day it was 7:48.

Throughout the day the trail offered a variety of difficulties. We climbed Mt. Success, Mt. Carlo, and the west, east, and north peaks of Goose Eye Mountain. And of course every time we ascended, we had to descend. Each mountain posed some type of challenge. From slippery, wet rockfaces that required pulling myself up ledges, to straight, dangerous rock slabs that I had to gingerly walk up or slide down, the trail didn't really offer up anything new. We left New Hampshire with a short rocky ascent and were greeted in Maine with a climb up Mt. Carlo. All in all, the trail still demanded respect and focus.

By far the biggest challenge of the day came on the west peak of Goose Eye Mountain. Some of the rocks were so steep that rebar had been drilled into the surfaces. After climbing up the rebar I still had to hoist myself up on top of the slab. When we finally reached the summit of West peak, the wind gusts had to be at least 60 MPH. I had a difficult time just standing.

Due to the wind I didn't pause. It was important to get back below tree-line as quickly as possible.

In addition to the wind, extensive bogs of squishy black mud appeared on almost every flat area of trail. Slim and I both made the mistake of stepping in the oozing substance. It literally came up to our knees. On numerous occasions I walked several yards off trail to try to avoid the quagmire. It was a downright nuisance. Plus many of the boards over the boggy sections were submerged due to yesterday's hard rain. As my mother has been known to say, "If it's not one thing, it's another." From slippery roots and rocks to jagged rockfaces, to the oozing mud and puddling water, it seems like there is constantly an obstacle around every bend.

Yet despite the challenges I have made it to Maine. Darkness is approaching and the shelter is steadily filling. Thru-hikers headed north meet hikers headed south. Trashcan, Hoops, Spacey, Burning Man, Hakuna Matata, and others whose names I didn't get are here. A pleasant group has assembled. Stories are being shared. The A.T. community is family. Everyone is willing to make a little shelter space for late arrivers. So as I settle in for the evening all is good. Tomorrow my buddies and I will tackle what many consider the most difficult mile on the A.T. as I hike my second day in Maine on the Appalachian Trail.

## August 11, Grafton Notch

It's past 9:00 PM. I'm at the brink of exhaustion, yet I need to write and post today's entry. I hope to be asleep within the next two hours. If I closed my eyes I would be in two minutes. It has been a physically and mentally tiring day. With only 267.2 miles until the finish line, it seems like I should be getting ready to celebrate. Instead I continue to find myself facing difficult challenges and often in precarious situations every day. There's no way to enjoy what I am doing due to the stress I am under. If folks really want to know what thru-hiking the A.T. is all about, I can sum it up in one word: hard. Make that HARD.

After a restless night's sleep at the Full Goose Shelter, I awoke at first light. Molar Man was already dressed and ready to hike. Susquehanna

Slim was getting ready. Pilgrim still snoozed in his sleeping bag. Begrudgingly I forced myself from my cozy bedding to ready myself for a day I had been dreading. My fears would soon be realized as I hiked what easily was one of my five toughest days on the trail. A good description would be somewhere between treacherous and brutal. For those who have hiked this section and describe it otherwise, my apologies.

So after a less than nutritious breakfast my buddies and I headed up the trail toward the Mahoosuc Notch, reputedly the hardest mile on the Appalachian Trail. As we walked I thought about a message Banzai had sent a few days earlier.

"DB, just a warning – the days before and after the Maine border are intense. I did Mahoosuc Notch in the rain which was a bad idea. On other places I fell twice and got minor cuts. Do not do this section while it's wet. There are lots of sheer rockfaces. I'm headed to buy grippier shoes." – BANZAI

The duration of the notch from the south end to the north end actually covers 1.3 miles. It would take us almost two hours to complete the infamous section. Some call it a fun mile. I may have too in my youth when I still possessed agility. It was definitely different climbing through, over, and under the boulder maze. We stayed together during the scramble, each offering suggestions for the most passable route. For the most part we chose to go over the giant rocks. Only once did we have to remove our packs to crawl through.

When the traverse finally ended we were immediately confronted with the Mahoosuc Arm, a lengthy ascent with long segments of sheer rockface to walk, climb, or crawl up. Like many other times, I clung to trees on the erosion line when the opportunity existed. Pulling myself up using spindly trees or roots afforded me the safest passage up the mountain. Within about a half mile from the summit we paused for lunch. Sitting in the middle of the trail on a rock, I thought about how tired and miserable I felt with over half the hike remaining. It was a challenge getting going again.

After the Arm there was no break. We then had to deal with Old Speck, a mountain I had not even expected to be a challenge. I was dead wrong. Exposed rockface near the summit required precision rock climbing. There appeared to be no room for error. At one point I stood almost petrified staring upward at a jagged rock that had to be climbed. As I pondered what to do, Burning Man happened to show up. The route he took looked like the safest so I followed. It was a relief to get past this section. The beauty of Speck Pond offered the only positive for the entire day.

Eventually we reached Speck Pond Shelter which left 3.8 miles to Grafton Notch. Those miles proved to be the most agreeable of the entire day. With a sane trail again, we quickly made our way to the notch and road. Sweet Tooth had not yet arrived, so Slim, Pilgrim, and I waited while Molar Man hitched a ride to Bethel where he could get cell service to call her. When we finally did get back to the Cabin, Honey had gratefully saved us some supper. Four tired hikers ate well.

So far Maine has been just as difficult as New Hampshire. I knew it was going to be tough. I just thought I would be able to hike without stress again. So far agreeable trail has been limited. It has been fortunate for me, however, that every time I find myself in a very real predicament, someone comes along to help. When I saw Speck pond today I thought of Don. I know that when others aren't around, he is. Today was again a challenge. Tomorrow may be as well. But regardless of the difficulty, I'm still making my way northward, slowly but steadily, on the Appalachian Trail.

### August 12, East B Hill Rd.

On another beautiful, sunny, mild Maine day I found myself hiking happy again. With a less difficult trail to traverse today, and a slackpack for the first time in over two weeks, Molar Man, Susquehanna Slim, and I covered the 10.3 miles from Grafton Notch to East B Hill Rd. in right at seven hours. That even included a thirty minute break for lunch at the Frye Notch Lean-to. Throughout the day I enjoyed the company, I enjoyed the views, but more importantly I just enjoyed hiking. All in all, it was a good day to be on the trail.

From the outset at Grafton Notch my hiking buddies and I were faced with the only challenging part of the day, the climb to the west peak of Baldpate at 3662 feet. Most of the ascent consisted of "regular" trail even though an occasional sheer rockface appeared. I regained some of my hiking composure and walked up most rather than hugging the tree-line. Since the rocks were relatively dry and not too slanted, this method of hiking proved somewhat easier. Even over a few rocks that were still slightly wet, I maintained this approach, following closely behind Molar Man and Slim. I missed Pilgrim, however, who had stayed behind to have a medical issue addressed.

After reaching the west peak of Baldpate we crossed a short notch before climbing up the east peak. The east peak posed more of a challenge, but not one I wasn't up to today. I put my head down and steadily walked up the creviced rockface to the summit at 3810 feet. Views from the top extended for several peaks to the west, including the Presidential Range in the Whites. Mt. Washington was even visible with only its summit in the clouds. I don't know how many miles could be seen, but it had to be close to one hundred with blue skies in all directions. I stared into the distance with awe. Again, the views were beyond spectacular.

From the east peak of Baldpate we descended about 1500 feet to the Frye Notch Lean-to, where we stopped for lunch. In Maine the word Lean-to is used in place of shelter. They are still the same three-sided wooden structures that usually sleep between six and twelve. After the break we ascended briefly a "no-name" mountain. I like these mountains without identities. They mostly are nondescript and pose little difficulty. Views are nice; however, sometimes it's also good to have a break from the challenging ascents. All the mountains that may be dangerous have names. After the short climb we descended another agreeable section of trail to Dunn Notch and Falls. Several water crossings occurred, but all had well-placed rocks for hopping across. I managed to stay vertical and dry throughout the hike.

We took our last break at the falls. As usual I leaned my hiking poles against a tree. Apparently a gust of wind knocked one down toward the water. Fortunately it hung up on the way down and Slim was able to retrieve it. While there we met Blondie, a southbound thru-hiker doing a northbound slackpack today. He passed us on the walk to East B Hill Rd. and rode back to the Cabin with the rest of us. The only northbound thru-hiker I saw all day was Spacey, a quiet young man who seems to enjoy his solitude.

So I'm suddenly just as encouraged about hiking today as I was discouraged after yesterday's more treacherous section. With 256.9 miles still remaining I certainly needed a morale boost. I think Baldpate gave it to me. It's only a little before 5:00. I've had a good hike, showered, and will join others at the supper table of Honey and Bear in about an hour. A cool breeze filters through the trees. All is well because I'm hiking happy again, headed north on the Appalachian Trail.

### August 13, South Arm Rd., Andover, Maine

I'm sitting at the lunch counter of the General Store and Diner in Andover. Susquehanna Slim occupies the stool to my left. Molar Man and Sweet Tooth are to my right. Our feet relax on red plastic milk crates. The crates keep our legs from dangling. It is 6:15. I've been awake since 5:30. The weather reporter on the wall-mounted TV notes that rain is in the forecast. Radar indicating a band of dark green, yellow, and orange verifies her statement. The rain will begin around noon. Our planned hike today should conclude before 2:00. We will most likely get wet.

To Sweet Tooth's right is a "regular." In fact, all the customers except the four of us are. We are the interlopers. Still I feel welcome among these western Mainers. We are easily recognized as hikers. Many of the customers have lived here their entire lives. The man next to Sweet Tooth talks about driving up to northern Maine today on business. Caribou, he mentions. I tell him I spent a week there several years ago. He talks about his state pridefully. My friends and I order breakfast, not really blending in, but accepted. The General Store and Diner is a good place to be on an overcast, cool August morning in Maine.

Too soon we drive away, toward the trail and another day of hiking. At 7:01 I take my first step into the woods from East B Hill Rd. Within a few steps I am climbing. The trail ascends over 600 feet to Surplus Pond.

I pause to take a picture, thinking about my brother. This looks like a perfect spot for a moose. I see none even though we have been told many inhabit the area. After the pond we continue to climb another 800 feet up Wyman Mountain. Despite the lengthy uphill, the trail is agreeable. There are still roots and long stretches of black mud. I try to avoid each squishy patch. Eventually I take a misstep. My right blue trail runner is transformed to a charcoal grey.

Molar Man and Slim hike ahead. I linger, enjoying the opportunity to finally let my mind wander. I have had to concentrate so often that my mind has felt fatigued. Today the gentle trail affords me the opportunity to daydream. With few views, my thoughts become a luxury. I remember other trail days, friends I have made along the way, places I have visited and will probably never see again. My thoughts and I hike alone down Wyman Mountain to the Hall Mountain Lean-to. I arrive there at 10:07, having hiked the six miles steadily. Molar Man and Slim are having a snack.

After a ten minute break we descend over 1500 feet sharply to Sawyer Notch. I suggest the name game again, but neither of my hiking buddies has an entry. Tom and Diane are the only two I can offer. So I suddenly find myself hiking deliberately again, needing to focus on every step as I carefully navigate the steep descent. Occasional rock steps help alleviate some of the stress on the knees. Slippery oozing mud lurks around every bend waiting to "suck up" an unsuspecting shoe. Then when I finally reach the bottom, the steep climb up Moody Mountain begins.

Near the summit of Moody we are treated to our only view of the day, and it is short-lived. Just when we reach the overlook, clouds engulf the area. The view disappears. The light rainfall increases as we start our descent. Like the downhill earlier in the day, this one also necessitates my utmost attention. Several times I come within a step of taking a fall on the slick mud. Each time I maintain my balance at the last instant. With some rock steps, all things considered, the descent goes well.

When I finally reach the bottom of the hill, a final stream crossing awaits. We had been warned that a fording would be necessary at this water crossing before the road. Molar Man and Slim, however, are on the other side, having rock-hopped across. With specific instructions on which rocks to use, I successfully make my way to the other side without stepping in the water. It really doesn't matter since my shoes are covered in wet mud. Still it feels good to have made my way over two streams and stayed dry. With Sweet Tooth waiting, the four of us are quickly on our way back to the Cabin.

Tonight I enjoyed another delicious meal prepared by Honey. Some hikers took a zero due to the rain and are still here. Other new ones have arrived. I have met Rocky and Steady State for the first time. Star Child, Splash, Sinner, Torch, Slow and Steady, Pumpkin Head, and Spacey also are in attendance. Sinner had to re-introduce himself since our paths had not crossed since Connecticut. Good company and great food abound. Tomorrow is supposed to be sunny. For that matter, sunny skies are predicted for the next few days. If the weather continues to be good, and the terrain remains agreeable, hopefully I'll be able to cover more miles as I move toward completion of the Appalachian Trail.

## August 14, ME 17, Oquossoc, ME

Old Blue conjures up the image of a docile, sleepy hound dog waiting for a pat on the head, kind of like Old Duke in *The Beverly Hillbillies*. Old Blue, the Appalachian Trail mountain in Maine, in no way resembled a lethargic canine. It greeted Molar Man, Susquehanna Slim, and me at 7:07 with an immediate steep rock-step incline. Despite the neatly arranged steps that had obviously required many hours of trail maintenance, Old Blue brought out the sweat early. When the steps diminished, the sheer rockface commenced. Some nice person had fortunately placed rebar ladders with railings in strategic places. When no rebar was available, I inched my way up the slabs, hugging the small trees for balance if I could find one.

Reaching the summit after climbing 2200 feet over 2.8 miles, I was already tired with 10.4 miles remaining to be hiked. Then a painstakingly slow descent followed. Every time a downhill occurs my pace decreases.

With massive amounts of mud to contend with, in addition to the steep slick rocks, deliberate hiking was a must. And when I slowed, my hiking buddies got ahead. It's just my method to try my best to ensure that I stay on my feet. On a few occasions I still needed to sit and slide down a slippery, mossy rock. I don't mind sitting when that's the best way.

After the slow descent I had to climb what seemed like a never-ending Bemis Mountain. We thought we had reached the summit about four times before we finally did. Even though there was no view due to cloud cover, we took our lunch break at the top. Pumpkin Head, Sinner, and Torch passed us as we ate. We also were passed by Stretch and Barking Spider later in the day.

The remainder of the day consisted of several ups and downs over the same tedious terrain. Like yesterday, both my shoes were caked in thick black mud. Wet roots contributed to the less than agreeable trail. Feeling tired early in the afternoon made the final four miles difficult. Molar Man hiked ahead while Slim and I lagged behind, taking our time on the final steep downhill. When it ended, the trail had one more special offering for our final mile of the day, another steep climb. This one, fortunately, ended at the road.

Slim and I walked up the highway to where the Volvo was parked. We quickly realized that Molar Man had fallen into the last stream crossing of the day. A haggard-looking man, who identified himself as a homeless trout fisherman, even offered Molar Man some dry pants. He declined. The fisherman kept insisting, saying that they were recently laundered. Sweet Tooth told the man they weren't the right size. If Molar Man had accepted the man's generosity, that would have been a different type of trail magic.

Today indeed was a tiring one. The trail threw some challenges our way, but we were up for them. As I hiked today I thought a lot about my brother. A year ago today Don had exactly two weeks left to live. A man of strong faith, he was ready to move on. I thought about the inner strength he continued to reveal up until the end. Daily as I walk I feel his strength with me. I'm getting close, brother. Just a little while longer on the Appalachian Trail.

## August 15, ME 4, Rangeley, Maine

I'm at a cabin in Rangeley, Maine. It is not to be confused with "the" Cabin of Honey and Bear in Andover. Molar Man, Sweet Tooth, Susquehanna Slim, and I will be here only one night. Tomorrow night Molar Man, Slim, and I will be back in the woods. But for tonight we're living in luxury, at least according to A.T. standards. A front porch looks out toward a scenic lake. A cool, autumn-like breeze reminds me to put on long sleeves before walking to the post office. The Blueberry Festival kicked off today. Much is happening in Rangeley, Maine.

Earlier this morning the group made its final appearance at the General Store and Diner in Andover for breakfast. Wanting to get to the trail before 7:00, we arrived at the diner at 5:00. The two cups of coffee, however, didn't keep me from getting drowsy on the drive up ME 17. That drowsiness wore off quickly as my buddies and I started up the trail at 6:42. With very little elevation change, today's hike proved to be about as agreeable as any I've experienced since Vermont. Mud continued to force various acrobatic maneuvers to prevent submersion, but it did appear a little firmer since there hadn't been any rain over the past 24 hours.

Ponds definitely highlighted the day. First came Moxie Pond, followed by the much larger Long Pond. We almost completely circled Long. At one point a sign indicating "Beach" stood just off the trail adjacent to a sandy spot with two benches. We chose to forgo swimming. We also walked past the trail to the Sabbath Day Pond Lean-to. Then at Little Swift River Pond we broke for lunch. I walked down by the water where two canoes were lying next to the bank. Torch, Sinner, and Pumpkin Head lounged by the pond. Still no moose were in sight.

Before reaching ME 4 to Rangeley we passed two more ponds in the afternoon: Chandler Mill and South Pond. As always I thought about Don and how much he loved to fish. I often think about the photos I have of my brother holding up a big bass. Don is what this hike is all about. He was a man who loved the outdoors all his life. As I walk I continuously remind myself of what a fine man he was in all respects. The A.T. provides the hiker with all that nature has to offer. Most of all it's about the woods, and Don loved the woods.

After a rather short 13.2 mile day we found ourselves in Rangeley before 2:30. After showering I walked to the post office to pick up my last pair of Brooks Cascadia Trail Runners. This shoe has served me well throughout the hike. I also bought another pair of SmartWool socks and treated myself to a large ice cream cone. Later in the afternoon Molar Man, Sweet Tooth, Slim, and I ate at a barbecue place. We also shopped for some groceries in preparation for our night in the woods. Sunshine and a morning in the 40's await us as we continue walking through Maine on the Appalachian Trail.

## August 16, Poplar Ridge Lean-to

I first met Pilgrim at a hostel near Front Royal, VA. He had twice been sick and was losing weight. I saw Pilgrim again at Bears Den and discussed my method of hiking with him. We again crossed paths in Pennsylvania. Then I ran into him in Salisbury, CT at Maria McCabe's. A couple of days later I received a text from Pilgrim telling me that he wanted to hike with me using what came to be called Don's Brother's Method or the DBM (light pack, big miles, and beds). So Pilgrim and I became hiking partners and friends over the next month. Through part of MA, all of VT and NH and into ME, we shared stories about our lives and the trail. It saddened me when Pilgrim left the trail earlier this week; however, I understood why. After finding out that he had Lyme disease, and with some other medical issues that needed to be addressed, he really had no other choice. It was a tough decision to go home, but Pilgrim knew it was time.

Today Molar Man, Susquehanna Slim, and I hit the trail at 6:05, anticipating a challenging day with three substantial climbs. The day began rather innocently with a brief gradual uphill before the serious ascent of Saddleback Mountain. With several segments of sheer rockface, I was able to walk right up most in my new shoes. When that method wasn't advisable, I meticulously worked my way up the edge. All in all, however, the ascent didn't create that much of a problem.

On the approach to the summit we noticed what looked like children playing. At the summit we met former thru-hiker Wendy, 7-year-old Noah and 5-year-old Juliet. All three were wearing sandals. Here we were, three men in boots or trail runners, working hard to keep from falling, while a couple of elementary kids were playing on the rocks in sandals. Wendy shared some cookies she had prepared just for thru-hikers.

From 4120 foot Saddleback we descended another minimally dangerous stretch until a second climb occurred. This one, the Horn, was over a shorter distance. At the summit we met a young man from New York, Ryan, who was working on bagging all 114 peaks of over 4000 feet in the northeast. The Horn climb and descent mirrored the previous mountain in terms of difficulty. The downhills again required deliberate hiking. After panoramic scenic views at the crests, it's always troublesome to have to descend so slowly.

After the Horn one more mountain remained, Saddleback Junior. Like the other two, some sheer rockface necessitated diligent maneuvering. And also like the other two, the descent was worse than the climb. Views prevailed again in all directions. With abundant sunshine and mild temps, the hike went really well despite the tough terrain.

Even though it was only 2:00 when we reached the Poplar Ridge Lean-to, we kept our plans for calling it a day. This shelter, which was constructed in 1961, is known for its baseball bat-like floor. Several other hikers stopped by before moving on. Pumpkin Head, Torch, and Spacey visited awhile before heading on up the trail. Stretch and Barking Spider showed up before dusk.

As we all began eating supper, I commented to Stretch, "Those Oreos sure look good"

"Would you like one?" the pretty blonde replied.

"No," I said, catching the one Stretch tossed in my direction.

Feeling a bit guilty for taking food from someone who almost always sleeps in the woods, I thanked her for the treat.

Slim chimed in, "With all the town food you're eating, DB, I can't believe you're yogiing cookies off of another thru-hiker." Stretch just laughed, saying she had plenty.

Rain has just begun, so it's good to be inside for the night, even if this is a rustic abode. A steady drizzle pattered on the roof as I settled into my comfortable bag on another day for which to be grateful. A peaceful calm came over me as I closed my eyes to rest. Perhaps I would sleep soon. I was in the company of many who shared my desire to reach the end of an odyssey. All was rather peaceful in the lean-to in Maine, close to our destination up the Appalachian Trail.

## August 17, Caribou Valley Rd.

Twenty-five years ago today I met the cross-country team that I coached for a hard interval workout at Cooper Creek Park. That fall sophomore Bobby Gardner and freshman Scott Teixeira would lead a young group of runners to a region championship. When I arrived home from the park that morning, Linda said she thought it was time. Later that afternoon our daughter was born. Some memories never fade.

So on my daughter's birthday I awoke at dawn in the Poplar Ridge Lean-to. Molar Man and I almost simultaneously began the ritual of breaking camp. Shortly thereafter Susquehanna Slim followed suit. Even though I've only stayed in around fifteen shelters, I have the morning routine down pat. I readied my pack, ate two pop tarts, and treated a 32-ounce bottle of water before exiting the shelter at 6:20. A bright sun filtered through the spruce trees as my hiking buddies and I ventured up the trail. I anticipated a good day's hike to accompany the crisp, sunny morning.

That anticipation quickly evaporated. My bright outlook was transformed into dismay shortly after I left the shelter. A perilous descent consisting of several steep rock slabs awaited us. So from the outset my stress level accelerated. Like with other similar sections, I slowed my pace and hiked deliberately. For about a mile it was slow going indeed. Finally, however, the trail leveled off to some degree with a few minimal ups and downs until we arrived at Orbeton Stream.

In the *A.T. Guide* several water crossings are designated for fording. Orbeton was one, but today the water level allowed us to rock-hop across.

This stream was the widest that I have crossed in this manner thus far. When I looked back to the other side I quite frankly wondered how I had managed to stay dry. For some time I've been dreading to some degree any fording; however, lately I've begun to look forward to trying one. I'm sure I'll get my chance soon.

After the stream crossing we ascended almost 1000 feet to the summit of Lone Mountain at 3260 feet. From there the trail again leveled nicely over two miles to the Spaulding Mountain Lean-to. We stopped for lunch and were joined by Barking Spider, Stretch, Captain Planet, and OB. When Slim brought up last night's Oreo episode, Barking Spider offered me another. I'm usually not one to accept food from young folks who spend most of their nights in the woods, but on these two occasions I appreciated her kindness. I hadn't seen OB since Pennsylvania. He sat on a rock, eating dry Ramen for lunch.

When we left the shelter Molar Man, Slim, and I were immediately faced with an almost 900 foot climb up Spaulding Mountain. With mainly a dirt trail, we made good time reaching the top. We decided to forgo a 0.1 mile side trail to the summit. After the summit the trail leveled again until an extremely precipitous downhill began just past Sugarloaf Mountain. Again I hiked with deliberation and focus as I slowly inched my way down the sheer rock slabs. The descent forced me to think every step that I took. Along the way we also spotted our first moose. He ambled about twenty yards away and parallel to the trail. Walking in the same direction as the moose, we kept him in sight for several minutes.

At the bottom the Carabassett River awaited. Also listed as a ford, again rocks and a plank were positioned so that a dry crossing was possible.

Slim commented as we prepared to walk the plank, "most people probably make it across."

Torch and Pumpkin Head provided an audience on the opposite bank as I eased my way over. I reminded them that one day they too would lose their agility.

Once Slim and I reached Caribou Valley Rd., we walked the half mile to where Sweet Tooth was waiting. Molar Man had hiked ahead and was already there. We then drove in to Stratton where we plan to set up a base for the next few days. Despite the challenging trail early as well as late in the day, the 13.2 miles passed quickly. Tomorrow we will hike a shorter day when we deal with two 4000 footers. Maine continues to be rugged, but I'm just taking it one day at a time as I continue northward.

## August 18, Stratton Brook Pond Rd.

I am sitting on the porch of the Stratton Motel in Stratton, Maine. There are five rooms here. Hikers fill every one. Slim and I occupy room 2. A hostel attached to the motel houses hikers as well. All the Way and Goose sit at a picnic table along with two hikers I don't recognize. Across the street Fotter's Market displays a sign stating, "Hardware Paint and Plumbing Supplies." Another says, "Groceries Meats Fresh Produce Beer & Wine." The local Lions Club solicits donations out front for some animal cause. Cars steadily arrive and depart. Business appears to be good on a lazy August afternoon in small town America.

Earlier today Susquehanna Slim, Molar Man, and I hiked what may be construed as a "nero," or almost zero, day of a mere 9.1 miles over mainly agreeable terrain. Other than a mildly strenuous climb up South Crocker Mountain to 4040 feet, followed by a less difficult ascent of North Crocker to 4228 feet, the day sailed by. The summits are only one mile apart with not much to be concerned with between the two. After the Crockers the trail gradually descended over 5.2 miles to ME 27. With few rocky sections, we covered the total hike in less than five hours.

Nothing really noteworthy happened during the hike's duration. One view and a nondescript trail made for a lackluster hike. It was just getting the miles done today. When we reached the road we had lunch and then walked an additional 0.8 miles to Stratton Brook Pond Rd. with no packs. Sweet Tooth was waiting there for the drive back to Stratton. Slim and I then decided to partake of a second lunch at the White Wolf Cafe. We also got laundry done and had the remainder of the day to relax.

While I have been writing other hikers have arrived at the hostel. I walked over to introduce myself to several whom I had not met. We have walked the same trail for almost 2000 miles and I'm meeting Wolfman, Timex, Toby, and Whistler for the first time. I am re-introduced to Red Knees whom I met near Max Patch over one-thousand miles back. Such is life on the A.T. One never knows who he might meet for a first time or who might reappear after not being seen for hundreds of miles. Perhaps a new northbound thru-hiker will greet me tomorrow as my buddies and I hit the Bigelows, a little farther up the Appalachian Trail.

## August 19, Bog Brook Rd.

On a beautiful, sunny, warm summer day, Molar Man, Susquehanna Slim, and I successfully conquered the Bigelows, the last major range on the A.T. in Maine. We knocked off a fairly challenging 16.1 mile day in less than ten hours. And more importantly I passed the 2000 mile mark in the early morning. I haven't used the word "awesome" to describe any hikes lately; however, today's hike was awesome. From the picturesque views of ponds from the peaks of 4000 foot mountains to gently rolling pine straw-laden segments, all was good today on the Appalachian Trail.

The most difficult part of today's hike occurred at the outset. Molar Man, Slim, and I faced a significant climb of 2600 feet over four miles. Several extremely steep sections made each of us stop occasionally to regain our momentum. Fortunately there weren't any technical issues with which to deal. It was just a long hard climb. Views of lakes and ponds were visible from several vantage points. Under perfect weather conditions, Cranberry Pond and Horns Pond appeared crystal clear from the higher elevation.

After reaching South Horn at 3831 feet, we continued working our way up the Bigelows. Bigelow Mountain west peak challenged us with an exposed summit and high winds. Even though the trail traversed close to a precipitous drop off, I never felt like there was any danger. For the most part I was able to walk up the rock ledges without having to use my hands. We took a brief break at the top, but needed to move on quickly due to the wind.

From the 4145 west peak the trail dipped slightly before ascending again to Avery Peak at 4090 feet. At the summit of Avery a sign designating the 2000 mile mark stands. The peak is actually about six miles past that milestone according to this year's standards. Even though the trail changes periodically, signs remain in their original places. Some old ones provide inaccurate distances. At the peak I talked with two hikers from New Hampshire, Jeff and Ray, who were climbing all the New England 4000 footers.

From Avery peak the trail descended to Safford Notch and then leveled before ascending again to Little Bigelow Mountain. The trail then descended 1200 feet before leveling off over the last two miles to Bog Brook Rd. where Sweet Tooth was waiting. On the descent from Little Bigelow we met section-hiker Abe and his young son Abel. Although he was out for only five days, Abe was carrying about the biggest pack I have ever seen. He said it contained beach towels and goggles along with dog food and other sundry items. I'm not quite sure why he needs all the things he mentioned carrying.

So as my day winds down I feel a sense of relief over having no more major mountains except Whitecap and Katahdin. Tomorrow's trail looks agreeable on the map. With sunny skies in the AM predicted, we should be able to get in another longer mileage day, headed north on the Appalachian Trail.

## August 20, Harrison's Pierce Pond Camps

I'm sitting on the porch of Harrison's Pierce Pond Camps. Rustic could be construed as an understatement for the primitive wooden structures just off the A.T. Four hummingbird feeders hang from wooden beams. Tim, the proprietor, says that based on the amount of sugar water consumed, there are probably as many as sixty birds feeding daily. Molar Man sits to my right. Next to him Sweet Tooth relaxes. At the end of the line of an eclectic assortment of chairs, Susquehanna Slim sits. We are all fascinated by the hummingbirds. As they fly in to enjoy the sweetness of the sugar water, Slim and I try to take pictures. I successfully record four birds in one photo. We aimlessly while away the afternoon, each subconsciously focused on finishing the hike.

Our day began eight hours earlier at Bog Brook Rd. Unlike recent hikes, today's trail consisted of the easiest terrain we have encountered since, well, since a long time ago. I almost miss the treacherous mountains that we have painstakingly climbed over the past few weeks. What I did truly miss were the views from the high elevations. None were to be found today. We did, however, experience a number of lakes and ponds. The trail almost completely circumvents Flagstaff Lake. I could see my brother standing on the rocky shore casting into the lapping waters. On this clear warm morning Flagstaff epitomized serenity and peace. I would have liked to just sit for a spell, but miles needed to be hiked.

The trail also skirted West Carry Pond and East Carry Pond. Even though there were almost no noticeable elevation changes throughout the day, rocks, roots, dirt, and of course mud, still existed. Occasional dried leaves and pine needles made for comfortable walking. For the most part today's hike came as close to any the trail has offered up to being simply a walk in the woods. It felt nice to be able to daydream while hiking once again.

So as I walked along at a two miles an hour pace, I did a lot of thinking. I reflected on many aspects of the hike as well as on those who have hiked along with me. And I thought a lot about Don. He would have loved all these ponds. I think East Carry was my favorite. Molar Man, Slim, and I had our lunch overlooking the peaceful waters of East Carry. The water appeared too shallow for any fish to be swimming near the bank. I imagined big ones under the surface farther out.

A little farther up at the north end of East Carry the trail crosses a small beach. I imagine a number of hikers over the years have paused for a swim in the warm August water. Not today. We moved on, picking up the pace slightly in anticipation of getting to the Camps by 3:00. With the agreeable trail and no distractions, we reached the sign indicating the turn at our designated time. The short side trail travelled over Pierce Pond by way of a rickety bridge that appeared to need some serious repair.

For the remainder of the afternoon we visited with other hikers who had stopped by to make breakfast reservations. Tim's pancakes are said to be some of the best on the entire A.T. Hikers who don't stay in the cabins can still come in for a reasonably priced meal. Pumpkin Head, Spacey, Steady State, Tobey, and Hangman were hanging around. After eating a supper that we had packed in, Slim and I played some pool before working on our journals in the dining room.

Tim walked over and asked, "Do you mind if I play some music?" We didn't.

After a few minutes he joined us at the table with a glass of wine.

As soon as he sat down Tim looked me in the eye and said, "Tell me about your brother."

And so I did. Tim listened intently as I talked about Don's life, his faith, his illness, and his death. He showed genuine compassion. Then Tim spoke of losing his brother in his early 50's. And I listened. I think talking about our brothers was therapeutic for both of us. Tim also discussed Parkside, the young hiker who had drowned in Pierce Pond while thru-hiking last year. It was obvious that Tim was still shaken by Parkside's death. Slim and I sat past our bedtime to listen and share. Tim's candor and sincerity affected us both.

So shortly before ten we retired for the evening. The pond runs right in front of our cabin, so the watery sounds will be within earshot all night. I hope they lull me to sleep so that I'll be able to hike strong tomorrow up to Caratunk. Tomorrow will also be bittersweet because it will be my last day hiking with Susquehanna Slim. Slim has decided to move on a little faster since he needs to go back and pick up a section he left out in Vermont. It has been a pleasure and an honor hiking through New Hampshire and part of Maine with Slim. So once again after tomorrow things will be back to where they were in Tennessee and Pennsylvania as Molar Man and I make our way toward Katahdin on the Appalachian Trail.

## August 21, Pleasant Pond Rd., Caratunk, ME

I first met Susquehanna Slim in Erwin, Tennessee when we shared a shuttle with Tom "10K" Bradford. I wouldn't see him again until near Race Mountain in Massachusetts. He was hiking southbound that day, so we chatted briefly on the trail. Then our paths crossed in Salisbury later that evening. In his trail journal Slim posted an entry talking about my method of hiking. So when he sounded somewhat despondent in a post, I sent him an email inviting him to join me to Katahdin. He sent a response accepting the invitation. From just south of Hanover until today we hiked every mile together until we parted ways at Pleasant Pond Rd. From there Slim headed on up the trail as Molar Man and I joined Sweet Tooth for the ride into Caratunk and rooms at the Sterling Inn. I'll miss my good hiking buddy, Susquehanna Slim.

The day started with a remarkable breakfast served up by Tim at Harrison's Pierce Pond Camps. Molar Man, Slim, Sweet Tooth, and I had been given the 7:00 time slot. Tim is a one man operation, so he serves breakfast in shifts when he is especially busy. Today there were seventeen hikers scheduled to dine. The standard breakfast includes 12 pancakes, eggs, sausage, juice, and coffee. The pancakes contained blueberries, raspberries, and apples. I opted for the half order of six. They were delicious. After our meal we walked across the shaky wooden bridge back to the trail.

It was important that we covered the 3.2 miles to the Kennebec River quickly in order to beat the large group of hikers behind us to the ferry. The Kennebec is the only river on the A.T. in Maine where fording is prohibited. A canoe transport is provided between 9:00 and 11:00 AM and 2:00 and 4:00 PM across the Kennebec. When we reached the rendezvous point two hikers were already waiting. One was Fancy Pants. The other was the young man whose trail name I can never remember or pronounce when I see it. OB just calls him "Boy." They rode over together while Molar Man, Slim, and I waited our turn.

Since the ferryman could only carry two hikers at a time, Slim and I went together. We first had to sign a waiver and put on life vests before the transport. Slim sat in front and paddled. I sat in the middle and watched.

Due to the currents the ferryman paddled north before veering the canoe toward the landing area. Molar Man took the next ride along with Torch. A troop of Boy Scouts waited to be shuttled across southbound. Once Molar Man reached the bank the three of us continued our hike up a very agreeable trail for the remainder of the morning. We eventually reached Pleasant Pond Rd. where Sweet Tooth was waiting. After bidding farewell to Slim, Molar Man and I headed towards Caratunk and the Sterling Inn.

Later in the afternoon we drove to Bingham for lunch at Thompson's Restaurant and then into Monson for some reconnaissance work. We talked with Phil at 100 Mile Wilderness Adventures and Outfitters about accessible roads in the wilderness. Currently Phil is constructing a hostel-like series of cabins for hikers. The information Phil provided should prove extremely helpful as we negotiate the 100 miles between Monson and Katahdin. After our meeting with Phil, we also drove into Greenville to look for a lodging base for the next few days.

Then it was back to Caratunk. Despite hiking only an 8.8 mile day, we accomplished a good deal. In fact, we discovered that there's a good possibility that Molar Man and I can hike the entire Wilderness without sleeping in the woods. That is of course with Sweet Tooth's assistance. Tomorrow night, however, we will be back in the woods for what could be one final time as we continue to make our way north up the Appalachian Trail.

## August 22, Moxie Bald Mountain Lean-to

I'm sitting on a boulder overlooking Bald Mountain Pond. Molar Man and I arrived at the Moxie Bald Mountain Lean-to at 2:00. Now I have to find something to do until dark. Watching the calm waters of the pond and listening to the silence are options. The rain that was predicted for 3:00 has not arrived. It's very warm and humid for Maine. A frog sits near my feet. I believe that I've seen more frogs in Maine than the other thirteen A.T. states combined. This one blends in with the crumpled leaves on which he is perched. Only a foot away from the pond, he appears to be pondering whether or not to leap. I look up occasionally, hoping to spot a moose in the distance.

Several hikers have gathered at the shelter about fifty yards away. Besides Molar Man, All the Way, Goose, Tracker, Bane, Heart Rock and two section-hikers without trail names relax. Some will move on; others will stay the night. The shelter supposedly sleeps eight. It looks crowded with five sleeping pads already laid out. I secured a spot next to the wall, which gives me a little more room. If the rain comes, the shelter could get busy. Hikers walk the path to the pond for water and then return to the shelter. Sleeping Beauty was here earlier. He decided to hike on with Jesse, a section-hiker from Boston.

This morning the more challenging A.T. of Maine returned for a while. When Molar Man and I hit the trail at 6:40 we walked almost a mile on a flat surface before being confronted with Pleasant Pond Mountain. The 1000 foot ascent brought out the sweat on our brows quickly due to the humid conditions. In fact we both struggled to reach the summit. Maybe it was because we hadn't been faced with a climb in a couple of days, or maybe it was the early hour, but for whatever reason, I was beat at the top. Fortunately a long, less-severe descent followed.

When Molar Man and I reached Moxie Pond we were expecting our first ford. Alas, no fording was needed again today. Even though the pond was considerably wider than most streams, a lengthy rock hop brought us to the other side. After Moxie Pond the trail leveled again until Bald Mountain Brook Lean-to. We decided to forgo the 200 yard walk to the shelter. Instead we strolled on up the trail and found a spot to stop for lunch.

"I miss Slim," I told Molar Man as we dined, sitting on rocks in the middle of the trail.

From the lunch spot the trail again ascended up Moxie Bald Mountain. Like the earlier climb today, this one offered somewhat of a challenge, at least near its end. We weren't sure why but this mountain offered a summit bypass trail. We chose the tougher, white-blazed route. About 0.1 mile before the summit, angled rock slabs began to appear. Because they were dry we were able to walk up the center without any problems. The trail dipped back into the woods shortly after the summit which the trail missed crossing by about thirty yards. Since clouds indicated approaching rain, Molar Man and I chose not to take the blue-blazed trail up to the top. As we started the descent a light rain forced us to affix our rain covers. The shower was short-lived. We continued to hike a very agreeable trail for two miles to the shelter.

The highlight of today's 13.6 mile hike was meeting a southbound hiker who sported a sign on his pack declaring, "Save Olympic Wresting." I asked CT Medic if I could take his picture, which resulted in a spirited conversation. In a couple of minutes CT Medic and I discovered that we had much in common. He had run the Boston Marathon, was wearing Brooks Cascadia trail runners, and more coincidentally, had recently lost his brother at an early age. CT Medic said his last birthday (37) was the first he had experienced without his twin. We shared about our brothers in the middle of the Appalachian Trail. I continue to believe that I have crossed the paths of many for a reason.

Well, it's now 6:20 and bedtime is approaching in the woods. All the Way and Molar Man have already been snoring. Goose is tenting near the pond. Tracker, Heart Rock, and Bane have set up hammocks under a tarp. Dag, their dog, is jumping between the hammocks. He became my friend this afternoon when I gave him the broth from some Vienna Sausages. The section-hikers, Allen and Alex, have returned from the lake and are getting in their bags as well. The rain has temporarily subsided. Another day is winding down in a shelter near a pond out in the woods on the Appalachian Trail.

### August 23, ME 15, Monson, ME

Five months ago today I signed in at Springer Mountain and began my walk north toward Maine. At times it feels more like five years. I've said before that time is irrelevant on the A.T. Sometimes I don't even know what day of the week it is. At others the whole experience seems more like a dream. Have I actually hiked 2071.4 miles? Do I only need to hike 114.5 more miles to complete a thru-hike of the Appalachian Trail? The answer is "yes" to both questions and I'm getting pretty excited about it.

Still, there's hiking yet to be done, and to be perfectly honest, I'm tired. So tomorrow I'm going to take one final day off to rest up for the 100 mile wilderness and Katahdin.

Today started like most when I've spent the night in a shelter. At first light I packed up quickly and started up the trail with Molar Man at 6:20. Due to last night's rain, mud made its presence known again today. And in addition to the mud, streams and rivers were at higher levels. As a result of these higher levels of water, I got the opportunity to do my first fording today. One took place at a stream while the other two occurred at the West Branch and the East Branch of the Piscataquis River. All went smoothly.

I must admit that I have been somewhat apprehensive over fording for some time. Today's events, however, alleviated any fears. When I arrived at the first stream I removed my trail runners and socks and the then put on my Vivo barefoot camp shoes. The flexibility of the plastic shoes made the crossings seem easy. At the West Branch of the Piscataquis, Goose and All the Way had arrived just before Molar Man and me, so I watched as they made their way across the wider river. A rope was affixed to trees on each side for balance. The water only came up to mid-calf at the deepest part.

The third and final ford occurred at the East Branch of the Piscataquis River. Even though the river was wider, the depth of water was about the same as the second crossing. Again I easily made my way across. On the other side Molar Man and I sat on a couple of rocks and had lunch. While dining, we watched Sleeping Beauty and Jesse cross using the rock hop approach. They only got a little wet. Since we were ready to move on, they took our rocks for their lunch. We would see no other northbounders throughout the afternoon; however, we did meet Fifteen who was walking south.

As the afternoon faded Molar Man and I both struggled to keep any momentum. I believe I felt sluggish due to poor nutrition. I never eat well when I sleep in the woods. So for the final 3.3 miles we pushed as best as we could. I also think the cumulative miles are getting to both of us. I know that my body is ready for a rest. Even with a slower pace we finished the 17.9 mile day over very agreeable terrain in less than nine hours. Considering we took three breaks and had to change shoes to ford three water crossings, we made good time. When we reached the parking lot off ME 15 we chatted briefly with Bane's dad. He has driven up from Arkansas to support his son and his buddies over the last one hundred or so miles.

So tonight I'm once again out of the woods and at a motel in Greenville, ME. The waters of a picturesque lake ripple nearby. I relaxed in an Adirondack chair by the lake for a while in the afternoon. Relaxation is something I hope I'll have more time for soon. Tomorrow, however, will be a day of scouting, as Molar Man, Sweet Tooth, and I go looking for roads in the 100 Mile Wilderness on the Appalachian Trail.

## August 24, Resting in Maine

I'm in the back seat of the white Volvo station wagon with Ohio plates. On a beautiful 50 degree sunny Maine morning, Molar Man, Sweet Tooth, and I are on a scouting expedition of sorts. It would have been a perfect day to hike; however, we both needed a day off. It's the first for me in three weeks. For Molar Man it has been over a month. Our bodies are grateful for the respite. We need fresh legs for the final push. Strangely, I'm starting to feel a little sad that the adventure is about to come to an end. Did I really just write that?

The stretch of trail from Monson, ME to the Abol Bridge is referred to as the 100 Mile Wilderness, mainly because there are no towns or significant highways between the two. Roads do exist in the wilderness; however, they are remote. If one hopes to navigate them effectively it helps to have a reliable atlas and a GPS. Molar Man has both, so we not only found all the roads today, but we devised a strategy to hike the entire wilderness with only one night in the woods. The DBM (or maybe it should be changed to the MMM) is in full swing for the remainder of Maine.

The three of us first located a road that leads to the Otter Pond parking area where we plan to end a 15.3 mile day tomorrow. From there we moved on to the more easily accessible Katahdin Ironworks Rd. where the A.T. also crosses. The downside to this route is that a $12 fee per person is charged for access to the logging road. Folks using this road must stop and pay at a checkpoint where an old iron smelting community existed in the 1800's. $12 a person seemed kind of exorbitant, but then again, it is private land. The fee also allowed us into the other logging road, Jo-Mary, so at least we got two for one. When Sweet Tooth picks us up on these roads, only she will have to pay.

When lunch time rolled around we stopped at a small town America general store for a burger. The establishment sported an inventory that included everything from bread, to homemade canned goods, to fishing lures. A wide assortment of adult beverages was arranged nicely behind the counter. The lady at the check-out called every customer who entered while we were there by first name. I've been very impressed with all the friendly folks in Maine. It truly seems that their sincerity is genuine. That is a trait this southern man appreciates.

After the lunch stop we began the trek up Jo-Mary in search of two additional A.T. access points. The lady at the Jo-Mary gate offered highlighted maps and solid information regarding our destination. Still, the gravel roads with crudely constructed signs posed some difficulty in finding the A.T. crossings. Nevertheless, displaying a goodly amount of patience, we managed to locate the trail in two strategic places. After the successful reconnaissance, we headed back to Greenville.

So with a plan in place for the 100 Mile Wilderness, Molar Man and I hope to reach Baxter next Sunday after spending only one more night in the woods. If all goes according to plans, we will summit on Labor Day. Our backup plan is a Tuesday climb. Either way, as my grandmama used to say, "Good Lord willing and the creek don't rise," there's only a little over a week remaining on the Appalachian Trail.

## August 25, Trail to Otter Pond Parking

When I think of the 100 Mile Wilderness, the final lengthy stretch on the Appalachian Trail between Monson and Millinocket, Maine, an old Cat Stevens' song comes to mind. "Miles From Nowhere" could certainly be applied to this section of trail. Some people zip through the wilderness in five days. Molar Man and I plan to take eight. That will put us in position for a summit date of September 2, hopefully. Today we walked into the "wilderness" at 7:20 and hiked 15.3 miles, plus an additional 0.8 on a side trail, to the Otter Pond parking area where Sweet Tooth was waiting.

From the outset the trail today didn't look any different from other sections of trail we have hiked. Ups, downs, rocks, roots, mud, rock slabs, jagged rocks, more roots, blowdowns, streams to rock-hop across, streams to ford, ups, downs, more roots, more rocks......need I say more. Ponds again made their presence known. There was Spectacle Pond, Bell Pond, Lily Pond, North Pond, and Mud Pond. Not to be outdone were the brooks. James Brook, Thompson Brook, and Wilber Brook required crossings. Then there were the streams. Little Wilson Stream, Big Wilson Stream, Vaughn Stream, and Long Pond Stream gave Molar Man and me ample opportunity for rock hops and fords.

If my brother had ever hiked this section of trail, it would have taken him a week to cover the 15.3 miles. He would have gotten himself a Maine fishing license and made a stop at each pond. Don loved the woods, but he loved fishing more. I have no clue what kind of fish might have been swimming in those ponds, but Don would have figured it out and known what lures to use for a big catch. I paused to think about my brother and take a photo at each of the ponds I passed today.

Sometime around mid-morning I noticed a familiar hiker up the trail. Funnybone, whom I hadn't seen since Salisbury, CT, was engaged in a conversation with Molar Man. He hiked along with us for a while until we stopped for lunch. Yesterday we happened upon our first McDonald's since Gorham in Foxcroft, so I decided to bring along a double cheeseburger for lunch. I also carried a coke to make my first meal in the 100 Mile Wilderness a memorable one. Mountain Goat and Klutz walked by as Molar Man and I ate.

Klutz smiled her cute smile and said, "Mickey D's."

Mountain Goat asked, "Where did you find that?"

They both good-naturedly laughed at the old guy with a burger on the trail.

About the time we finished lunch two section-hikers stopped to chat. Steve and his teenage son Sam were out to do the wilderness. They sported some mighty large packs, telling Molar Man and me that they just couldn't figure out what to leave behind. Steve said he had climbed Katahdin years ago, so I quizzed him a little regarding some concerns I have. He offered some appreciated positive assurance that I could make it. Later in the day I would see Steve slip from a rock, winding up in Big Wilson Stream almost to his waist. Sam had managed to stay dry on the rock hop.

Late in the afternoon Molar Man and I both tired. We had begun the day strong after yesterday's rest; however, all the ups and downs kind of tuckered us both out. At the final water crossing, Long Pond Stream, Molar Man somehow figured out a passage across using rocks. Some in fact were submerged. I chose to ford after almost slipping in from a rock in the rushing waters. According to the *A.T. Guide* there are only three fords remaining. Thus far none have caused any real challenges. I just take my time, use my trekking poles for balance, and make sure I have a solid plant before taking the next step.

After what seemed like a long tiring day, Molar Man and I finally reached the blue-blazed trail to the Long Pond Stream Lean-to. Two-tenths of a mile past the turn to the shelter we located the unmarked side trail to the Otter Pond Parking area. A little apprehensive since we weren't positive that the trail we had taken was the right one, we hiked quickly, hoping that it was. When the white Volvo came into sight, we were two relieved, happy hikers. Within minutes we were on our way back to Greenville.

Tomorrow will offer us a day with more elevation, five mountains to climb, and several views. Molar Man suggested a very early start and I agreed. So a little after sunup we'll be back out in the wilderness as we make our way toward a mountain a little farther north in Maine on the Appalachian Trail.

## August 26, West Branch, Pleasant River

This constitutes the second opening paragraph that I have construct-ed today. I decided to trash the first due to negative attitudinal content. It began with the statement, "I hate this trail." That's exactly how I felt much of the day. In the other opening, however, I proceeded to go into a tirade over my frustration with all the obstacles the A.T. keeps throwing in my direction. I'm no different from any other hiker. Everyone who steps foot on this oftentimes brutal "footpath" faces the very same trail condi-tions. So I deleted the draft that made me sound like a whiner. Regardless, today's trail was no fun. It aggravated me from the first climb, taunted me with a smooth surface for about ten yards, laughed, and tossed a nostalgic White Mountain-like descent at me near the end of the day. Sometimes, and I did say sometimes, I hate this trail.

The A.T. set the mood for today's hike early when it placed a root in a position for my foot to snag. Before I had shed my rain jacket, I found myself face down in the dirt. Fortunately my head didn't hit. My hands saved me. Still the fall from the trip on the root established an irritable at-titude that, for whatever reason, I embraced throughout the day. Today's hike was hard. I wasn't looking for hard. I wanted the path to return. Af-ter all, we are in the 100 Mile Wilderness, which I thought was supposed to be known for its fast terrain. Maybe the young folks are able to whiz right through, but this old body needed nine hours to cover the 15.0 miles. When two southbound hikers said hello, I just frowned in their direction, muttering, "I hate this trail."

The first challenge occurred on Barren Mountain. Molar Man and I started the day at a pretty good pace, arriving at the summit in less than two hours after a 1600 foot ascent over just under three miles. Like other days and climbs, roots, rocks, and mud all made their presence known. What I had not expected was the need to use my hands a few times to pull myself up a rockface or balance myself by holding to a tree. With four more mountains still to be climbed, I was already bordering on exhaus-tion after the first. The 4:30 alarm might have also been a factor regarding my early fatigue.

After descending Barren Mountain we were confronted with Fourth Mountain. I'm always a bit leery of these "unnamed mountains." Not only was Fourth another tough climb, but on the way up Molar Man and I had to deal with Fourth Mountain bog. A board walk helped us with that. From Fourth Mountain we moved to Third Mountain. I suggested to Molar Man that we name the two Joe and Henry respectively. He failed to see the humor. At least the climb up to Monument Cliff on Third Mountain wasn't quite so steep.

After Third we came to my favorite mountain of the day. After almost a 500 foot ascent, we reached the peak of Columbus Mountain. Finally, after hiking 2100 miles, I have discovered in Maine a mountain that shares its name with my hometown. I took a picture of the sign designating its name and elevation before starting another descent to the Chairback Gap Lean-to. The only northbound thru-hiker we had seen all day, Sleeping Beauty, was taking a break there. Sleeping Beauty agreed that the trail had been tough today.

From the lean-to we only had to climb 200 feet to the summit of Chairback Mountain. Despite some rock slabs, the climb wasn't too bad. The descent, however, was downright treacherous. Slim even sent me a text warning. For about a tenth of a mile I thought I was back in the Whites. A very dangerous, steep, rocky trail forced me to hike with deliberation again. On more than one occasion I sat down to inch my way down a rock slab. It was tedious.

When we finally reached a dirt trail, we were able to hike at a faster pace all the way to the Katahdin Ironworks Rd. Sweet Tooth had arrived earlier and was offering some trail magic to Sleeping Beauty.

As I approached, Sweet Tooth said, "Sleeping Beauty has already warned me about your irritability, DB."

I acknowledged it before dropping my pack to hike another half mile to the West Branch of the Pleasant River packless. Molar Man followed suit. Sweet Tooth drove up the road to meet us for the ride into Milo.

Tonight we are staying in the home of Everett and Frieda Cook. I have not met a more delightful couple in Maine. When we arrived, one of their great-granddaughters was over for a visit. For a while I sat on a front porch bench swing thinking of my brother. I remembered a front porch swing that we had shared as children on the porch of our grandparents. I also remembered sitting by Don's side a year ago when we both knew that his death was near.

⁓

On that hot August afternoon, Don was at the point where he could not talk at all and resorted to an alphabet chart for communication. It proved to be a challenge to understand what Don wanted or needed. I tried to remain patient as I pointed to letters on the chart as he spelled. It took a tremendous amount of fortitude on Don's part just to nod when I verbalized what he could not. As we sat in silence, I continuously reminded myself that it was my brother, not I, who needed compassion and understanding.

This particular day was different from the many others I had spent with him over the past several weeks. Normally we were in the great room of Don's home, often watching daytime television. It gave us both some degree of joy if there happened to be an afternoon baseball game to view. At other times we resorted to the History Channel, Don's preference over the other cable choices. Even in what Don knew were his last days, he would smile and even laugh at Larry the Cable Guy. We also became somewhat hooked on *Pawn Stars*, a show that neither of us would have considered watching under other circumstances.

But on the aforementioned afternoon we sat in his and Lisa's bedroom. Don faced the gun case that for many years had hung in a room in our parents' home. After our father's death in 1996, our mother had insisted that Don take the heavy, wooden cabinet. It contained the guns that Don had used to kill many a deer. One was the same gun that our father had hunted with when Don and I were children. I'm sure that as he stared at the encased shotguns, he must have occasionally thought of other days, days before an illness had deprived him of a sport he had loved so well.

When the silence became too difficult to handle, I talked. A healthy Don might have asked me to lower my voice or not to repeat a story that I had told before, but a somber Don, deprived of the ability to speak, merely stared and listened. At one point I asked if he would rather me talk or sit quietly. He nodded that he wanted me to talk. For some reason, John Donne's "Holy Sonnet 10" or "Death Be Not Proud" came to my mind. This was a poem that I had taught to senior English students for three decades, but at this moment the theme that I had attempted to instill into their adolescent minds did not seem to apply to my brother. Donne implies that there are many difficulties that men go through in life more than once, but that death is a one-time occurrence. Therefore, Donne states that all men must die no matter what their state in life happens to be. Furthermore, he says that since we will wake eternally right after death, that death is really not that big of a deal.

I talked to Don about the poem. I told him that I regretted relating this theme over the years because death could be a struggle. Don had suffered for months and continued to suffer daily, yet he couldn't seem to die. Knowing that a place in heaven was reserved for his soul, he asked for deliverance from this world to the next even though he trusted God as the only One with the power to make that decision. For Don and others who suffer with a debilitating terminal illness, death **is** a big deal. While waiting for it to happen, they must wake up daily knowing that a daunting perseverance will be necessary throughout their waking hours. And when the night arrives, and they try to sleep, they know that the same degree of determination will be required the next day as well.

After I told Don about John Donne's poem, he nodded toward the alphabet chart, wanting to spell something. As I pointed to the various lines and letters, he indicated first a P followed by an R, and then an A, and at that time I asked, "Do you want me to pray?" Don nodded yes. It was the first time that my brother had ever asked me to pray. So I prayed. In that solitary room that certainly conjured up so many pleasant memories for my brother, we sat together and I prayed. I don't remember exactly everything I prayed, but I do know that I prayed for Don, his peace, his comfort, and for Lisa, and Brent, and Lori, and for our mother, a mother who was grieving so for her dying son.

As I have hiked the Appalachian Trail, I have thought daily about my brother Don, and I have prayed. I have prayed a prayer of thanksgiving for my brother's life, for all that he contributed for the good of mankind while here on this earth, and for all the wonderful times we shared as brothers. Often when I have faced a challenging section of trail, I have thought of my brother who bravely confronted an illness with no cure, every day, for 15 long months. I have prayed, and I have moved on, for I really haven't been hiking alone. There have been other sojourners with me. But more importantly, God has been with me, and my brother has been with me as well. The three of us have walked together. I have stumbled at times; I have encountered difficult stretches that have seemed insurmountable; I have felt defeated. Despite all of these obstacles, we have walked on. I have admired the beauty of all that God has created and I have been thankful......for every day that I have had the opportunity to hike the Appalachian Trail.

## August 27, Logan Brook Lean-to

Molar Man and I just rolled into the Logan Brook Lean-to after another day filled with ups and downs. We had thought about moving on to the next shelter; however, we are both tired. So after only 12.8 miles we have called it a day. As I sit on a mossy rock about three feet off the trail heading north from the shelter, I am being serenaded by Logan Brook. Running only about twenty yards from the front of the shelter, the brook will provide my water source as well as offer a pleasing sound throughout the evening. This setting is quite nice in all respects.

Our day began at 7:20 with an immediate ford of the West Branch of the Pleasant River. Molar Man and I both managed to get across without a problem even though the ford is listed in the *A.T. Guide* as having a slick, rocky bottom. It was the widest ford that we've encountered. After the river we began a long gradual ascent of over 1600 feet up Gulf Hagas Mountain. The final half mile was steep. From there we briefly descended before climbing up to West Peak at 3178 feet. Neither of these mountains offered a view. After another descent we next climbed Hay Mountain with the same result.

From the beginning of the hike today, I promised myself that I would attempt to hike with a more positive attitude. Even though I fell three times on slippery rocks, none resulted in any blood loss. I apologized to the trail and promised not to be too critical of what it throws at me. That was just before one of the falls. It didn't matter. I wanted to at least try to befriend the trail again. Hopefully the old guy has forgiven me for hating him yesterday.

The highlight of the day definitely came at the summit of White Cap Mountain. Panoramic views on a beautiful afternoon made the tough climb worthwhile. Then on the rocky descent we were greeted with our first view of Katahdin, majestically appearing 72 miles in the distance. As I descended I alternated looking down in an effort not to fall and staring at the Big K, transfixed against a blue sky surrounded by puffy white clouds. I looked in awe at the mountain I'll be confronted with in only a few days.

So tonight should be the last I spend in the woods. Molar Man and I plan to move into Millinocket tomorrow afternoon and slackpack the remainder of the trail with Sweet Tooth's assistance. I'm definitely ready for the hike to end. I'm about as physically and mentally depleted as I can ever remember being at any time in my life. This journey has challenged me in so many ways. The mental aspect has by far been my greatest challenge.

So as I prepare to spend my last night in a shelter, I'm thinking about one year ago tonight. That was my brother's last night on Earth. Don knew, like I knew, that his death was near. Lisa and I tried to make him comfortable, but our efforts were to little avail. The Braves game was on in the background, but in his depleted state, Don couldn't even enjoy his beloved team.

This trail has been hard, but my difficulties pale exponentially to how hard Don's existence was over those last few weeks and at its end. So as I lie in the shelter tonight, in the woods that Don loved, I'll remember my brother. I'll think about our last night together, but more importantly, I'll think about all the good times we shared. Tomorrow there's a hike to be continued. Only 71.4 miles remaining on the Appalachian Trail.

## August 28, Jo-Mary Rd.

When I started this epic journey in March, my plan was to summit Katahdin on August 28, the first anniversary of my brother's death. Those plans were not meant to be. I realized that I would need a little longer when I was back in New Hampshire. Two days ago I figured out why. August 26 and 27 last year were two of the most difficult days of Don's life. Then one year ago today he was released from his agony. At 7:55 A.M., the time he was officially pronounced dead by a hospice nurse in his home, I stopped in the middle of the trail and said a prayer. And I felt my brother right there with me.

The past two days have been hard. I think they were supposed to be for a reason, just like so many things that have occurred on this hike. Not to in any way compare with Don's last two days, but mine too have been challenging. I've tripped; I've fallen; I've bled; I've feared that my next step might lead to disaster. But through it all, I'm OK. Today all went well. For Don, one year ago today, he too was OK. His faith sustained him during those last agonizing days because he knew that soon he would be OK. With Don on my mind and his spirit by my side, I hiked strong throughout the day. As I walked today, everything was OK.

After a peaceful night's sleep in the Logan Brook Lean-to, I awoke at 5:20 to see Molar Man already stirring. When my watch alarm sounded ten minutes later, I was stuffing my sleeping bag into its sack. A few minutes later All the Way roused himself and also began packing up. The one "young kid" in the shelter, 23-year-old McJetpack, even stirred despite the early hour. I took an instant liking to the lad from a Chicago suburb when he arrived at the shelter last night. An affable fellow, he said this would be the earliest that he would be the last to leave. I told him I would see him up the trail as Molar Man and I headed for the white blazes at 6:04.

With an exceptionably agreeable trail, we hiked at a better than two miles an hour pace for the first four miles. A ford had been listed in the *AT Guide* at the East Branch of the Pleasant River; however, we were able to rock hop without difficulty. Shortly thereafter we began our only climb of the day, a 700 foot ascent up Little Boardman Mountain. Even though the little guy only stood at 1980 feet, the last 400 feet were steep. At the top we ran into Double Nickel and a section-hiker, Rich, from St. Simons, GA, who was completing a section-hike he started back in 1979. Now that's perseverance. Rich carries a trumpet which he plays every night. Kind of made me think of Gabriel.

After Little Boardman the trail became (to quote Slim) "a walk in the park." Sure there were a few rocks and roots, and some boggy areas with board walks, but mainly it was a fast path. At the Cooper Brook Falls Lean-to we stopped for lunch. McJetpack was also there. Since I won't be staying in the woods anymore I offered him a salmon packet. He graciously accepted and then filled my water bottle from the brook for me. As Molar Man and I returned to the trail for 3.7 more miles, Goose and All the Way showed up. I've been around them regularly now since early in New Hampshire.

Those final short miles of the day sped by. In fact, the whole day did. On the gentlest trail I've seen in weeks, we knocked out 15.4 miles in seven hours, thirteen minutes. At Jo-Mary Rd. Sweet Tooth was waiting. She said she had just provided some trail magic for McJetpack before we arrived. Who says this is a 100 mile wilderness? It did, however, take us 35 minutes on the logging road to reach the main highway. From there we made our way to Millinocket. So tonight I'm in a motel. Tomorrow and the three days thereafter, Molar Man and I will return to the A.T. to slackpack the remainder of the trail.

Today turned out to be a good day to hike. I passed two good fishing ponds on this day especially dedicated to Don. He would have liked them both. I smiled as I thought about memories we shared. I became emotional when I thought about our baseball conversations that are no more. I regretted that he is missing the Braves' successful season. I thought about

Lisa and Brent and how much they miss a kind and loving husband and dad. But most of all I was grateful as I hiked for Don's life and for his faith. My brother is OK and I will be too as I hammer out 56.0 more miles on the Appalachian Trail.

## August 29, Somewhere in the Wilderness

If I had to use one word to describe today on the Appalachian Trail it would be "wet." From light rain to wet slippery rocks, to wet slippery roots, to wet slippery mud, it was all wet. And as a result of a wet trail, by day's end, I was a bit wet myself. Wet shoes, wet socks, wet fording shoes, and, to some degree, damp pants accompanied me throughout the later stages of today's hike. After last night's heavy rain many sections of the A.T. had become streams themselves. Other portions, quagmire-like, waited patiently to quickly turn a blue shoe black. All day there was as Coleridge may have said, "water, water, everywhere."

For the first time in a long time, Molar Man and I started the day not sure of where our final destination would be. We knew that Sweet Tooth would be parked at a road crossing the A.T.; however, it was uncertain to us whether the road crossed the trail at 12 miles or at 15. When we got to the Nahmakanta Stream Campsite and found no road, we realized we would be walking three more miles. Still we covered today's distance in right at seven hours with two breaks. Considering the delays when we reached two water crossings, we made good time.

Like other recent days we passed several bodies of water. Mud Pond was the first. It looked like the perfect place for a moose to inhabit due to its swampy appearance. I stared in all directions but sighted none. A little later the trail curled around the banks of Jo-Mary Lake for nearly a mile. A sandy beach area practically touched the trail. On a sunny warm day this would have been a great place for a swim. Even in the light rain, it seemed very peaceful. As Molar Man and I passed a ray of sunlight tried feebly to peek through the clouds.

Next we stopped at the Potaywadjo Lean-to for a short break. Rich and Double Nickel were there as well. The shelter's roomy privy was about as nice as any I've seen on the A.T. Complete with a window curtain and sky light, it also sported an interesting sign inside. "Latch door when leaving or porcupines will eat this building." Funny, I haven't seen one of those critters the entire hike. After leaving the shelter we passed Twitchell Brook, Pemadcook Lake, and then Deer Brook. I already said it was a wet day.

The first major challenge of the day caught us by surprise when we reached Tumbledown Dick Stream. Listed in Awol's *AT Guide* as a ford, we did not anticipate what we found. Due to the excessive rain last night the stream had swollen to the point where there appeared to be no place to safely walk across. There were also no rocks above surface to hop. Molar Man walked about a hundred yards up stream to try to find a suitable place to cross without success. So reluctantly I followed my friend's lead as he walked out over the rushing water on a blowdown to a boulder in the middle of the stream. From there he hoisted himself up on the rock and then positioned himself to gingerly slide on his pants across another blowdown. We didn't take any action photos because I think we were both too petrified. I did get one of the spot after I was safely on the other side.

As I was crossing in the same manner as Molar Man, Birdman, an older section-hiker, arrived at the stream. He followed me across and gratefully thanked me as I offered him a hand for the final step. The whole process was a bit unnerving. This trail just never lets up. On a day when it looked completely flat, it taunted us with swollen streams and relentless mud. The hiker can never win. We just have to try and compete. Thankfully, all three of us succeeded with the trial thrown at us today.

A little later we reached a branch of the Nahmakanta Stream which was fordable. Molar Man and I changed into our "water" shoes and easily walked across the narrow stream that was only ankle deep. On the opposite side metal steps were placed against the bank due to its steepness. While we were putting our hiking shoes back on Birdman showed up and just walked across in his boots. I suppose they were already wet, or maybe he didn't carry fording shoes.

From the stream we hiked on through the puddles and mud to the pick-up location. I tripped on a root and fell during the final three miles. It was my second fall of the day. The other was on a slippery rock. That makes seven falls in the last three days. I'm trying to stay vertical. It's just sometimes hard to do so. None of the falls have been serious. I've gotten up right away each time and have only bled once from a small scrape on my elbow.

So today was an OK day despite the trail conditions. After we reached Sweet Tooth we all drove up to Abol Bridge to check out day after tomorrow's rendezvous point. On the drive up on Golden Rd. we were treated to an even closer look at a partially cloud-covered Katahdin. The view gave me a little queasy feeling when I realized I would be climbing up that majestic mountain in a few days. The scouting trip proved successful as we found out all the details regarding checking in at the ranger station for our summit. From there we headed back to Millinocket where I've had a relaxing evening. Tomorrow it's back to the wilderness where I hope to stay dry for just a little while longer on the Appalachian Trail.

## August 30, Pollywog Stream

With the four-day countdown officially underway, Molar Man and I started today's hike with a mere 8.7 miles planned. When one is slack-packing the 100 Mile Wilderness, there are obviously limitations regarding the availability of roads. So today's hike turned out to be a half-day hike since we finished around noon. That gave us, along with Sweet Tooth, the remainder of the day to drive into Baxter State Park to check out the Katahdin Stream Campground. Now with all logistics in place, we just have to hike the final 27.2 miles leading up to summit day.

From the logging road where we ended yesterday, Molar Man and I started up a pretty level trail for the first mile. At Prentiss Brook we were able to rock hop across since yesterday's raging waters had subsided. In fact, there would be no perilous water crossings today. Most of the water we saw was in Nahmakanta Lake early, and later in Crescent Pond. Part of the trail along Nahmakanta Lake travelled along a sandy beach. Some pebbles mixed in with the sand, but it still made for fast walking.

After passing the lake we stopped briefly at the Wadleigh Stream Lean-to. Then we crossed another unnamed stream before beginning a climb of Nesuntabunt Mountain. Even though the ascent covered only 700 feet, it was steep.

I told Molar Man, "I suppose the trail is offering us one final practice climb before Katahdin."

With his usual stern countenance, my hiking buddy offered no reply.

Unfortunately we were unable to see the Big K from the summit due to cloud cover. We did get a nice view of another pond. I'm not sure which one it was.

As we descended the mountain there were a couple of other places where the lake was visible. After leveling off, the trail almost circled Crescent Pond. At one point a small boat had been tied to a tree. At another a few other boats and a canoe lay near the bank. Still no moose were to be seen even though this pond looked like the perfect habitation. I paused by the boats for a few minutes to watch, listen, and reflect in the stillness of the picturesque setting. Quiet prevailed. From the pond we made our way along another body of water, Pollywog Stream, toward the logging road where Sweet Tooth was waiting.

At the car Double Nickel and Rich were enjoying some trail magic in the wilderness. Birdman also arrived to join us. I told Rich that I hoped we were on the summit together because I wanted to hear him play his trumpet. He said he definitely planned to play. As we drove up the logging road we also saw Bane's dad, who had parked near a rushing, boulder-filled stream to take some photos. This may be called the 100 Mile Wilderness, but we sure have seen a lot of traffic over the past few days.

After a quick stop in Millinocket the three of us headed up to Baxter. All the rangers we spoke with were extremely helpful. They exhibited great patience since I imagine they have been asked the same questions many times. From the first ranger station we drove back into the campground and saw where the A.T. crosses on its way up Katahdin. I felt the excitement, knowing that I'm only three days away from walking up that path.

When we got back to the motel in Millinocket, I spotted Barking Spider and Stretch getting out of a car. Stretch introduced me to her dad, Peter, who had come from Baltimore to pick them up. Peter thoughtfully mentioned Don when he told me he had been reading my journal. Stretch and Barking Spider are two of the nicest young folks I've met on the trail. I congratulated both for summiting today. I have also seen others at the motel, that I had hiked with or around, who have now summited. Burning Man and Hakuna Matata were here Wednesday and I spoke with Torch and his dad yesterday. All were excited to be finished. For me, however, there are still a few miles to be hiked. Early tomorrow Molar Man and I plan to hike our last big mileage day as we put ourselves in position for the last big climb on the Appalachian Trail.

## August 31, Abol Bridge/Penobscot River

One year ago today my family laid Don to rest. Along with his good friends Steve and Mike, I had the privilege and honor to eulogize my brother at his memorial service. With a heavy heart I spoke of Don's love of the outdoors. Of how he loved to fish and hunt and walk in the woods. I spoke of his love of baseball and how much he loved the Braves. I talked of how much he loved his family, and above all I spoke of his faith, especially in the last weeks of his life. Our family mourned Don's death, but more importantly we celebrated the life of a truly good man. A good husband, a good father, a good son, and a good brother. On the one-year anniversary of my brother's service I hiked throughout the day with Don on my mind.

The one thing that I recall most vividly after Don's diagnosis of ALS was how he regretted not having a disease he could fight. My brother never quit. His opponent just overwhelmed him. In some ways that's what the Appalachian Trail has done to me. It has tested every physical muscle in my body. It has attempted to get in my head and invoke almost a mental torture. It has left me bruised, cut, scraped, battered, and so tired that I could hardly think. But unlike Don's bout with ALS, The A.T. has given me the opportunity to fight back.

Today I think I made my peace with this trail that I've had a love/hate relationship with since I first stepped foot onto it. I promised myself at 7:00 this morning that I would enjoy hiking today, whatever the trail had to offer. The A.T. rewarded me with about as agreeable a 17.2 miles as any I've confronted over the past several weeks. Sure, the rocks and roots and mud continued; however, I just took them in stride and focused on the bigger picture. For the past five months and eight days I have enjoyed a privilege that not many get. I've had the opportunity to spend each of those days with nature. Today I appreciated that opportunity.

Molar Man and I hiked with a purpose today. We reached the Rainbow Stream Lean-to, a distance of 2.2 miles, in less than an hour. With confidence, I walked the log bridge across the stream and snapped Molar Man's picture as he made his way to the other side. That first hour set the tone for the remainder of the day. After the brief break at the shelter we didn't stop again for almost four miles until we reached the Rainbow Lake Campsite. Some section-hikers were breaking camp at the beautiful setting. The trail then continued to wind around the lake for a while. I looked over my left shoulder often, expecting to catch a glimpse of an isolated fisherman on a boat. None appeared.

When the trail finally moved away from the lake, it elevated over 400 feet to Rainbow Ledges. With cloud cover in all directions, Molar Man and I had no views while we took a short lunch break. The climb up the ledges, over some almost level rockface, actually seemed easier hiking than over the roots and through the mud. We stopped again at the Hurd Brook Lean-to where Funnybone, Double Nickel, and Rich were also taking a break. We all talked of our Monday summit plans. From there Molar Man and I hiked strong, reaching Golden Rd. before 2:30.

The A.T. turns right at the road and heads toward Abol Bridge. From the middle of the bridge we were treated to a view of Katahdin. Clouds rolled over the mountain as I paused to admire its enormity. Below in the Penobscot River a fisherman appeared to be fly-fishing for trout. After crossing the river we passed a trading post on our way to the parking area where Sweet Tooth was waiting. From there it was back to Millinocket. Later in the evening the three of us joined Susquehanna Slim and his lovely wife, Jodie, for dinner. It was the first time I had seen Slim since he summited on Friday. For Molar Man and me that event will have to wait until Monday. Just two more days on the Appalachian Trail.

## September 1, Katahdin Stream Campground

I'm sitting in the lobby of the Katahdin Inn in Millinocket, Maine, pondering. For a little over five months every one of my days has revolved around a hike. After tomorrow, hopefully, that will change. So with only the 5.1 miles to the summit of Katahdin remaining, I'm reflecting a little over my time on the A.T. For a while there I didn't think this day would ever arrive. Now that it's here, it feels more like a dream in many respects than reality. To be quite honest, I just want to get it done and go home to Georgia.

While I have been hiking the A.T. many have referred to this hike as a "dream." If I'm honest with myself, thru-hiking the Appalachian Trail has never really been a dream of mine. It's something I've thought about at times; however, I've always come back to my senses rather quickly when I examined the enormity of the task. There is no doubt that if my brother had not died, I wouldn't be sitting in Maine the day before a planned summit of Katahdin. If Don were alive I would be Don's brother. I would never have become Don's Brother. It was only his illness and death that prompted this adventure.

Prior to March 23, 2013, I had not done any section-hiking of the A.T. since 2009. On that last trip I stopped after about 25 miles of a scheduled 160 mile stretch with a sore back and no enthusiasm. I went home with a total of a little over 1000 miles of section-hiking, vowing to never hike the trail again. I really didn't like hiking that much. So as I sit here on the eve of a completed thru-hike, I'm thinking about a spring afternoon, on a breezeway, overlooking the Chattahoochee River with Don. I did this hike because I told my brother I was going to do it.

Today Molar Man agreed to start a little later with only the 10 miles remaining from north of the Abol Bridge to the Katahdin Stream Campground. When we did hit the trail at 7:30 we had an easy road walk for about a mile before the A.T. crossed Katahdin Stream and headed back into the woods. Other than the usual rocks, roots, and mud, nothing differed. The trail did remain relatively level until we reached the lower fork of the Nesowadnehunk Stream. After the recent rains, fording looked too treacherous, so Molar Man and I opted for the "high water level" trail around the lower and upper forks of the stream. I think my buddy would have attempted a difficult ford had I not urged him to follow the safer route.

A little later we walked up a side trail to Big Niagara Falls, a pretty impressive cataract I must admit. After a short break we followed the same path back to the white blazes for an extremely agreeable walk the rest of the way. At the Daicey Pond Trail parking area, some couples and their small children were headed up the trail toward the falls. From there we crossed Perimeter Rd. before the A.T. followed another short road to where it turned back into the woods.

Before leaving Baxter we visited the ranger station to fill out our paperwork for tomorrow's summit. The ranger also gave Molar Man and me a form to complete and mail to the ATC headquarters in Harper's Ferry documenting our completed hikes. We next drove back to Millinocket, had lunch, and returned to the motel where we saw Goose and All the Way, who finished yesterday. I got a much needed nap before joining the two for supper. Tomorrow I will be confronted with the most challenging day thus far, as I try to wrap up my thru-hike on the Appalachian Trail.

## September 2, Katahdin

When Molar Man said he would like to stick with our plans to summit Katahdin on Labor Day, regardless of the weather, I felt just a bit concerned with our decision. With a 90% chance of rain by early afternoon, I seriously wondered if we were doing the smart thing. I had been somewhat apprehensive and a little anxious about the climb for the past week.

Due to the potential for a nasty day, my anxiety increased. So with almost a certainty of no views, Molar Man and I signed the trailhead register at 6:30 before taking our first steps toward the summit of Katahdin and the end of my thru-hike of the Appalachian Trail.

For about the first mile the agreeable trail only minimally elevated as it traversed over more roots, dirt, and small rocks up to Katahdin Stream Falls. From there the more severe climb began. Like some of the climbs in the Whites, portions of trail required us to use our hands. When possible I chose to take advantage of the erosion areas to navigate around more challenging rock slabs. Eventually, however, rock scrambling was necessitated. As the wind speed increased and the cloud cover expanded, we hit the most severe section of the ascent.

For about a mile the climb became dangerous and unnerving, especially considering that a light rain had begun and the temperature was dropping steadily. As Molar Man and I neared the final few hundred feet of the 2000 foot ascent to the Tableland, he stopped, stooping down behind a boulder to shield himself from the sideways rain and wind.

Surprisingly he asked, "Do you want to turn around here?"

When I asked, "Why?" Molar Man stated, "It's not going to get any better."

For a brief moment I wondered if we were in danger due to the elements. If we turned around I would either have to try to summit another day or end my hike without seeing the summit. Neither choice appealed to me.

"Let's keep going," I replied.

When we returned to our full posture the wind almost knocked us over. So with Molar Man leading the way we continued the climb. While pulling ourselves up onto and over large rocks, we sporadically caught glimpses of cloud-encircled pieces of surrounding ledges. In a way I think not seeing all the exposed areas may have been advantageous. A part of me was disappointed that we were almost entirely engulfed in clouds. Another sighed relief that the precipitous ledges remained invisible. We just followed the white-blazed boulders up the mountain. By the time we got to the Tableland the winds made it almost impossible to remain upright. I kept Molar Man in sight as I hunched over to keep from being blown off of the mountain.

That last mile past Thoreau Spring proved "foggy" in more ways than one. I had limited visibility and my mind was clouded with interspersed thoughts of finishing the trail and hypothermia. At the end of his life, Don couldn't take one step, so I realized that every step I took was one he couldn't take. He was on my mind. He was with me. I felt strong with his presence. I think that gave me a sense of calm at times I might have felt some danger. There was no doubt I was enveloped in prayer then, a sense of strong connectivity with God and just the whole concept of being watched over.

So many thoughts were running through my mind that the summit actually came upon me before I expected it. Due to the adverse conditions I could not see the summit sign until I was practically on top of it. The entire hike I had expected to get emotional at the summit. I didn't. I simply wanted to get my picture taken and get off that mountain. Thankfully, there was one other hiker there. Ben, who said he had hiked up on another trail, took shots for Molar Man and me. It was exactly 10:00 at the summit.

Because of the deteriorating weather we did not linger. In less than five minutes we began the descent. About a half-mile down we met three other hikers that we did not recognize. Later we met a young man and lady. That was it. Katahdin was a lonely place on this bleak day. We needed to hike safely, but we also needed to hike quickly to get back below tree-line. Twice on the Tableland the wind literally knocked me over. Each time, I quickly regained my feet and continued. I walked in a crouched position to maintain my equilibrium. It was beyond challenging to navigate the steep ledges, now wet, in what had to be 70 to 80 MPH winds.

Rain pelted us from above and wind blew us from behind. Through it all my hiking buddy and I just kept moving, knowing that we had to get down that mountain. Getting past the Tableland, Molar Man paused briefly behind a boulder. He was shivering. We were both drenched and cold. There was no way to eat our lunch, so we didn't even try. We just kept moving, sliding down, easing down, painstakingly inching our way down the wet boulders. My gloves helped on the rebar even though they were also soaked. I just kept reminding myself of all those who were praying for me and a calming sense remained with me through the storm.

Time passed rapidly, or did it stand still, as we just continued to make our way down the wet boulders. Finally we got back to tree-line and then below. The terrain still demanded our attention; however, wind became less of an issue. Because of the steady cold rain and wet rocks, I had to be careful not to slip. Molar Man and I stayed together as we moved closer and closer to Katahdin Stream. When we did reach the level section of trail, standing water covered large segments. Since our feet were already soaked, we just sloshed through the puddles.

With each step I felt a sense of relief, knowing that we were so near to warmth and safety. Then what we were about as anxious to see as the sign on Katahdin appeared. We stood before the trailhead register where we had stood seven and one-half hours earlier. Molar Man's glasses were so fogged over that he could not see to sign out. I signed 2:00 for both of us. We had safely made it to the summit and back down. I could finally feel good about having thru-hiked the Appalachian Trail.

Within minutes Molar Man and I were inside the Volvo, getting warm and headed back to Millinocket. We met my family on the way out of the park. I had gotten off the mountain so quickly that their arrival was late. It didn't matter. When I saw Linda, Lisa, Brent, and Lori, all was well. After I took a hot shower, we all dined at the A.T. Cafe before my family and I drove to Bangor. Later in the evening Rachel arrived, which made the end of the day even more special.

So surrounded by those I love I said a prayer of thanksgiving for all that had happened during my five months and eleven days on the Appalachian Trail. I also thought about my brother. If not for Don's life and memory, I would not have successfully accomplished this thru-hike. He had been with me in spirit every step of the way from Springer Mountain in Georgia to Mount Katahdin in Maine. Maybe I still wasn't as much of an outdoorsman as my brother was, but I had come to respect and appreciate all that nature had presented me. Don loved the woods. After 164 days I had begun to embrace them as well.

Over the next few days my mind journeyed through Don's life. I replayed memories of childhood baseball, fishing with our dad, Braves games, and holidays. I thought about the healthy Don. The husband, the father, the son, and the brother. I thought about his illness and his death, but more importantly, I thought about his faith. And I thought about a late afternoon overlooking a river when I told my brother of my plan. I saw the smile on his face then which I continue to see today. It's a smile that I'll always see every time I recall a time in my life when I walked 2185.9 miles from Georgia to Maine on the beautiful and challenging Appalachian Trail.

# Afterwards

## 15

# Back to the Regular World

A few weeks ago, on a wet, cold, potentially hypothermic day, I summited Katahdin. Almost regretfully, it feels strange to allude to the hike in the past tense. For so long I thought about how many days had passed from the beginning of the hike. Now I find myself contemplating the number of days since it ended. This, the third week since its conclusion, coincides with the six month anniversary of its beginning. I deemed time irrelevant while following white blazes. In the present, time again marches on. Moments exist when I feel as if the hike didn't actually occur, but instead resides merely in my imagination. The reality of the regular world has for now replaced the gossamer existence on the trail.

The adjustment back to my "real life" has proven challenging at times. At others it seems almost as if I had never been away from my home. When I walked into my church sanctuary the first Sunday after returning home, I felt as if I had attended the previous week. I sat on the same pew. The same parishioners surrounded me. Then when the pastor welcomed me back, for a second I wondered where I had been. Many wanted to hug my neck or shake my hand. I smiled, thanking each for his or her prayers while I was away. When the service ended I attempted to make a quick exit, not really wanting to talk about the hike. As it simmered in my subconscious I desired to keep it to myself, only reluctantly sharing tidbits with those who asked. I had openly written about each day while on the trail; now I wanted instead to protect the memories. Verbalizing my feelings seemed more difficult than typing them. After all, who would really understand?

I have met with some of my friends. I shared a lunch with some of my running buddies, answering a variety of A.T. questions, but more importantly fellowshipping with good friends that I had missed. I've exchanged emails or text messages with Banzai, Molar Man, Pilgrim, Susquehanna Slim, and Steady and Spirit. I miss my A.T. pals. I also miss the trail. While hiking I just wanted to finish. Now I find myself contemplating being back in Virginia or Vermont or New Hampshire. Just like in this paragraph, my mind fluctuates constantly. I pick up my cell phone to make a call to only find myself scrolling through trail photos. I wonder how others who shared their hikes with me are adjusting to the "regular world." I debate whether or not to make a phone call. I replay in my mind the good times, the times of excitement and joy. But just as often, I recall days of duress and fatigue. Equally, I bask in the memories of both.

I've gone to the beach and thought about the mountains while walking barefoot in the sand at dusk. I viewed the setting sun over the waves and remembered a twilight in Pennsylvania. I ate seafood on a weathered, wooden deck and recalled a restaurant in Maine. I strolled down tree-lined streets at sea level with a vision of roots and rocks transfixed on my brain. I thought of Don and how he loved to fish, and of how much he loved the woods. I spoke often of the hike. Linda patiently listened, reminding me that we could go to the mountains in October. I wondered if a brief visit to the Smokies would satisfy a longing for white blazes.

Sometimes I think of Ulysses when he returned home to Ithaca. Tennyson was right. How does one truly "adjust" after a great adventure? As my hike neared its end, I kept repeating, "Each step I take is a step I'll never have to take again." I suppose the key words here are "have to." No, I'm not contemplating another thru-hike. I'm not even planning a return to the trail anytime soon. I'm not ruling out, however, other hikes on the A.T. or even other trails. They just won't occur in the immediate future. For now, I'm happy in this "regular life" in the "regular world." Still I will daily cherish the many fond memories that have forever become a part of me because I chose to go for a hike on the Appalachian Trail.

# About the Author

Mike Stephens is a retired high school English teacher and cross-country coach who resides in Columbus, Georgia. He has hiked over 3000 miles on the Appalachian Trail, including a 2185.9 mile northbound thru-hike in the spring and summer of 2013. Also an avid runner for over thirty years, Mike has completed forty-two marathons including the Boston Marathon eight times. *Don's Brother* is his first book.

Made in the USA
San Bernardino, CA
27 July 2014